ARTHUR GOLDWAG

Arthur Goldwag is the author of *The Beliefnet Guide to Kabbalah;* *'Isms and 'Ologies; Cults, Conspiracies, and Secret Societies;* and *The New Hate.* A freelance writer and editor for more than twenty years, he previously worked at Book-of-the-Month Club, as well as Random House and *The New York Review of Books.* He lives in Brooklyn, New York.

ALSO BY ARTHUR GOLDWAG

*The New Hate: A History of Fear and Loathing
on the Populist Right*

*Cults, Conspiracies, and Secret Societies:
The Straight Scoop on Freemasons, The Illuminati,
Skull and Bones, Black Helicopters, the New World
Order, and many, many more*

*'Isms and 'Ologies: All the Movements, Ideologies,
and Doctrines That Have Shaped Our World*

The Beliefnet Guide to Kabbalah

THE POLITICS

OF FEAR

THE POLITICS
OF FEAR

The Peculiar Persistence
of American Paranoia

ARTHUR GOLDWAG

VINTAGE BOOKS
A Division of Penguin Random House, LLC
New York

Library of Congress Cataloging-in-Publication Data
Names: Goldwag, Arthur, author.
Title: The politics of fear : the peculiar persistence of
American paranoia / Arthur Goldwag.
Description: New York : Vintage Books, 2024. |
Includes bibliographical references and index.
Identifiers: LCCN 2023028513 | ISBN 9780593467060 (paperback) |
ISBN 9780593467077 (ebook)
Subjects: LCSH: Political culture—United States. | Conspiracy theories—
United States. | United States—Politics and government—Public opinion. |
United States—Politics and government—21st century.
Classification: LCC JK1726 .G6525 2024 |
DDC 306.20973—dc23/eng/20230927
LC record available at https://lccn.loc.gov/2023028513

Author photograph © Grace Lile
Book design by Steven Walker

vintagebooks.com

This book is dedicated to Richard Torregrossa, Jr. (1957–2020), who would have found much to argue about in its pages.

Oppositions have the illimitable range of objections at command, which need never stop short at the boundary of knowledge, but can draw for ever on the vasts of ignorance.

—George Eliot

Contents

THE POLITICS
OF FEAR

Introduction

On October 27, 2018, Robert Bowers, a forty-six-year-old truck driver with a clean criminal record but a social media footprint that was rife with angry Holocaust denial and conspiracy theories, came to the end of his rope. One target of his vitriol was the Hebrew Immigrant Aid Society, which, he believed, "likes to bring invaders in that kill our people."

"I can't sit by and watch my people get slaughtered," he posted on the alt-right platform Gab. "Screw your optics, I'm going in." One hour later, he burst into a bris at the Tree of Life Congregation synagogue in Pittsburgh, Pennsylvania, shouted, "All Jews must die!" and opened fire with an AR-15.[1]

As shocking as a shooting at a synagogue was, it was also a little surprising that it had been so long since one had occurred in the United States, where military-grade automatic weapons are commercial commodities and mass shootings are nearly daily occurrences (there had been 383 in 2016 and 348 in 2017).[2]* Church

---

* For those keeping score of attacks targeting Jews, a Klansman opened fire on a Jewish community center and retirement community in Kansas City in 2014, killing three; in 2009 a white supremacist killed a security guard at the Holocaust Museum in Washington, D.C. In 2006, a Pakistani American shot six

shootings were becoming increasingly common (there had been three in 2017, including one in Sutherland Springs, Texas, where twenty-six died), and the climate of fear and hatred, whether online or in the real world, was at a constant simmer.

The midterm elections were just ten days away, and Fox News and other conservative outlets had been running stories about the Hispanic invasion of the southern border for months. Less than a week before, Donald Trump had tweeted that immigrant "caravans" from Central America posed such a clear and present danger to Americans—some of those would-be émigrés, he claimed, were terrorists from the Middle East—that he had "alerted Border Patrol and Military that this is a National Emergy [sic]."[3]* But what did the eleven worshippers Bowers killed, most of them elderly (the oldest was ninety-seven) have to do with any of that? A lot, if you were as marinated in paranoid conspiracy theory as

women at the Seattle Jewish Federation, one of them fatally. An anti-Semite sprayed the lobby of a Los Angeles Jewish community center with submachine gun fire in 1999 (the victims survived, but the gunman murdered a Filipino American postal worker at a different location a few hours later). In 1977, a white supremacist opened fire on a bar mitzvah in St. Louis, killing one. In 2019, a year after the Pittsburgh shooting, an African American couple who were active in the Black Hebrew Israelites—a group that believes that Blacks, Hispanics, and Native Americans are the true heirs of the ancient Israelites and that the people who call themselves Jews are Amalekite and Khazar impostors—attacked a kosher grocery store in Jersey City, killing three. One of them left a note that said, "I do this because my creator makes me do this and I hate who he hates." That same year, a Chabad synagogue in Poway, California, was attacked by a nineteen-year-old with an AR-15. A woman was killed and three others, among them an eight-year-old child, were seriously wounded. In a letter the gunman posted on 8chan, he said the Jews were "meticulously [planning a] genocide of the European race."

* It is unlikely that Trump's warning inspired Bowers directly, as Trump was an object of his vitriol as well. Bowers called him a closet globalist, controlled by Jews.

he was. He didn't so much believe that they were aiding hostile invaders as that they—and all Jews—were hostile invaders themselves.

The idea that rootless Jews weaponize immigrants, minorities, and the poor against their host countries has been in the air for more than a century, but it gained renewed currency in 2012, after the publication of Renaud Camus's book *Le Grand Remplacement,* which proposed that nonwhite immigrants from Africa and the Middle East were "replacing" white Christians and their civilization. Camus's book focused on Muslims, but he had also written about the troubling over-representation of Jews in French culture. When his ideas traveled to this side of the Atlantic, they gave American white supremacists a new buzz-phrase, "white genocide," and a rallying cry to go with it: "Jews will not replace us!" In what immediately became an infamous event, torch-wielding neo-Nazis chanted it as they marched across the campus of the University of Virginia in Charlottesville during the Unite the Right rally in August 2017, along with *"Sieg heil!";* "Blood and soil!"; and "Hail Trump!" There was street fighting the next morning, and a counterprotester was deliberately run down by a car.

While Trump had temporized for days before condemning the organizers of the Unite the Right rally, the statement he issued in the wake of the Pittsburgh killings was prompt and unequivocal: "Antisemitism and the widespread persecution of Jews represents one of the ugliest and darkest features of human history. . . . There must be no tolerance for antisemitism in America or for any form of religious or racial hatred or prejudice."[4] But almost four years to the day later, on October 16, 2022, the now ex-president posted what many took to be a thinly veiled threat to the large majority of American Jews who hadn't voted for him. "No President has done more for Israel than I have," he wrote on his Truth Social platform. But "our wonderful Evangelicals are far more appreciative of this than the people of the Jewish faith. . . . U.S. Jews have to get their act together and appreciate what they have in Israel—Before it is too late!"[5] It was a new twist on the old accusation that Diaspora Jews can't be true patriots because their loyalties are divided between Israel and the countries where they reside. But this time, the complaint was that so many Jews were putting Israel second.

October 2022 was a busy month for people who track anti-Semitism. On the eighth, the billionaire rap and fashion mogul Ye, formerly known as Kanye West, an outspoken Trump supporter with presidential ambitions of his own, had tweeted that he was ready to go "death con 3 On JEWISH PEOPLE." Why? Because "you guys have toyed with me and tried to black ball anyone whoever opposes your agenda."* A few days before, while being interviewed by Tucker Carlson, Ye told Fox News's prime-time viewership that he would rather his children celebrate Hanukkah than Kwanzaa, because "at least it will come with some financial engineering."[6]

Ye was spouting views that are not just held by neofascists, but are all too common in some African American communities (most notably the Nation of Islam). But the likeliest trigger for his outbursts was an investment that Ivanka Trump's Jewish brother-in-law Josh Kushner had made in Ye's ex-wife Kim Kardashian's Skims, a lady's lingerie venture. A few days before Ye's "death con" post appeared, he'd posted an open message to Kushner on Instagram: "WHAT IF I HAD 10% OF KARLIE KLOSS UNDER-

---

* Ye infuriated many Blacks too, when he wore a "White Lives Matter" T-shirt to a French fashion event. Two years before, he had donated $2 million to the families of George Floyd, Ahmaud Arbery, and Breona Taylor; now he insisted that Floyd was a victim of fentanyl abuse rather than police violence.

WEAR LINE WITHOUT YOU KNOWING" (the supermodel and entrepreneur Karlie Kloss is married to Kushner). "JARED WAS HOLDING TRUMP BACK," he added, a bit enigmatically. "IVANKA IS FIRE."[7]

But if Ye's anti-Semitism is undeniable—a widely accepted definition of racism is "any set of beliefs (ideology) that members of a specified group(s) possess certain immutable characteristics . . . that justify their inferiorisation,"[8] and Ye's "you guys," "your agenda," and "financial engineering" clearly suggest that he puts all Jews in the same bad basket—his political thinking (and much of his other thinking as well) is too murky to spend much time on, as his paranoia likely has clinical origins. Though he insisted he was "mentally misdiagnosed," he had been medicated for a bipolar disorder.[9]

Ye paid a steep price for his verbal incontinence in the form of canceled endorsements and branding deals, but what was striking at first was how few Republicans spoke up to condemn his words. Some actively defended him—not because he couldn't help himself, but because they seemed to believe he'd said nothing wrong. "If you are an honest person, you did not think this tweet was antisemitic," the Republican activist Candace Owens argued.[10] Trump ran interference for him as well, during an interview on Salem News. "Well, I haven't really seen the statements," he said. "I did watch the Tucker Carlson interview and he was really nice to me. . . . Sometimes he'll make a statement and a lot of people will think it's worse than he means it to be."[11]

As if to underline how comfortable he was with Ye's views, a few weeks later the former president had dinner at Mar-a-Lago with Ye and his new friend Nick Fuentes, the twenty-four-year-old founder of the America First Foundation, which runs the America First Political Action Conference (AFPAC). An incel and white nationalist* who'd marched in Charlottesville, Fuentes's proposed cure for America's ills is a "white uprising." "Here's the pathway," he told his followers. "We have one more election where white people can make the decision. . . . It's time to shut up, elect Trump, and then stop having elections."[12] As for the Jews, "Don't tell me that they're entitled to their religion," he said on another occasion. "Oh, I'm antisemitic? Yeah, I piss on your Talmud. . . . You think I care what an antichrist believes?"[13]

It wasn't just Trump, Ye, and Fuentes. In Pennsylvania, Doug Mastriano, the Republican candidate for governor, alluded darkly to the "privileged, exclusive, elite" Jewish day school his opponent Josh Shapiro had attended, where he learned "disdain for people like us."[14] But if Shapiro was too Jewish to lead real Pennsylvanians, he wasn't Jewish enough to be considered a "real" Jew. Mastriano's senior advisor Jenna Ellis, who had been a lawyer for Trump's 2020 presidential campaign, tweeted that a *Washington Post* story about Shapiro's faith was "disingenuous" because Shapiro, who keeps kosher and observes Shabbat, is "at best a secular Jew in the same way Joe Biden is a secular Catholic."[15] A few days later, Mastriano's wife chimed in. "As a family," she said, "we so much love Israel. In fact I'm going to say we probably love Israel more than a lot of Jews do."[16]

And there was more. On October 21, the Jewish Telegraph

---

* "Incel" is short for "involuntary celibate"; incels blame the hyperfeminine "Stacys" they are attracted to (as well as the athletic "Chads" those Stacys prefer) for their own lack of romantic success. Fuentes denies he is a white nationalist, but only because of the stigma it carries. As he explained on a YouTube political talk show in 2018, "The reason I wouldn't call myself a white nationalist—it's not because I don't see the necessity for white people to have a homeland and for white people to have a country. It's because I think that kind of terminology is used almost exclusively by the left to defame." (https://www.rightwingwatch .org/post/nick-fuentes-denies-being-a-white-nationalist-by-explaining-that-hes -a-white-nationalist/)

Agency noted that Michele Reynolds, a Republican candidate for the Ohio state senate, had self-published a manual for small-business owners that included the phrase "Jew you down" (Jewish culture, she explained, "has a reputation for not wasting resources"). Her campaign responded that she was merely sharing "what she learned from the wisdom of the Jewish community and how they are reputable for building successful businesses with a foundation of solid money principles."[17] Ten days later, the JTA reported that Johnny Teague, an evangelical pastor and businessman who was running for Congress in Texas, had published a novel entitled *The Lost Diary of Anne Frank,* in which Christian prisoners at Auschwitz told Anne about "Jesus and all He faced in His dear life as a Jewish teacher," inspiring her to wonder whether the Messiah had "come already, and we didn't recognize Him."[18]

If the overt Jew-bashing and its seeming lack of political consequences were new (I'm old enough to remember when Jesse Jackson's private remarks about "Hymietown" ignited a firestorm in the Democratic Party in 1984, and how Pat Buchanan's syndicated column about Israel's "amen corner in the United States" in 1990 earned him a book-length rebuke from his fellow movement conservative William F. Buckley[19]), attacks on Blacks, immigrants, and their progressive allies had become all too common in the Trump era, and they were continuing apace.

During that same month, at a Trump rally in Nevada, Alabama senator Tommy Tuberville said that Democrats are definitionally pro-crime and anti-white because they are pro-Black. "They want crime because they want to take over what you got. They want to control what you have. They want reparations because they think the people that do the crime are owed that."[20] The next day, Georgia representative Marjorie Taylor Greene took to the rostrum at another Trump rally to declare that "Joe Biden's five million illegal aliens are on the verge of replacing you, replacing your jobs and replacing your kids in school. . . . They're also replacing your culture. And that's not great for America."[21] In Wisconsin, where the Black lieutenant governor, Mandela Barnes, had challenged Republican incumbent Ron Johnson for his seat in the Senate, the National Republican Senatorial Committee ran an ad that juxtaposed Barnes's face with those of three Democratic House members, all of them women of color, and the words "different" and "dangerous."[22]

The shooting in Pittsburgh was neither the first nor the last to be explicitly motivated by an us-versus-them ideology. All the way back in 1994, a Brooklyn-born Jewish doctor named Baruch Goldstein celebrated Purim by carrying an IMI Galil assault rifle into the Cave of the Patriarchs in Hebron, Palestine, and killing twenty-nine Muslim worshippers. On December 2, 2015, Syed Rizwan Farook and Tashfeen Malik, a married Muslim couple from Redlands, California, attacked a San Bernardino County Department of Public Health Christmas party, killing fourteen. In March 2019, Brenton Tarrant murdered fifty-one Muslims in Christchurch, New Zealand, after publishing a manifesto entitled *The Great Replacement*.

In August 2019, twenty-one-year-old Patrick Wood Crusius posted his own manifesto about the Hispanic "invasion" on an 8chan message board, in which he paid tribute to Tarrant. "The Hispanic population is willing to return to their home countries if given the right incentive," he wrote. "An incentive that myself and many other patriotic Americans will provide."[23] Then he drove the more than six hundred miles from his home in Allen, Texas, to a Walmart in El Paso, where he killed twenty-three customers (as it happened, thirteen of them were American citizens and one was German). In May 2022, eighteen-year-old Payton S. Gendron posted a 180-page manifesto about white genocide and the Jewish role in the Great Replacement on Google Docs. His "immediate plan," he wrote, was to kill Black people, but "the real war I'm advocating for is the gentiles vs the Jews. We outnumber them 100x, and they are not strong by themselves."[24] Donning body armor and a military helmet with a webcam mounted on it, he drove to a supermarket in a Black neighborhood in Buffalo and opened fire, live-streaming the attack on Twitch. Ten people died.

When Anders Behring Breivik set off a car bomb in Oslo and machine-gunned students at a progressive summer camp on the island of Utoya in 2011, killing seventy-seven, he claimed it was to turn back the tide of cultural Marxism ("It is better to kill too many than not enough, or you risk reducing the desired ideological impact of the strike," he wrote in his fifteen-hundred-page manifesto).[25] When Elliot Rodger went on a killing spree in Isla Vista, California, in 2014 because of his sexual frustrations ("All of my suffering on this world has been at the hands of humanity, particularly women. . . . If I can't have it, I will destroy it. . . . I will arm myself with deadly weapons and wage a war against *all women and the men they are attracted to*," he wrote in his 141-page autobiography);[26] and when Dylann Roof killed nine worshippers at the Emanuel African Methodist Episcopal Church in Charleston in 2015 because "Black people are killing white people everyday . . . what I did is so minuscule compared to what they do to white people,"[27] I'd made it my business to read their writings and try to make sense of them. But soon after Trump was elected, I'd stepped back. After spending a decade tracking religious, racial, and misogynistic conspiracy theories, I'd had enough.

I never wanted to be a "hateologist," as a reviewer of one of my books once called me; the work was dispiriting, the pay nearly nonexistent, and, beyond seeing my name under headlines like

"Conspiracy Theories Explain the Right" from time to time, and being asked to opine about one or another of those theories in the nether reaches of radio, TV, and the internet (*no, I don't think the military's HAARP is altering the weather; fossil fuels are a much likelier culprit*), the satisfactions were few and far between. Sometimes, when careless bookers hadn't bothered to read past the word "conspiracy" in my mentions, those media appearances could be downright awkward. I'll never forget the look a Russia Today correspondent flashed me after she invited me to expound on the U.S. government's plot to poison the country with toxic flu vaccines and I didn't take the bait. Watching myself on YouTube and reading the comments the next day, I learned that my eye movements betrayed the fact that I had been drugged or hypnotized.

I knew I wasn't changing any hearts or minds. My progressive friends told me my obsession with the revanchist right was not just paranoid in its own right but politically counterproductive, as it diverted attention and energy from the very real policy work that needed to be done. The people I was writing about were dead-enders, they said; demographically and politically, they were on their way out.

Irony of ironies, the people who took me the most seriously were those same dead-enders, and I certainly wasn't changing any of their minds. They hate-read my articles and blog posts because doing so fed their sense of self-importance. Some of them returned the favor by "outing" me as a Jew, a communist, or even a tool of the Rockefellers (the Metapedia, which billed itself as the white nationalist alternative to Wikipedia, branded me a "Jewish propagandist and Europhobic scribbler . . . a Jewish supremacist who masks his Talmudic fear of his nearest competitor; European man"), or more creepily still, sending me long manifestos like the ones I just wrote about, cut and pasted together from a hodge-podge of sources, some of them centuries old.

I've always tried, as both a writer and a human being, to put myself in other people's shoes, to make a good-faith effort to understand why they think as they do. But opening myself up to programmatic racists, anti-Semites, xenophobes, misogynists, and delusional paranoids of other stripes exacted a steep psychic toll—not just because their ideas were so repugnant, but because so many of the people expressing them seemed like such sad, damaged souls. When I just listened to the sounds of their voices—the music, not the words—what I heard was discordant, to be sure, but it was almost always pitched in a minor key. Nobody constructs a whole worldview out of resentment, anger, and sanguinary revenge fantasies because they feel well loved and secure. If their ideas were grotesque and fantastical, their pain was clearly real. It affected me in ways that often caught me off guard. My wife used to tell me that I was showing the signs of Stockholm syndrome.

Then Donald Trump descended that golden escalator. Trump said a lot of the same things those haters did, but he had far more celebrity than they or indeed any other politician did, and an almost unprecedented genius for homing in on his followers' lowest common denominator. Looking at the crowds he attracted to his rallies and his poll numbers, it was clear the angry right had found a champion who could bring them fully into the mainstream. That said, Trump wasn't a guttural white nationalist in the mold of American Nazi Party founder George Lincoln Rockwell or former KKK grand wizard David Duke, or an eggheaded "race realist" like Jared Taylor and his bookish colleagues at the New Century Foundation think tank; his politics were purely transactional and self-serving. But if a white supremacist, a Gamergate misogynist, or even a rabid 9/11 truther like Alex Jones wanted to say "nice" things about him that could help him win votes, he wasn't about to stand in their way.

Like Aristotle's unmoved mover, Trump devoted most of his mindshare to blissful contemplation of himself. But when a news story about race, immigration, the sexes, or law and order did manage to break through and capture his attention, he would share his thoughts about it with the public via talk show appearances, ghostwritten books, and tweets. Though he sometimes contributed money to Democrats, a thread of casual, Archie Bunkeresque bigotry (*Jews are good at money; Blacks excel at sports, entertainment, and, sadly, criminality; Asians are smart but they talk funny*) ran through most of his pronouncements.

All the way back in 1989, not long after he'd sent up his first presidential trial balloon, Trump had taken out full-page ads in four New York newspapers to demand the death penalty for the Central Park Five, the Black and Hispanic youths who were falsely accused and wrongly convicted of raping and beating a white jogger nearly to death.* Ten years later, in 1999, he formed a committee, headed by the political dirty trickster Roger Stone, to explore another presidential run, this time as the standard-bearer of Ross Perot's Reform Party. The campaign book he released, *The America We Deserve,* included some policy proposals that ran against the grain of the Republicanism of the day, like a one-time supertax on the wealthy to reduce the national debt and—ironically, given his later crusade against Obamacare—a call for universal healthcare. Though he said he was against "partial-birth" abortions, he styled himself as pro-choice. Oprah Winfrey, he told CNN's Larry King, would be his ideal running mate.[28]

But by 2015, Trump had forged a more coherent political identity around his instinctual America-first nativism, his disdain for

---

* Their convictions were vacated in 2002 after DNA evidence confirmed a serial rapist's confession.

the political establishment in general, and for Barack Obama in particular, who he claimed was more inclined to play golf and especially basketball than run the country. "I heard he was a terrible student, terrible," he told the Associated Press in 2011. "How does a bad student go to Columbia and then to Harvard?" In case anyone missed the implication that Obama was an affirmative action president, Trump spelled it out more clearly: "I have friends who have smart sons with great marks, great boards, great everything and they can't get into Harvard."[29]

While it seemed unlikely that Trump truly believed Obama was a citizen of Kenya and hence ineligible to be president, or that hordes of other undeserving immigrants were stealing everything that wasn't nailed down and raping and murdering white women wherever they found them, saying that he did won him the support of a lot of people who resented having to sit through Spanish-language instructions when they called customer service, or who couldn't bear to see a Black family living it up in the White House when their own children could no longer afford to live in the neighborhoods they'd grown up in.* While Trump's personal brand was all about tacky excess and self-aggrandizement, his ardent fans among the white working class felt that they knew him, and, stranger still, that he knew them too, and loved them.

Vulgarian and serial adulterer that he was, a significant swath of evangelical Christians also embraced Trump as the messianic

---

* Undocumented immigrants do commit crimes, of course, but evidence gathered in Texas suggests that on average, they are more law-abiding than native-born Americans. A peer-reviewed study of arrests in that state found that "US-born citizens are over 2 times more likely [than undocumented immigrants] to be arrested for violent crimes, 2.5 times more likely to be arrested for drug crimes, and over 4 times more likely to be arrested for property crimes." (https://www.pnas.org/doi/10.1073/pnas.2014704117#sec-6)

redeemer they'd been waiting for. That's not hyperbole, but a plain fact that helps explain why so many artists of the far right, the kind who paint muscular Jesuses cradling AK-47s, also turn out paintings of Donald Trump receiving his blessing, and why you see so many people at Trump rallies wearing T-shirts emblazoned with a flag and a cross and the words "Jesus is My Savior / Trump is My President."

The Trump Prophecies was a best-selling book, published in 2017, in which Mark Taylor, a retired firefighter, shared the visions he began having in 2006 about God's plans for Donald Trump. "For I will use this man to bring honor, respect and restoration to America," God told him. "America will be respected once again as the most powerful and prosperous nation on earth (other than Israel)." A prophecy Taylor received in 2015 was about the Supreme Court:

> The Spirit of God says, The Supreme Court shall lose three, and My President shall pick new ones directly from my tree. Are you still not convinced that he's my anointed, and that he's the only I have appointed? . . . Those who attack him, their numbers go low, even to the point of a big, fat zero.[30]

With his focus on polling numbers, God sounds a lot like Trump.

Of course, most of Trump's religious followers understood that he wasn't exactly an advertisement for Christian humility and virtue. As the evangelical leader Mike Evans put it after Trump moved the American embassy from Tel Aviv to Jerusalem, Persia's Cyrus the Great "was used as an instrument of God for deliverance in the Bible, and God has used [Trump], this flawed human being like you or I, this imperfect vessel . . . in an incredible, amazing way to fulfill his plans and purposes." Benjamin Netanyahu also compared Trump to Cyrus; to commemorate the new U.S. embassy, Israel's Mikdash Educational Center minted a thousand collectable coins stamped with images of Cyrus and Trump.[31]

Trump's and his supporters' Christianity is not about turning the other cheek and loving thy neighbor as thyself; its primary focus is retribution. When Jake Tapper asked Trump if he had ever asked the Lord for forgiveness, Trump couldn't understand why he would be expected to do such a thing. "I like to be good," he replied defensively. "I don't like to have to ask for forgiveness. And I am good. I don't do a lot of things that are bad."[32] When another interviewer asked him to quote his favorite Bible verse, Trump said it was "an eye for an eye." To be clear, he wasn't referring to the verses in the Gospels that reject Hammurabi's principle, but the ones in Exodus, Leviticus, and Deuteronomy that endorse it. An eye for an eye is "not a particularly nice thing," he explained. "But you know, if you look at what's happening to our country . . . how people are taking advantage of us, and how they scoff at us and . . . laugh at our face, and they're taking our jobs, they're taking our money . . . we have to be very firm and have to be very strong. And we can learn a lot from the Bible, that I can tell you."[33]

Many of Trump's eye-for-an-eye Christians went on to embrace the QAnon movement, which looks forward to a final judgment and a new dispensation, when Trump will exterminate the traitors who have robbed real Americans of their birthrights and reign over a purified nation. In QAnon's telling, Democratic politicians are not just irresponsible with the nation's tax dollars, or soft on crime and national defense—they are the leading edge of a vast movement of pedophiles who literally cannibalize innocent children. As bizarre as that may sound, QAnon has attracted allies who wield real power. Though only a handful of elected politicians openly display their allegiance, more than a few drop allusions to it that true believers will understand.* By August 2022, Trump himself was reposting Q content on his Truth Social website and playing a Q-inspired song at his rallies.[34]

You didn't have to have a PhD in psychology to register the vast hurt and insatiable neediness that fueled Trump's grandiosity. On the very first day of his presidency, Trump sent his new press secretary out to claim against all evidence that his inauguration had attracted larger crowds than Obama's. In their book *Peril,* Bob Woodward and Robert Costa reported that House Speaker Paul Ryan spent the weeks between Trump's election and his inauguration researching techniques for dealing with people with narcissistic personality disorders, because he was convinced Trump suffered from one. Psychiatrist Bandy X. Lee ascribed to Trump and his supporters a syndrome she called "narcissistic symbiosis," a leader-follower relationship in which the leader, "hungry for adulation to compensate for an inner lack of self-worth, projects grandiose omnipotence—while the followers, rendered needy by societal stress or developmental injury, yearn for a parental figure."[35]†

* This explains why Elise Stefanik, a Republican representative from New York and the chair of the House Republican Conference, addressed a temporary shortage of baby formula with this tweet: "The White House, House Dems, & the usual pedo grifters are so out of touch with the American people that rather than present ANY PLAN or urgency to address the nationwide baby formula crisis, they double down on sending pallets of formula to the southern border." In other words, Democrats are baby rapists who literally take food out of the mouths of American infants and give it to undeserving foreign ones.

† Lee would pay a price for her bold (or reckless and irresponsible, depending on your view) violation of the Goldwater Rule, the American Psychiatric Association's guideline, adopted after *Fact* magazine surveyed twelve-thousand-plus psychiatrists on the question of Goldwater's psychological fitness to hold office, that it "is unethical for a psychiatrist to offer a professional opinion unless he or she has conducted an examination." Thanks in part to pressure from Alan

Whether he was a programmatic racist or just a casual one, an autocrat by conviction or merely by temperament, Trump set about remaking the presidency in his own image, shattering the surprisingly fragile norms that had held the country more or less together since the end of the Civil War and turning Republicanism into a cult of personality. The only thing preventing a complete collapse into strongman authoritarianism, it seemed, was his incuriosity, ignorance, impulsiveness, and lack of strategic discipline. Half a year into his presidency, when those Nazis marched through the streets of Charlottesville, I figuratively threw up my hands. Trump had already welcomed white nationalists into the West Wing.[36] Now that the fox is in the henhouse, I thought, what's the point of writing about all those lesser threats still lurking in the woods?

Though Trump had failed to secure a popular majority, his victory had been seen as a mandate to vastly curtail immigration from non-European nations ("shithole countries," as he called them),[37] rebuild the nation's infrastructure, restore its manufacturing base, cut working people's taxes, and provide even more generous health coverage than Obamacare. With the exception of immigration restrictions, none of those things came to pass, though Speaker Ryan—guided, no doubt, by the insights he'd gleaned about the care and feeding of malignant narcissists—successfully orchestrated the passage of massive tax cuts that were largely tilted to corporations and the well-to-do.

That Trump had so little in the way of concrete policy accomplishments to point to by the time he was running for reelection

___

Dershowitz, who claimed Lee had implicitly defamed him as mentally ill since he was a Trump supporter, her contract with Yale School of Medicine was not renewed.

in 2020 was a feature, not a bug, of his populist appeal. Populist politicians win when enough voters feel like they're losing,* and Trump knew how to ride the waves of discontent. Both the social and economic disruptions of the COVID-19 pandemic and the widespread demonstrations following the police murder of George Floyd in Minneapolis seemingly buttressed his case that the country was falling apart. It wasn't his fault that China had manufactured and inflicted a plague on the world while government agencies like the Centers for Disease Control and Prevention (CDC) and the National Institutes of Health (NIH) stood by complacently—or worse still, he implied, were actively complicit in the crime. As for those police killings, if he had a problem with them, it's that the corrupt Democrats that run America's urban hellholes won't let the police shoot more of the illegal immigrants and minorities that commit all the crimes. Robert Mueller's yearslong Russia investigation and the impeachment sealed Trump's case—the elites were all lined up against him, he said, because they hate Trump voters. The fact that he was president, that his party still controlled the Senate, and that he had secured a conservative majority on the Supreme Court that would likely stand for a generation or more did nothing to change his underdog status. MAGA Republicans know that the real power in this country is wielded by urban Blacks, poor immigrants, leftist college students, Antifa thugs, and progressive female politicians like Hillary Clinton and Nancy Pelosi.

---

* As William G. Howell and Terry M. Moe wrote at the time in their book *Presidents, Populism, and the Crisis of Democracy* (University of Chicago Press, 2020), "the essence of populism is a rhetorical framing of democratic politics as an apocalyptic battle of 'the people' against 'the system'" and "the status quo," which are defined as intrinsically "corrupt, unresponsive, morally reprehensible, and democratically illegitimate."

Trump badly wanted to win reelection, of course, but he could make hay out of losing too. His powerful connection with his voters turned on their shared sense of victimization, and as he said repeatedly, the system was rigged against them. But concession was not an option. To concede would be to acknowledge the system's legitimacy, and, worse still, to taint his brand identity with weakness.

Four days after the polls closed, on November 7, 2020, the TV networks finally called the election for Biden. People in my Brooklyn neighborhood were literally dancing in the streets. But a month later, it had become clear to all but the starriest-eyed pundits that Trump did not intend to leave office voluntarily. There would be no formal transition process, no sit-down with the Bidens for tea. Even more distressing was the near certainty that most Republicans would support him if he found a way— legal or extralegal—to remain in power.

Though I lost some sleep worrying that Trump and his team would pull off a soft coup by convincing enough states to disqualify enough electors to throw the election into the House, I never imagined he would dispatch a mob to the Capitol. What motivated me to write this book—and I had begun planning it well before January 6—was the selective nature of memory. Assuming the courts rejected Trump's fantasies about voting machines that had been hacked by a dead Venezuelan dictator, paper Biden ballots that had been preprinted in China, and truckloads of valid Trump ballots that were diverted to landfills, and that he would finally be pried out of the White House, I was afraid we'd forget how perilously close to the brink our democracy had come, and that all too soon, QAnon, MAGA, and Stop the Steal would seem as remote to us as WIN buttons and Jimmy Carter's cardigan sweater do today. We could not afford such complacency.

Trump is living proof of Alexander Hamilton's warning in Federalist No. 1: "That of those men who have overturned the liberties of republics, the greatest number have begun their career by paying an obsequious court to the people; commencing demagogues and ending tyrants." And like Sartre said of Jews and anti-Semites, if Trump hadn't existed, he would have had to have been invented, because he is a symptom of problems that are hardwired into America's geography, economy, and culture, and that have bubbled up to the surface of our politics every few decades since the Constitution was ratified. He wasn't the first and he won't be the last politician to harness our discontents to his ambition. And the next demagogue that comes along will have likely learned from his mistakes.

I was certain that the populist, authoritarian genie Trump released would not go back into its bottle. Like the California forests that Trump said were burning because their floors hadn't been raked as thoroughly as Finland's, America's political culture is a tangled mess and would continue to be even if Biden managed to restore a semblance of normalcy. Going forward, it seemed to me, the names "Dominion" and "Smartmatic" (the companies that supplied the voting machines that were wrongly said to have erased Trump's winning votes) would have the same emotional valence for future MAGAs that "Yalta" did for John Birchers when my baby boom cohort was growing up, and that "stab in the back" did for a certain generation of Germans. I conceived this book as a wake-up call, an antidote to "the system works" euphoria that pervaded the media in the wake of the Watergate hearings and Nixon's resignation, and that I feared would follow the conclusion of Trump's chaotic presidency.

But even the illusion of normalcy stubbornly refused to come. Six months after he slunk off to Mar-a-Lago with his hoard of classified documents, the first president since Andrew Johnson to boycott his successor's inauguration, Trump was not only still sucking up a wildly disproportionate share of media attention, he was a political center of gravity, endorsing loyalists and purging apostates and holding rallies to ensure that the 2022 midterms would be a referendum on Biden's legitimacy, and even more important, that when he formally announced for 2024, there would be no viable Republican challengers.

In the meantime, he beguiled his MAGA followers with suggestions that he might return to office much sooner. Vote audits in red states could still negate Biden's victory, he and his loyalists said. And there were other paths. If the Republicans retook the House in 2022, they could elect Trump Speaker. Biden and Kamala Harris would be impeached, and as third in line to the presidency, Trump would then return to the White House. Mike Lindell, the My Pillow entrepreneur and Trump super-supporter, wasn't prepared to wait even that long. He announced a date certain for Trump's second inauguration: the morning of August 13, 2021. "It'll be the talk of the world," he said.[38] When August 13 came and went without any notable returns or departures in Washington, he doubled down. "It's Trump 2021," he said, adding, a little bit mysteriously, "If we don't solve 2020, there is no 2022 and 2024."[39]

Trump issued calls for the immediate release of every January 6 rioter in federal custody and argued that the Black Capitol police officer who shot and killed Ashli Babbitt should be lynched. Had what happened to her happened to someone on "the other side," he said—implying that the Capitol police were not carrying out their duty to protect the members of Congress and their staffs from a violent mob, but choosing political sides—"the person that did the shooting would be strung up and hung."[40] By September 2021, as mainstream a columnist as *The Washington Post*'s Robert

Kagan was writing that Trump had already plunged the country into as grave a constitutional crisis as it had experienced since the Civil War, "with a reasonable chance over the next three to four years of incidents of mass violence, a breakdown of federal authority, and the division of the country into warring red and blue enclaves."[41]

Would Trump's comeback efforts work? From day to day, it was impossible to say. Trump's businesses and he himself were in serious legal and financial jeopardy, and he no longer enjoyed the protections and immunities that come with the presidency. He remained broadly unpopular in huge swaths of the country, and since his sole agenda seemed to be personal restoration and revenge, it was hard to see how he could convince substantial numbers of new voters that electing him would change their lives for the better. As it turned out, the 2022 midterms were not the rout for Joe Biden and the Democrats that Trump and the Republicans had been counting on and that most pundits predicted. The Democrats held on to the Senate, and though the Republicans did win the House, their majority was razor-thin. Trump's announcement a week later that he would indeed run in 2024 landed with something of a thud.

But the country remained as polarized as ever.

Quantitative political scientists and pollsters rightly point to education and race as our greatest dividers. In 2020, Biden won 68 percent of congressional districts in which 30 percent or more of voters held bachelor's degrees. Donald Trump won 64 percent of districts where less than 30 percent held four-year college degrees ("I love the poorly educated," he famously crowed when he won the Nevada primary in 2016).[42] If those districts were at least 70 percent white, Trump won 96 percent of them. After the

2022 midterms, Democrats controlled 77 percent of the congressional districts with the highest shares of college graduates while Republicans controlled 64 percent of the districts with the lowest shares.[43] The numbers are undeniable, but while they help make sense of broad voting trends, they don't account for the extreme behaviors and beliefs of so many elected officials. If education and wealth inoculated people against paranoid conspiracism, our political class would be largely immune to it.

What follows is not a postmortem of Trump and Trumpism, which would be premature for as long as he remains in public life, or an attempt to predict his political future, which is beyond my own or anyone else's ken. Think of this book instead as a set of reflections, developed in real time, about the American right wing's politics of fear. Its overarching argument is that Trumpism is what happens—and what has always happened, albeit under different circumstances and with different names—when two of the main wires that feed into the American identity cross. One of them is Protestant religiosity. The other is the worldly individualism that we associate with the eighteenth-century Enlightenment. Each is bottom-up and anti-aristocratic, and both are compatible with capitalism. But they are not compatible with each other; touch them together and they spark. When that happens, an infrastructure of cable TV news, talk radio, podcasts, and social media, aided and abetted by Vladimir Putin's army of trolls, who work assiduously to inflame whatever divisions they find, ensures that the fire catches and spreads. Still another structural factor that plays into Trumpism are the eternal conflicts between town and country and agriculture and finance, exacerbated by our society's rising inequalities and the status anxieties that afflict its left-behinds.

The first three chapters or essays, "Conspiracies and Conspiracy Theories," "The Paranoid Style and the Art of the Deal," and

"Through the Looking Glass," recount the re-emergence of America's paranoid style over the last several decades, starting on the farthest fringes of the right, whose die-hard denizens had never given up their hopes of seeing the New Deal, the civil rights movement, the sexual revolution, and the First, Thirteenth, Fourteenth, Fifteenth, and Sixteenth Amendments to the Constitution repealed, and who eventually colonized and annexed the Republican Party. In the chapter entitled "Cognitive Dissonance," I identify that well-known bias as a tool to help understand thought contagions, from 1950s-era flying saucer cults to the QAnon movement today.

"The Deepest Bias(es)" includes a thumbnail history of American anti-Catholicism, which is both older and more hardwired into our national identity than anti-Semitism and maybe even anti-Black hatreds. And finally, in "Farm and City, Church and State," I look at the long-standing conflicts between urban businesses and rural farmers, and the rise of Christian nationalism, while exploring a surprising twist on the term "witch hunt." Along the way, I share some of my personal observations of MAGA America during a pivotal moment in 2022, gleaned at a Trump rally I attended in Pennsylvania.

Richard Hofstadter's essay "The Paranoid Style in American Politics," published first in *Harper's* in 1964, remains the most penetrating and readable account of America's long history with far-right conspiracy theories that I know of, but the great mystery today is not why a deracinated few still cling to their hateful delusions, but why the many are as susceptible to those delusions as they are—and how authoritarian both the leadership and the rank and file of the party of Lincoln has become. "If conservatives become convinced that they cannot win democratically," the Never-Trump conservative David Frum warned in his 2018 book *Trumpocracy: The Corruption of the American Republic,* "they will not abandon conservatism. They will reject democracy." Many of them already have. A former speechwriter for George W. Bush (Frum famously coined the phrase "axis of evil"), he hoped to shock the patriotic sensibilities of the great middle that conservativism once appealed to. Whether that middle even exists anymore is an increasingly dubious proposition.

My modest hope for *The Politics of Fear* is that it can help explain the peculiar persistence of America's paranoid style. My immodest hope is that in doing so, it might help to dispel it to some small degree—or rouse some of Frum's sane but complacent majority to come to our democracy's defense.

1

Conspiracies and Conspiracy Theories

There are conspiracies, there are theories about conspiracies, and there are conspiracy theories.

The conspiracy that Catiline hatched in 63 BCE to kill Cicero and burn Rome was real, even if the niceties of his prosecution remain matters for scholarly debate. When Pope Sixtus IV, the archbishop of Pisa, and members of the Pazzi family conspired to assassinate Lorenzo de' Medici and seize control of Florence's government in 1478, that was no theory; dozens of participants were arrested, tried, and executed after the plot failed. Robert Catesby really did plot with Jesuits to blow up the House of Lords while King James presided over the opening of its new session in 1605; Guy Fawkes was caught red-handed in its cellar with thirty-six barrels of gunpowder. Abraham Lincoln's assassination was the fruit of a botched conspiracy to decapitate the U.S. government and restore the Confederacy—Vice President Andrew Johnson and Secretary of State William Seward were also its targets. Eight of John Wilkes Booth's co-conspirators were eventually arrested and four of them were hanged.

The so-called Business Plot, or Wall Street Putsch, to unseat

FDR and replace him with Major General Smedley Butler in 1933 is more ambiguous—and as such may fall under the category heading of a theory about a *possible* conspiracy. Allegedly bankrolled by J. P. Morgan Jr., Irénée du Pont, and the CEOs of General Motors and General Foods, among others, it was dismissed as a "gigantic hoax" by *The New York Times* after Butler testified about it before Congress. But Congress itself was less certain; its investigation concluded that "there is no question that these attempts were discussed, were planned, and might have been placed in execution when and if the financial backers deemed it expedient."[1]

But the idea that no airplanes were involved in the attacks of September 11, 2001—that Israeli intelligence operatives, working with Jewish real estate developers and their allies within the U.S. government, detonated explosives that had been pre-positioned inside the walls of the Twin Towers and 7 World Trade Center and then attacked the Pentagon with a cruise missile, and that they did all this to prevent Secretary of State Colin Powell and Saudi Arabia's Prince Bandar from meeting on September 13, lest they discuss the possibility of an independent Palestine—is an unalloyed conspiracy theory (and just one of the many that have proliferated around those terrible events). So are claims that the 2012 shooting at Sandy Hook Elementary School in Newtown, Connecticut, or the bombing at the Boston Marathon in 2013 were false flags in which no one was really killed, perpetrated by the U.S. government to give cover to its efforts to abolish private gun ownership. All of them require their thousands of moving parts to mesh seamlessly and their countless participants to maintain an unbroken wall of silence over an indefinite period. All of them presume the absolute power and discipline of the plotters—and at the same time, the breathtaking arrogance or incompetence that compels them to scatter clues in their wakes that even a YouTube detective couldn't miss.

A large share of the stories that the Trump team put out about the theft of his "landslide victory" in the presidential contest of 2020, which turned on everything from renegade voting machine companies to Italian satellites, pallets of Iranian cash, and corrupt local election officials, were conspiracy theories as well. Most of the people promoting them didn't really believe them; they floated them to assuage Trump's wounded pride, or to provide cover for the real but ultimately unsuccessful conspiracy they'd hatched themselves, which was to get slates of fake electors appointed in Arizona, Georgia, Michigan, Nevada, New Mexico, Pennsylvania, and Wisconsin so they could steal the election from Biden.*

People who believe conspiracy theories already hold a very low opinion of the supposed plotters; they embrace them because they make emotional sense. If you believe that the government is evil, then you will be open to the idea that its officials do terrible things. If you believe that governments are controlled by hidden cabals, then you will see their handiwork everywhere. That doesn't mean that governments don't do terrible things sometimes, or allow others to do so with impunity. If you are looking for something to be outraged about, you don't have to take a red pill, crack a Bible code, or parse the telling similarities between ancient Mesopotamian rites and the "Cremation of Care" pageant that the rich and famous members of San Francisco's Bohemian Club stage at

---

* When Dominion, the voting machine company whose software was said to have deleted millions of Trump votes, sued Fox News for defamation, Fox was compelled to release internal documents that showed how little credence its executives, journalists, and talk show hosts really gave to the story, despite promoting it endlessly on the air. In a note to the *New York Post's* Col Allan, Rupert Murdoch, News Corp's executive chair, admitted that much of what Trump was saying was "bullshit and damaging." "Read What Murdoch Said in His Deposition in the Fox-Dominion Case," *New York Times,* February 27, 2023. (https://www.nytimes.com/interactive/2023/02/27/business/media/dominion-fox-news.html)

their annual retreats in Northern California, like the young Alex Jones famously did to prove that America's elites sanction or even practice human sacrifice.

White genocide may be a myth, but genocide certainly isn't; America's forefathers really did exterminate most of America's indigenous inhabitants, making and breaking treaties with them willy-nilly during the intervals between asymmetrical military campaigns. For nearly two-hundred-fifty years, Americans bought and sold African men, women, and children to work their plantations, and for more than a hundred years after that, treated their nominally free descendants as second-class citizens. And there's more: government doctors in Tuskegee deprived dying African American men of the antibiotic treatments that could have easily cured their syphilis. Federal Housing Administration (FHA) programs in the 1930s, '40s, '50s, and '60s systematically deprived Black Americans of access to the subsidized mortgages that fueled the explosion of suburban homeownership, exacerbating and perpetuating the vast inequalities of wealth between the races.*

Thanks to the Pentagon Papers, the Church Committee report in 1976, and many other sources from within and without the government, we now know that U.S. intelligence and military officials, working on their own and under orders from their civilian leaders, committed all kinds of atrocities, both in secret and in full view, around the world and right here at home. They arranged foreign leaders' assassinations; surveilled and harassed American intellectuals, activists, and celebrities; irradiated young soldiers and fed psychoactive drugs to civilians without their knowledge. Private actors have done terrible things too. Tobacco companies conspired to quash the evidence that smoking causes can-

* White families average eight times the wealth of Black ones today, in large part because of home equity.

cer; pharmaceutical companies deliberately addicted hundreds of thousands of their customers to deadly opiates; fossil fuel conglomerates have worked to discredit the scientists who are sounding the alarm about anthropogenic climate change.

As depressing as all those real-life conspiracies may be to contemplate, they don't require any magical thinking. Conspiracy theories, on the other hand, reflect a view of the world in which the secret machinations of a shadowy "they" fill the roles that gods and demons held for pagans, or that millennial end time prophecies still do for some Christians. The term "conspiracy theory" came into common use as a pejorative in the 1940s and '50s, but its origin dates back to at least January 11, 1863, in a letter to *The New York Times* from Charles Astor Bristed, a gentleman scholar and a grandson of John Jacob Astor.[2]

The week before, the *Times* had printed a letter from a reader who presumed to explain why England had chosen to remain neutral in America's Civil War, despite its long-standing opposition to slavery. The answer was obvious, the correspondent said: because England's landowning aristocrats understood how crippling a protracted civil war would be. The United States had not only begun to rival England as a military and economic power; its democratic institutions threatened to "revolutionize [England's] . . . leading on to the emancipation of the masses of the British population." This they could not allow.

Bristed agreed that the English were hypocrites. But he denied that they had anything like a conscious plan where America was concerned:

Any man who has made European politics his study . . . sees fast enough that since 1849 (to go no further back) England has had quite enough to do in Europe and Asia, without going out of her way to meddle with America. It was a physical and moral impossibility that she could be carrying on a gigantic conspiracy against us. But our masses, having only a rough general knowledge of foreign affairs, and not unnaturally somewhat exaggerating the space which we occupy in the world's eye, do not appreciate the complications which rendered such a conspiracy impossible. They only look at the sudden right-about-face movement of the English Press and public, which is most readily accounted for on the conspiracy theory.

A likelier explanation for England's behavior, Bristed went on to say, was old-fashioned bad faith. England's leaders believe that slavery is wrong, but they also understand that severing their ties with the Confederacy would mean the loss of southern cotton for England's mills (not to mention an end to its lucrative trade in smuggled munitions), and hence economic pain. "When their philanthropy came home to them in this shape," Bristed wrote, "they found it an immense bore, and were too anxious to get rid of it." To help the English thread the moral needle, Confederate apologists made an energetic case for the laughable proposition that the war was not about slavery at all, but turned on knotty questions about states' rights. The North had imposed tariffs that advantaged its own manufacturing interests while hurting southern planters' and otherwise threatening the economic and political sovereignty of southern states. "John Bull eagerly swallowed the suggestion," said Bristed, and applying "this salve to his conscience . . . gave himself up unreservedly to that party whose success he imagined would be for the interest of his own immediate necessities."*

* Bristed would gain some measure of fame in the post–Civil War era because of his fear that the victorious Union would retain the emergency powers it had granted itself to fight the Confederacy. His 1867 book *The Interference Theory of Government* made a proto-libertarian case against government intrusions into

Bristed's "salve to his conscience" uncannily anticipates the theory of cognitive dissonance—the phenomenon, first identified by the psychologist Leon Festinger, in which people seek to relieve the psychic distress they experience when a deep-seated belief comes into conflict with objective facts by distorting, ignoring, or rejecting those facts—which I will have much more to say about in chapter 4. It also captures the casuistry of many a Lost Cause neo-Confederate today, who insist that the Civil War was only tangentially about the institution of slavery and the status of the enslaved—despite Alexander Stephens's unambiguous assertion that the Confederacy's inviolable first principle was white supremacy, that its "foundations are laid . . . upon the great truth that the negro is not equal to the white man; that slavery, subordination to the superior race, is his natural and moral condition."[3] As the Confederacy's vice president, Stephens knew whereof he spoke.

Eighty-some-odd years after Bristed's letter was printed, in 1945, the philosopher of science Karl Popper formally defined conspiracy theory as "the view that an explanation of a social phenomenon consists in the discovery of the men or groups who are interested in the occurrence of this phenomenon (sometimes it is a hidden interest which has first to be revealed), and who have planned and conspired to bring it about."[4] Popper, of course, was thinking about the foibles of communism and Nazism, which interpret history in the light of global theories about the malign intentions of certain groups and classes. Both look forward to great reckonings—communism's "end of history," when the work-

---

the private sector, like tariffs and liquor prohibition, and more generally "the meddling, narrow, and intolerant Puritan spirit" when it is "possessed of almost unlimited political power." Friedrich Hayek's seminal *The Road to Serfdom,* published in 1944, was inspired by a similar concern, that England would retain its command economy after World War II came to an end.

ers seize the means of production from the bourgeoisie and the state melts away, and Nazism's triumph of the Aryan race and the thousand-year Reich.

How does the paranoid style of conspiracism play out in practice? When trying to understand the causes of a war, a historian might document, among a host of other factors, the role that the machinations of arms traders and international bankers played in the breakdown of diplomacy. Confronted with the same information, a conspiracist would look past what the industrialists and financiers on both sides of the conflict did to who they were. What did those "merchants of death" and "evil Shylocks" have in common? They were greedy and rapacious and cared more about capital flows than the interests of their own nations. And who does that sound like? Why, the Jews, of course, a nationless people who deal in weapons for the same reason they lend money at interest and promote miscegenation and vice—in pursuit of a deliberate plan, conceived and put into motion by their leaders millennia ago, to undermine the foundations of Christianity and Christendom. Thus, as Henry Ford declared in 1920, in an interview with J. J. O'Neil of the *New York World*, "international financiers are behind all wars. They are what is called the international Jew. German Jews, French Jews, English Jews, American Jews."[5]

Show those conspiracists a non-Jewish arms trader or banker—or the statistical evidence that the overwhelming majority of Jews have neither riches nor power—and cognitive dissonance kicks in. To relieve the discomfort, they mentally rearrange reality, justifying their thinking and assuaging their consciences at the same time. Jews control money and arms trading to such an extent that some gentiles have no choice but to take up the business themselves, they might say—but only to ensure that their own nations can feed, clothe, and defend themselves. If some gentile officials appear to have behaved badly, well, that is because Jews manipulated them with bribes, just as the chief priests of the Temple paid Judas to betray Jesus. The only reason this isn't more widely understood, they might continue, is because of the iron grip that Jews hold on the media. As for those Jews without money, if they want to avoid the fate that their leaders so richly deserve, they should overthrow them. The fact that they have not makes them complicit in their treachery, and so just as culpable. All is set right again in the mind of the conspiracy theorist.

Nineteenth-century conspiracy theorists looked at the precarious state of Europe's old empires and saw in it the hand of the Rothschilds, the fabulously wealthy Jewish banking dynasty, and by extension the recently emancipated Jewish populations of Europe. Twenty-first-century conspiracists look at the problems of our world today and pin the blame on George Soros, the Hungarian-born Jewish billionaire and supporter of progressive causes, and by extension, the minorities and less-advantaged people who are those causes' beneficiaries. As Glenn Beck put it in a three-part special program he produced for Fox News back in 2010, "Who's the puppet master? George Soros. . . . But what is it that he believes in? He has tens of billions of dollars all flowing in, pulling strings. His tentacles are everywhere. What is he going through all of this trouble for to achieve? Well, globalization."[6]

What raises the paranoid style above mere bigotry is its systemic scope and illusive scientism—the belief that the hated other's malignancy is not just inborn and immutable but contagious, infecting everyone it touches, especially in the boardrooms of leading industries and at the highest levels of state. Conspiracy theorists accuse their enemies (who are not always Jews, of course, though they are almost always something alien and other) of the ghastliest crimes, not because of their supposed beliefs (socialism and anarchism in the nineteenth century; cultural Marxism, "wokeism," critical race theory, and globalism today), but because of who they are, whether that is Jewish or Catholic, Masonic, Black, Muslim, gay, trans, Asian, atheist, foreign-born, communist, a member of the "Deep State," or if any or none of those apply, satanic.

Glenn Beck's view of the world in 2010* was paranoid to be sure, but its politics were internally consistent and mostly consonant with the Republicanism of the time. That's no accident. In his short book *Conspiracy Theories,* the English philosopher Quassim Cassam noted that as strange and even hallucinatory as conspiracists like Beck's theories may be, it's important to pay attention to the programs they support, because conspiracy theories "are first and foremost forms of political propaganda." They perform this function by elevating "a political objective in a special way: by advancing seductive explanations of major events that, objectively speaking, are unlikely to be true but are likely to influence public opinion in the preferred direction."[7] If, like Steve Bannon once said, the best way to neutralize a skeptical or hostile

---

* Beck's political views have changed more than once since 2011, when Fox canceled his contract (Beck had already been a lightning rod; the backlash to the Soros documentary from Jewish groups might have been the last straw). In 2017, he apologized for helping to create Donald Trump, whom he compared to Hitler; two years later, he enthusiastically supported Trump's reelection efforts. It's important to note that the demonization of Soros did not begin or end with Beck. When Donald Trump was indicted in New York in March 2023, Trump and many of his Republican backers and rivals, including Florida governor Ron DeSantis and Ohio senator J. D. Vance, claimed that Manhattan's Black district attorney, Alvin Bragg, was funded and controlled by Soros. On May 15, 2023, Elon Musk, the owner of Tesla, SpaceX, and Twitter, one of the world's richest men, posted that Soros "wants to erode the very fabric of civilization. Soros hates humanity."

media is to "flood the zone with shit," then there is no better way to do that than by promoting conspiracy theories. In Jonathan Rauch's words, the tactic "is not about persuasion: [it] is about disorientation."[8]

While there are any number of haters with equally distorted views on the far left (the pro-Hamas declarations of some in the wake of the atrocities in Israel on October 7, 2023, a case in point), I focus on the right in these pages because, despite what you hear on Fox News, their politics have not penetrated very far into the Democratic mainstream. Most of the handful of democratic socialists in Washington have more in common with the political center of a generation ago, which also included some Republicans, than the anarchists and Marxists they are wrongly conflated with. Just as "communist" is a misnomer for progressive Democrats, "conservative" is a misleading description of today's Republicanism.

In the post–World War II era, the eighteenth-century Irish-British politician and thinker Edmund Burke was revered by conservative theorists like Russell Kirk. In the *Concise Routledge Encyclopedia of Philosophy*, Anthony O'Hear aptly described Burke's as an "approach to human affairs which mistrusts both a priori reasoning"—meaning grand theories—"and revolution, preferring to put its trust in experience and in the gradual improvement of tried and tested arrangements."[9] Republicanism today is an angrier affair and far less squeamish when it comes to revolutions. Awash in nostalgia for its fading certainties about class, race, and gender, it is energized by an atavistic urge to simply burn things down. In the immortal words of the longtime Republican operative and Trump supporter Roger Stone, captured in footage shot by Danish documentary filmmakers on the eve of the 2020 election, "Fuck the voting, let's get right to the violence."[10]

The notion of a "loyal opposition" has disappeared entirely

from contemporary Republicanism. Congressional Democrats are not "learned colleagues" but implacable foes who must be destroyed. The rhetoric used to describe them is deliberately dehumanizing. As Dan Bongino, who seems poised to inherit the late Rush Limbaugh's niche in right-wing talk radio, put it, "Liberalism is a cancer, it's a forest fire, it destroys everything it touches."[11] In September 2022, Georgia Republican Marjorie Taylor Greene ran a campaign video in which she compared Democrats to feral hogs, since both, she said, prevent farmers from providing food for American families. After shooting one from a helicopter with a high-powered rifle, she invited viewers to enter a raffle whose first prize was the privilege of accompanying her on a hog hunt.[12] Lest anyone accuse her of fomenting violence against Democrats, in a speech at a Trump rally she explained that the Democrats are guilty of a lot more than verbal violence themselves. "Democrats want Republicans dead," she declared, "and they've already started the killings."[13]

When a disturbed MAGA supporter broke into then-Speaker Nancy Pelosi's San Francisco home in 2022 and bludgeoned her octogenarian husband with a hammer, fracturing his skull, right-wing social media lit up with unfounded claims that his attacker was a leftist and his gay lover, and/or that the attack was a false flag, staged to discredit the right. Even more disturbingly, a number of prominent Republicans cracked ghoulish jokes about it. "Not only are we not BUYING the wacky, implausible Paul Pelosi story," Dinesh D'Souza tweeted, "but we are even LAUGHING over how ridiculous it is." As Halloween approached, Donald Trump's son Don Jr. tweeted a picture of a hammer and a pair of underwear captioned "Got my Paul Pelosi . . . costume ready."[14]

Quoting Daniel Bell in 1964, Richard Hofstadter wrote that "the modern right wing . . . feels dispossessed: America has been largely taken away from them and their kind."[15] That is even more the case today. Glenn Ellmers, a onetime senior fellow and research director of the Claremont Institute, the think tank that claims to have done more than any to create an "intellectual case for Trump,"[16] articulated those feelings in its flagship publication *The American Mind:*

> Most people living in the United States today—certainly more than half—are not Americans in any meaningful sense of the term. I don't just mean the millions of illegal immigrants. . . . I'm really referring to the many native-born people—some of whose families have been here since the Mayflower—who may technically be citizens of the United States but are no longer (if they ever were) *Americans.*

The only real Americans, he goes on to explain, are the "75 million people who voted in the last election against the senile figurehead of a party that stands for mob violence, ruthless censorship, and racial grievances.* . . . Practically speaking, there is almost nothing left to conserve. . . . Overturning the existing post-American order, and re-establishing America's ancient principles in practice, is a sort of counter-revolution, and the only road forward."[17] So much for Edmund Burke's cautious meliorism.

To give you a sense of how deeply this sense of dispossession has taken hold, here's Fox News's Bill O'Reilly, in 2015: "Traditional American values are under siege. . . . If you're a Christian or a white man in the U.S.A., it's open season on you."[18] Replace-

---

* To be clear, he was referring to Joe Biden and the Democrats, though after January 6, a reader might wonder if that isn't a clear case of the pot calling the kettle black—or of what a Freudian would call "projection."

ment theory has risen to the level of doctrine. "Now, I know that
the left and all the little gatekeepers on Twitter become literally
hysterical . . . if you suggest that the Democratic Party is trying
to replace the current electorate, the voters now casting ballots,
with new people, more obedient voters from the Third World,"
Tucker Carlson, who succeeded Bill O'Reilly in his eight o'clock
time slot, told Fox News viewers in April 2021. "But they become
hysterical because that's what's happening actually. Let's just say
it: That's true."[19]

And I was not exaggerating about the role that Satan and
Satanism play in far-right thinking. "For two years, the left has
claimed that schools are unsafe for children due to Covid," Fox
News's Rachel Campos-Duffy declared in January 2022. "But
there's something much more terrifying lurking in the halls of one
school in Illinois." The Jane Addams Elementary School, she went
on to report, recently held its first-ever after-school Satan Club.
"That isn't an isolated incident," she said. "Satanists are taking up
cultural space all across America."[20]

Hungary's authoritarian prime minister, Viktor Orbán, is
a great hero of the American right. In 2017, András Aradszki,
his secretary of state for energy, delivered a speech entitled "The
Christian Duty to Fight Against the Satan/Soros Plan," which he
claimed was to forcibly settle "tens of millions of migrants" in
Europe. "The fight against Satan is a Christian duty," he said. "Yes,
I speak of an attack by Satan, who is also the angel of denial,
because they are denying what they are preparing to do—even
when it is completely obvious."

But, just in case it wasn't obvious enough, the next day Hungary's deputy prime minister Zsolt Semjén took to the airwaves
to explain Satan/Soros's motivations. "Look at this migration,"
he said. "Fundamentally, the root of this hundreds of years ago

started from Freemasonry's inspiration, which later had a Jacobin version and a Bolshevik version, and one of its many branches is the Soros-type extreme-liberal thing, which from its heart hates Christian traditions, the Christian Europe's traditions and civilization, and if possible even more hates the nation-states."[21] What's notable here is how Semjén looks across time and space and sees the same sinister plots against the sovereignty of Christian nation-states, centuries ago and today, whether carried out by Jacobins or Masons, Bolsheviks or rootless cosmopolitan financiers of a certain faith. From inside the bubble, the persistence looks like confirmatory proof. From outside, it looks definitionally paranoid.

Donald Trump endorsed Orbán enthusiastically when he ran for reelection in 2022. In his victory speech, Orbán identified his enemies by name: "The left at home, the international left all around, the Brussels bureaucrats, the [George] Soros empire with all its money, the international mainstream media, and in the end, even the Ukrainian president."[22] For all the David and Goliath appeal of Ukraine's brave resistance to neo-imperial Russia, for all its citizen-soldiers' resemblance to our own Minutemen and the Spirit of '76, many on the American right also share Orbán's disdain for Ukraine and its Jewish president, Volodymyr Zelensky.

On February 22, 2022, as Russia massed tanks, missile launchers, and troops along Ukraine's borders, Tucker Carlson ticked off a litany of grievances against Democrats, the Chinese, global corporations, diversity initiatives, and so-called left-wing cancel culture to explain why he was "rooting" for Russia and its white, Christian, and decidedly unwoke president, Vladimir Putin, in the coming conflict. "Has Putin ever called me a racist?" he asked rhetorically. "Has he threatened to get me fired for disagreeing with him? Has he shipped every middle class job in my town to Russia? Did he manufacture a worldwide pandemic that wrecked my business and kept me indoors for two years? Is he teaching my children to embrace racial discrimination? Is he making fentanyl? Is he trying to snuff out Christianity? Does he eat dogs?"[23] Ukraine and its Democratic supporters, apparently, had done all of those things and more.

The next day, at a fundraiser at Mar-a-Lago, Donald Trump praised Putin's savvy and smarts, referring to his threatened seizure of Ukraine, a country of more than forty million souls, as if it were a real estate coup. "He's taking over a country—a vast, vast location, a great piece of land with a lot of people—just walking right in."[24] When Trump delivered the keynote address at a Conservative Political Action Conference (CPAC) meeting in Orlando three days later, the Russians had already walked in. Trump drew a bright red line: "The tyranny we have witnessed," he thundered, "should shock and dismay people all over the world." Except the tyranny that Trump was so outraged about was not Russia's invasion of a sovereign country, but the arrests of some two hundred demonstrators who had camped out on the streets of Ottawa, Canada, for several weeks to protest vaccine and mask mandates. As for Putin and Ukraine,* "the problem is not that Putin is smart, which of course he's smart, but the real problem is that our leaders are dumb." [25]

The interplay of conspiracy theories, the paranoid style, and the status anxieties that are at their roots are as old as humanity. At one time or another, they have risen to the forefront of the politics of virtually every country and culture. It's not hard to understand

---

* Trump, of course, had personal reasons to dislike Ukraine's current regime, given his campaign's connection via Paul Manafort to its pro-Russian former president, and the role that his "perfect phone call" to Zelensky had played in his first impeachment. As for his own history with Putin, there is much more to be said about it than I could do justice to in a footnote or, indeed, an entire book.

why. Unlike science, economics, and law, conspiracy theories are intuitive and easy to grasp and apply. The reason you are suffering, almost all of them say, is because someone who is not like you wants to hurt you. Politicians who position themselves on the side of people who believe this—and nearly all people do at one time or another, when they are feeling especially beleaguered and sorry for themselves—can reap tremendous rewards.

Reduce conspiracy theories to their essence, and they are bedtime stories, whose narratives simultaneously frighten and reassure, because they present a world without moral ambiguity, where causes are clear and effects are never ambiguous. With their hooked noses and their bags of ill-gotten money (or substitute another invidious stereotype as appropriate), the villains of classic conspiracy theories are immediately recognizable. Their heroes may be larger-than-life icons like Trump, but they are also the conspiracy theorists themselves, who, having swallowed the red pill that allows them to see things as they really are, now share the hero's quest. The prospect of a happy ending—when truth ultimately triumphs and the righteous few who kept the faith receive their rewards—gives their lives meaning and purpose.

Consider QAnon, whose followers believe Trump is secretly working to defeat an international cabal of child rapists and killers led by Soros, Hillary Clinton, and a host of other well-known political figures and celebrities. It is perhaps the most florid and at the same time the most influential conspiracy theory of the Trump era. Writing in *The Atlantic* in the fall of 2020, Adrienne LaFrance speculated that it could also turn out to be its most enduring legacy. "A movement united in mass rejection of reason, objectivity, and other Enlightenment values," she wrote, "[it is] not just a conspiracy but the birth of a new religion."[26]

Even if Trump makes a really spectacular comeback and returns to the White House (which is hardly out of the realm of possibility), QAnon seems unlikely to me to survive as a movement for very long, much less mature into a religion. It will probably seem as weird and inexplicably of its time to our grandchildren, if they read about it in their history books at all, as nineteenth-century American political movements like the Anti-Masons and Silverism do to us today. But the underlying structure of its narrative will abide. Much older than Trump and Trumpism, it is almost infinitely adaptable.

Any film lover will tell you there are only a handful of archetypal storylines. Adventure movies send young men off on dangerous quests; rom-coms turn on foolish misunderstandings; horror films play variations on the legend of Faust and the Golem of Prague; war movies replay Homeric tropes. It's the same thing with conspiracy theories. The tradition that QAnon comes out of tells just one story, though its heroes and villains are swapped in and out as needed to suit the times.

Its ur-template can be found in the Gnostic writings that emerged in the first centuries of the Christian era, which argued, among other things, that virtually everything we think we know about reality is an illusion, and that the God of organized religion is an impostor. That was more or less the premise of the movie *The Matrix,* from which the red pill metaphor comes. Swallow it, and your eyes are opened to the horrible truth.

The atrocities that QAnon describes—dissolute people of vast wealth and high education, who, vampire-like, rape Christian children and drink their blood—are inspired not by Gnosticism itself but by canonical Christians' exaggerated attacks on Gnostic heresies in the early days of the church. One example of this can be found in the fourth-century church father Epiphanius's description of the Phibionite Gnostics, who, he claimed, not only shared their wives in common, but aborted any pregnancies that resulted from their unions, pounded the fetuses with pestles, mixed the paste with honey and spice, and ate it with their fingers in communal rites.[27] A more proximate source is the blood libels against Jews and accused witches that have been spread since the Middle Ages. The nineteenth-century Know Nothings also told lurid stories about Roman Catholic priests, who they said maintained sex dungeons beneath their convents and abbeys.

Michael D. Langone, the executive director of the International Cultic Studies Association, characterizes QAnon as less of a cult or religion than a "safe space for paranoid speculation . . . a sort of virtual-reality, fantasy world in which 'seeing connections' provides not only the thrill of a personal ah-ha experience, but also an opportunity to be rewarded by others via *likes* and *shares*," leading to a kind of social media addiction.[28] No matter how you categorize it, QAnon had permeated our politics to such an extent by 2020 that even some mainstream Republicans were referencing its themes and language in their campaigns. Trump's son Eric posted the letter Q and the group's slogan, "Where we go one, we go all," on his Instagram account.[29] Analyzing Donald Trump's reposts on Truth Social in August and September 2022, the AP found that "of nearly 75 accounts . . . more than a third of them have promoted QAnon."[30] When the billionaire Elon Musk purchased Twitter in 2022 and reinstated many of its canceled accounts, QAnon believers became convinced that he was one of them—and possibly as important a figure in its prophecies as Trump.[31]

The movement was born on October 28, 2017, when a poster on a 4chan message board with the username Q Clearance Patriot, who claimed to be a high-ranking member of the intelligence community ("Q" was said to stand for his clearance level), began dropping "breadcrumbs," a trail of cryptic clues that careful readers could follow to arrive at a clear view of the shocking truths that lurk beneath the deceptive surfaces of things. "HRC extradition already in motion effective yesterday with several countries in case of cross border run," the post began. "Expect massive riots organized in defiance. . . . Do you believe HRC, Soros, Obama etc have more power than Trump? Fantasy." [32]

Though Hillary Clinton was not in fact arrested or on the lam, many more posts followed. Each was parsed as carefully as if it had issued from an oracle. Special Counsel Robert Mueller, who was heading up the Department of Justice's Russia probe, wasn't Trump's Javert, Q and his interpreters revealed—the two were actually close allies, working together in secret to bring down the Satan-worshipping pedophiles who control the Deep State. Those elites don't just abduct, rape, and torture children, but harvest the ultra-powerful stimulant adrenochrome from their pituitary glands after they die, which they then inject into their own veins. "It's the drug of the elites," one Q believer explained.* [33] But a cleansing storm was coming. Once Mueller's report was released, Trump would reveal himself in all his glory, sweeping up his enemies and executing them.

A core theme in the QAnon universe is the notion of "the storm," which Trump inadvertently introduced on October 6, 2017, just a few weeks before Q entered the scene. Posing for a photograph with senior military leaders and their spouses at the White House, he asked, seemingly out of the blue, "You guys

---

* A Twitter thread from April 2018 introduced the "Frazzledrip" conspiracy theory: that a video recording of Huma Abedin and Hillary Clinton ripping off a child's face and wearing it as a mask while they drank its blood had been recovered from Anthony Weiner's laptop. (https://www.vox.com/technology/2018/12/12/18136132/google-youtube-congress-conspiracy-theories)

know what this represents?" He traced a figure in the air with his index finger that might have been the letter Q. Then he answered the question himself: "Maybe it's the calm before the storm."

When asked repeatedly what the storm was, his answer was cryptic: "You'll find out," he said. [34]

When the finished Mueller report failed to change the weather, Q believers looked ahead to the 2020 election—and to the Deep State's brazen efforts to steal it from Trump. The pandemic, they quickly realized, was one of its tools. "What is the primary benefit to keep public in mass-hysteria re: Covid-19?" a Q follower tweeted. "Think voting. Are you awake yet?"[35]

If Q and his followers' posts nudged believers in a certain direction, the movement wasn't exactly led—it was emergent and participatory, like a massive multiplayer online game. Anyone was free to interpret Q's breadcrumbs as they liked. Q invited followers' contributions with asides like "keep your eye on the ball," "follow the money," "find the connections," and "keep digging and keep organizing the info into graphics (critical)." Doing just that, a schismatic sect of Q believers emerged who said that Q was none other than John F. Kennedy Jr., who had faked his death in 1999 so he could help Trump battle the Deep State. He had been photographed at a Trump rally, some said, disguised with a beard and glasses. In another widely distributed photo, the same bearded man could be seen outside a DoubleTree hotel. Clearly he was sending them a message: that he was JFK's body double.

More sober-minded observers suspect that Q was the brainchild of one or more trollers in search of lulz and money. Back in 2016, Jack Posobiec, a well-known publicist for the alt-right, had helped to popularize the so-called Pizzagate conspiracy, the internet rumor, based on "decryptions" of John Podesta's hacked emails, that Hillary Clinton and the global elites kept a harem of juvenile sex slaves in the basement dungeon of the popular Washington, D.C., pizzeria Comet Ping Pong (in real life, the restaurant doesn't have a basement—as Edgar Maddison Welch learned in December 2016, when he entered the restaurant brandishing an AR-15, intending to liberate the children). In 2018, fearing that QAnon was getting out of hand, Posobiec attempted to put the brakes on the movement by debunking it in a report for the far-right-wing One America News Network.[36]

Posobiec interviewed a white nationalist troll known as Microchip, who confessed that he and a partner with the username Dreamcatcher had written the first Q post to "get people thinking," basing it on "all kinds of crazy theories" they'd gleaned from Alex Jones's Infowars and other conspiracist sources (like, ahem, Posobiec's Pizzagate). They took the name Q from Luther Blissett's novel *Q*, published in Italy in 1999. Set during the Protestant Reformation, its eponymous antagonist was a papal agent who controlled world events from the shadows. Luther Blissett, as it happens, is not a real person but the pseudonym for a group of anarchistic "culture jammers" who, like the Yes Men in the United States, engineer media hoaxes to make political points. One of the hoaxes they promoted was a series of false stories about satanic ritual abuse. Seeing how sticky they were, Microchip and Dreamcatcher adapted them as well.[37]

Picking up on Posobiec's exposé, the equally right-wing *Federalist* critiqued the increasingly blatant attempts of some Q posters to "monetize" the movement. *The Federalist* article closed with a plea from Microchip:

QAnon is not going to save you . . . you gotta go out and vote, you gotta go out and do activism. You can't just sit at home and hope that these magical guys behind the scenes are going to magically save the USA because they're not there.[38]

I don't know what made Posobiec become so fastidious about internet hoaxes. My guess is that he was motivated in part by professional jealousy (Q was stealing a lot of his thunder), but also by the recognition that Q's claims were so extreme that they were undercutting rather than amplifying Republican propaganda. What I do know is that Posobiec and Microchip weren't the first trolls to find themselves in the role of the sorcerer's apprentice.

In the 1880s and '90s, a French writer who went by the pseudonym Leo Taxil published sensational exposés of the Palladists, a supposed cult of Satan-worshipping Freemasons. In 1897, at what turned out to be the last of the many press conferences he had called over the years to hype his bombshell revelations, Taxil stunned the room with a confession: all of those press conferences, all of the books and articles he'd written over the last decade and more had been lies, concocted out of whole cloth to embarrass the Catholic Church. His confession didn't matter; a century later, conspiracy theorists are still writing about Palladism as if it is a real thing. Microchip's confession didn't matter either. Despite Posobiec's, OAN's, and *The Federalist*'s efforts, QAnon continued to spread like wildfire, and not just in the United States, but in Germany, England, and Japan—seventy-one countries in all, according to one tally[39] (though by early 2021, the editor of Japan's *Mu*, a magazine that specializes in stories about aliens, the occult, and worldwide conspiracies, had written off QAnon as a flop, saying it was "too naïve for our readership").[40]

Along with its lurid accusations of politicians and celebrities, QAnon offered a vision of a better world to come that combined features of the heavenly kingdom of the premillennial dispensationalists with the redistributionist programs of classic populism. *The storm will be a global tsunami*, the Q devotee Praying Medic posted in November 2019. *Afterward, the world will become a place of "lavish abundance. . . . Trillions of dollars in wealth that* has been stolen and squandered by the elites [will be] returned to the people from whom it was stolen . . . [and] cures for diseases which have been hidden from us to enrich those who own drug companies" will be made available, along with advanced forms of free energy. "Many such advances have been hidden from us, and I suspect Trump will force many of them to be disclosed."[41]

A month before the 2020 election, Trump tweeted a terse message: "Tonight @FLOTUS and I tested positive for COVID-19. We will begin our quarantine and recovery process immediately. We will get through this TOGETHER." Q believers celebrated, because they understood he was going underground to avoid the fallout from the storm, which would happen any day. The proof was the word "together"—TO-GET-HER. Hillary was finally going to be arrested. As if that wasn't obvious enough, Q himself had dropped an image of a clock with its small hand pointing to 10 and its big hand pointing to 2 a few weeks before; 10/2 was the date of Trump's "diagnosis."[42]

Lara Logan, a former CBS News correspondent whom even Fox News and Newsmax now consider too extreme to put on camera, has clearly been influenced not just by replacement theory but by Q. In October 2022, she told an interviewer about the "global cabal" that is planning to bring "100 million illegal immigrants" to the United States to "dilute what they call the pool of patriots."[43] The "open border," she said, is "Satan's way of taking control of the world" while the elites "dine on the blood of children."[44]

Logan also told a podcaster that the Rothschilds and 10 Downing Street had paid Darwin to invent the theory of evolution.[45] Her comment revealed the influence, whether through direct reading or osmosis, of an infamous text that also lurks behind Q: *The Protocols of the Elders of Zion*—the Beethoven's Ninth of conspiracy theory.

In 1903, members of Czar Nicholas II's secret police stitched together purported transcriptions of secret meetings held by Jewish leaders in the Prague cemetery and published them in a Russian newspaper. Two years later, the material was reprinted as the appendix to the notorious anti-Semite and mystic Sergei Alexandrovich Nilus's book *Velikoe v Malom I Antikhrist Kak blizkaya Politicheskaya Vozmozhnost* (*The Great in the Small; or, The Advent of the Antichrist and the Approaching Rule of the Devil on Earth*). In it, the Jewish leaders discuss the progress of their plan to undermine the prosperity, morality, and ultimately the sovereignty of Christian nations via the power of international finance from above and revolutionary workers' movements from below.

Much like a supervillain in a James Bond movie, the Jews laid out their plot in lurid detail. By manipulating the money supply to make some countries more powerful than others, they ensured that Christian Europe would continue to bleed itself in endless wars; by promoting labor unions and compulsory education, they had raised the lower class's aspirations above its capabilities, guaranteeing the establishment of communist and socialist regimes that would inevitably collapse. Through their control of the sin industries and popular culture, they were weakening Europe's moral fiber. Once their work of destruction was finished, they would "erect on the ruins the throne of the King of the Jews," who will rule the world with an iron fist from Jerusalem. "The Goyim are a flock of sheep, and we are their wolves," their leader cackles. In a later edition of the *Protocols* published in 1914, he is explicitly identified as Theodor Herzl, the father of Zionism.

Scholars have since determined that most of the *Protocols* was cut and pasted from older sources, specifically Sir John Retcliffe's anti-Semitic novel *Biarritz* and Maurice Joly's satire of Napoleon III's regime, *The Dialogue in Hell Between Machiavelli and Montesquieu,* which did not even mention Jews. Much of the original material in its pages—for example, the uncanny prediction that a world war would soon break out—was introduced in the numerous new editions and translations that began to appear in the 1910s and '20s.

The *Protocols* were not uniquely paranoid. John Robison's *Proofs of a Conspiracy Against All the Religions and Governments of Europe* and Abbé Augustin Barruel's *Memoirs Illustrating the History of Jacobinism,* both published in 1797, laid the blame for the French Revolution and other troubles on Adam Weishaupt's short-lived Bavarian Illuminati (the group had been exposed and disbanded in 1785, four years before the revolution began). Those books were influenced in their turn by seventeenth-century attacks on the Jesuits and fourteenth-century attacks on the Knights Templar, who were accused of everything from usury and sedition to Satan worship, witchcraft, and ritual sodomy, much as the Phibionites had been. As Umberto Eco wrote of the *Protocols* in his novel *Foucault's Pendulum* (he would later write an entire novel about the *Protocols* called *The Prague Cemetery*), "It was, again, the Plan of the Jesuits and, before that, of the Ordonation of the Templars. Few variations, few changes: the Protocols were self-generating; a blueprint that migrated from one conspiracy to another."[46]

Pat Robertson, the late chancellor of Regent University and chairman of the Christian Broadcasting Network, ran for president in 1988 and published a book in 1991, *The New World Order,** that explicitly wedded End Times Protestantism to *Protocols of the Elders of Zion*–style conspiracism. In it we learn how the Rothschilds funded the Illuminati's takeover of the Freemasons to carry out the French Revolution. "The satanic carnage that the

---

* Due to an internal glitch, Amazon sometimes lists me as its coauthor, which I assuredly am not.

Illuminati brought to France," he wrote, "was the clear predecessor of the bloodbaths and successive party purges visited on the Soviet Union." Another rich Jew named Moses Hess helped Marx and Engels write *The Communist Manifesto,* Robertson claims. Other European bankers paid John Wilkes Booth to kill Lincoln because he'd printed paper money during the Civil War instead of taking out high-interest loans; later, the Jewish bankers Paul Warburg and Jacob Schiff came to the United States with the explicit aim of destroying it by forming "an American equivalent of the German Bundesbank or the Bank of England." The plan came to fruition in 1913, with the formation of the Federal Reserve system. After that came eighty years of unnecessary hot and cold warfare, fomented by bankers so they could lend money at interest to both sides. "The result was so profound and the excuse for war so flimsy," Robertson wrote—even World War II, apparently—"that casual observers would have reason to suspect that someone had planned the whole thing."[47]

Donald Trump summoned the *Protocols* in 2016 with his infamous tweet of a photograph of Hillary Clinton over a background of hundred-dollar bills. Next to her is a star of David, in which the words "Most Corrupt Candidate Ever!" are printed (Trump insisted on Twitter that it was just an innocent "Sheriff's Star, or plain star!").[48] He did it again in a TV commercial, run at the close of his campaign, that featured images of shuttered factories next to pictures of Jews like then–Federal Reserve chair Janet Yellen, Goldman Sachs CEO Lloyd Blankfein, and of course George Soros. In his voice-over, Trump described the "global power structure that is responsible for the economic decisions that have robbed our working class, stripped our country of its wealth and put that money into the pockets of a handful of large corporations and political entities."[49]

Jacob Anthony Chansley, aka Jake Angeli, aka the Q Shaman,

the bearded, bare-chested man with the horned helmet and red, white, and blue face paint who was photographed standing at the House Speaker's dais with his fist raised during the January 6 Capitol insurrection (and whose image appears on the cover of this book), told interviewers that he'd been drawn to QAnon because its views sounded so much like what he'd read in Milton William Cooper's *Behold a Pale Horse.* Cooper built his conspiracist classic on the foundation of the *Protocols,* which was reprinted at full length in its appendix.

QAnon believers mix and match material from the *Protocols,* its ur-sources, and its descendants to explain today's events. In a Facebook post in 2018, Marjorie Taylor Greene speculated that the Camp Fire, the deadliest wildfire in California's history, was not caused by fallen power lines, as investigators claimed, but by a space-based laser deployed by the Rothschild-connected company Solaren, which was using it to clear the right-of-way for a bullet-train project run by California senator Dianne Feinstein's businessman husband, Richard Blum. "I didn't even know and didn't find out until recently that the Rothschilds were Jewish," Greene protested disingenuously, when critics accused her of anti-Semitism. Doubters wondered why she had also shared videos in her Facebook account that accused "an unholy alliance of leftists, capitalists, and Zionist supremacists" of scheming "to promote immigration and miscegenation, with the deliberate aim of breeding us out of existence in our own homelands."[50]

Though absurd and monstrous on its face, the story that the *Protocols* tells was inspired by an undeniable truth: that the emerging new liberal order of the nineteenth century was indeed threatening to churches and kings—and not just to their prerogatives, but to their very existence, just as the broader acceptance of gay and trans people poses a challenge to heteronormativity in our own day, and Black people's demands for reparative justice could spell the end to the default privileges that white people in the United States have enjoyed since the reversal of Reconstruction in the late 1860s and 1870s. As bizarre as the paranoid conspiracy theories that the *Protocols* and QAnon traffic in may be, as hurtful and destructive of civility and civilization, they wouldn't be as convincing as they are to so many if the people who believe them weren't sincerely aggrieved, and if the kinds of horrible things that they accuse their objects of—from greed, corruption, cannibalism, and torture to pedophilia, rape, treason, mass murder, and Satan worship—weren't behaviors that really do exist.

Of course, Jews as a category don't ritually torture and murder Christian babies, but human babies of all varieties—including Jewish ones—have been horrifically abused. Is it altogether delusional to imagine, as QAnon's believers do, that the elites who rape children often escape justice, when we know that some very elite individuals have paid hardly any price for doing just that? Comet Ping Pong may not have had a sex dungeon, but Jeffrey Epstein certainly had a harem of underaged women and a circle of socially and politically connected friends, including billionaires and royalty. His story—everything from the mysterious sources of his wealth, to the slap on the wrist he received in 2008 after pleading guilty to procuring a child for prostitution, not to mention his odd connection to Trump's attorney general William Barr (whose father was the headmaster of the Dalton School when it hired Epstein as a math teacher in 1974), and his mysterious suicide in jail in 2019—could have leaped fully formed from the head of an anti-Semitic conspiracy theorist, like Athena from the head of Zeus, but it was all too real. Donald Trump's affectionate comments about Epstein in a 2002 *New York* magazine profile shed an ironic light on QAnon's cult worship of him as a champion of exploited children. "He's a lot of fun to be with," Trump said. "It is even said that he likes beautiful women as much as I do, and many of them are on the younger side."[51]

Ultimately, there are only so many bad things that people can do, and human beings have done all of them. In the heat of war or under the influence of a mob or a charismatic leader, even the steadiest-seeming people may commit atrocities. When they return to their senses, some assuage their consciences by claiming self-defense *(the enemy straps suicide vests onto children; we had to shoot them)* or military necessity *(that hospital we bombed was a command center; they were using its patients as human shields)*. Or they cling all the harder to the unbelievable and deny that anything bad was ever done *(those so-called atrocities are false flags, carried out with crisis actors)*. If there are too many rapes, too many dead babies to deny, they might insist that their enemies cold-bloodedly killed them themselves in order to generate outrage—or double down and say that there are no civilians in war zones, just enemies and friends, and that those dead babies got what they deserved (the phrase "nits make lice" has been traced all the way back to 1683).* The right doesn't hold a monopoly on this. In 1992, as towering a figure on the left as Noam Chomsky lent his credibility to efforts to diminish the magnitude of Serbian crimes against Bosnian Muslims, grossly mischaracterizing the

---

* It first appears in *An Impartial Collection of the Great Affairs of State from the Beginning of the Scotch Rebellion in the Year MDCXXXIX to the Murther of King Charles I*. Its author, John Nalson, quoted a relative, a captain in the English army, who described the atrocities that occurred. "No manner of Compassion or Discrimination was shewed either to Age or Sex," he said, "but that the little Children were promiscuously Sufferers with the Guilty, and that if any who had some grains of Compassion reprehended the Soldiers for this unchristian Inhumanity, they would scoffingly reply, Why? Nits will be Lice, and so would dispatch them."

Serbian Trnopolje camp, where inmates were routinely starved, tortured, raped, and murdered, as a refugee center that anyone was free to leave.[52]

Trump voters' feelings of dispossession are not that far off the mark either, as a host of not-so-fun facts about economic inequality make clear. While there are over twenty million millionaires in America, more than half the country (56 percent) can't even cover a thousand-dollar emergency expense.[53] A 2017 study found that the richest three Americans (none of them Jewish, as it happens) controlled more wealth than the bottom 50 percent.[54] The rich really have gotten richer. A 2022 Congressional Budget Office report found that the total real wealth held by the richest families in the United States tripled between 1989 and 2019 while average earners' gains were negligible.[55]

All of that said, it's important to remember that while conspiracy theories can and do travel from the bottom up, they are more typically propagated from the top down. Not all conspiracy theorists are as powerless and put-upon as they claim. Autocrats frequently secure their power via real-life conspiracies and then hold on to it by inflaming the public's fears of imaginary or real ones led by immigrants, would-be political reformers, or foreign states, much as abusive parents and cult leaders keep their victims in a state of constant fear and dependency. As Hannah Arendt famously observed in *The Origins of Totalitarianism,* terror can be used as "an instrument to rule masses of people who are perfectly obedient." A former member of the Peoples Temple recalled the White Nights at Jonestown, when Jim Jones would tell his followers that "our situation had become hopeless and that the only course of action open to us was a mass-suicide for the glory of socialism. We were told that we would be tortured by mercenaries—were we taken alive."[56]

A huge part of the reason that conspiracy theories work as well as they do as propaganda is because of their explanatory power. To be human is to be incessantly brought up against the limits of our understanding. To add to our frustration, some things that are opaque to us are transparent to others. The mystery of money, for example—how the same dollar can buy so much more or less depending on when and where and how it's spent, saved, or invested, and for that matter, why a piece of printed paper with a number on it is accorded the same value as a gold bar or a house or some other tangible thing. There are people among us who understand those things very well and use their knowledge to become rich and powerful. George Soros understands money and the art of leverage; Bill Gates understands computers and money, and if you weren't suspicious enough already, he's also taught himself a lot about epidemiology. The explanations that conspiracy theories provide are easy to understand and emotionally satisfying; in that way, they even the playing field. In the conservative columnist Richard Grenier's oft-quoted phrase, they are the "sophistication of the ignorant."

None of that is new, either. Conspiracy theories have always given people who feel weak and powerless a way to regain the upper hand. The rage for bimetalism* in the nineteenth century was driven by paranoid claims about the role that the Bank of England played in the passage of the Coinage Act of 1873, which demonetized silver. The cryptocurrency fad in our own day was similarly driven by fears about banks and governments. The idea that citizens can mine money from computer servers may sound "high-tech and futuristic," as Paul Krugman put it in his *New York Times* column in early 2022, when the crypto bubble was still

---

* The idea that the remonetization of silver would cause inflation, and hence ease farmers' debt burdens and reduce income inequality.

inflating, but it ultimately "[plays] to political paranoia" because its aim is a currency that is untainted by the likes of the Rothschilds, the Bank of London, or the U.S. Treasury.[57] The scandalous collapse of a cryptocurrency company like FTX doesn't make true believers more skeptical; it just adds grist to the conspiratorial mill. FTX's founder Sam Bankman-Fried is a Jew, after all.

Knowing why you are politically and financially weak (or thinking that you do) may not be enough to restore your strength, but it feels like a start. Many people would prefer to believe that COVID-19 was Chinese germ warfare, or an evil plan by Bill Gates and his wealthy friends to depopulate the world while injecting mind-control microchips into the survivors via dangerous vaccines, than accept that it was a horrible stroke of bad luck that caught many governments off guard, forcing them to choose between bad and worse alternatives.

The illusion of understanding that conspiracy theories confer is so powerful that conspiracists often embrace more than one. Studies have shown that a person who believes that 9/11 was an inside job is also more likely to believe that Princess Diana faked her own death, or that she was murdered. Some conspiracists even claim to believe theories that literally cancel each other out, for example, that Osama bin Laden is still alive and that he was already dead when U.S. Special Forces invaded his compound.[58] The solvent that dissolves the contradiction is the principle that the official explanation is always a lie.

Our brains are wired to seek patterns and distrust strangers for sound evolutionary reasons—*rustling sounds in the bushes = saber-toothed tiger; strangers = competition for scarce resources*—but those adaptations entail negative externalities. Sometimes we see patterns where they don't in fact exist and think the worst of people simply because we don't know them. Unscrupulous power seekers know how to turn those foibles to their advantage. Our only defense against them is our common sense, which is a very thin reed indeed.

As I wrote a long time ago, Socrates said that "the only true wisdom is knowing that you know nothing." Conspiracism is the delusion that you know everything. As such, it is a kind of theology, or more precisely still, a demonology.

2

The Paranoid Style and the Art of the Deal; or, What Do Trump and MAGA Really Believe?

The American historian Richard Hofstadter coined the phrase "the paranoid style in American politics" to evoke the "qualities of heated exaggeration, suspiciousness, and conspiratorial fantasy" that characterize a politics that is wholly based on "suspicious discontent."[1] The essay in which he introduced it was his valediction for the John Birch Society and other reactionary groups that had coalesced behind Barry Goldwater's bid for the presidency in 1964. Lyndon Johnson's crushing victory, Hofstadter believed, had finally sealed their doom. Nearly sixty years later, one can only wonder what he would have made of Trump and his MAGA nation.

In May 2021, the End Times minister and QAnon believer Bishop Larry Gaiters appeared on the podcast *Up Front in the Prophetic* and told its listeners that he had it from well-placed sources in the FBI that Joe Biden's son Beau did not die of brain cancer as the media reported. In truth, he was sacrificed to Satan to ensure his father's political rise—exactly as Biden's first wife and daughter were in 1972, when the public was falsely told they'd been killed in a car accident.[2] A month later, when Gaiters was a guest on the *Patriot Streetfighter* podcast, he informed its listeners that the QAnon movement "was born on the first of April in 1860, a year before the outbreak of the Civil War, by twenty-five northern generals . . . whose objective was to design a Christian-constitutional movement to protect the first Constitution of the United States." That noble effort was foiled by Ulysses Grant, who "was paid off not just by the Vatican order . . . but the Rothschild British arm of the Rothschild dynasty." Biden was also in the pocket of those organizations, Gaiters said, but what's even more important to understand is that he "was actually executed two years ago."[3]

The Second Constitution Gaiter implicitly referred to was secretly foisted on the American people by Masons and Jewish bankers in London and pedophile priests in the Vatican after they annexed Washington, D.C., to their hidden empire of city-states in 1871, according to an article I found at the website of the National Liberty Alliance, a sovereign citizens group.* As for Biden's execution, Gaiters explains that he, Tom Hanks, and the Clintons were all killed and replaced by clones. Trump, on the other hand, is alive and well and surrounded by loyal military officers at Mar-a-Lago. He has the nuclear codes and the use of Air Force One and is still the rightful president of the United States.

---

* Sovereign citizens believe, among other things, that the only legitimate level of government in the U.S. is the county, and that county sheriffs are the only legitimate law enforcement officers. By refusing to accept federal benefits or acknowledge federal law, they believe they regain their individual sovereignty. I would provide a link to the article, but it has disappeared from the website. I did find a variant of it posted on a Turkish news forum, however. Its first sentences are worth quoting, as they perfectly capture the tone and content of classic conspiracy theory: "Did the world wars, revolutions & big events of human history happen naturally or coincidentally, or were they calculated & pre-planned? If they were pre planned [*sic*], who planned them?" (https://www.turkishnews .com/en/content/2012/11/23/the-hidden-empire/)

Bizarre, libelous, and altogether delusional conspiracy theories like Gaiters's typically begin and end on the farthest fringes of the political spectrum; most of the time, they have exactly the same impact on mainstream policymaking that whispers about FDR being a secret Jew did in the 1930s; that Eisenhower was a "conscious, dedicated agent of the Communist conspiracy" did in the 1950s; or the rumors about the Clintons murdering their enemies did in the 1990s, which is to say, almost none at all. If you want to take the temperature of the right, we're typically told, you need to find out what conservative business leaders, military officers, elected officials, and opinion columnists are saying.

But as it turns out, many of those supposedly reputable people are saying the same kinds of things. Around the time that Gaiters was pontificating about Biden, Grant, the Rothschilds, and Tom Hanks, one hundred twenty-four retired generals and admirals were posting an open letter to the nation in which they warned that we were in "a fight for our survival as a Constitutional Republic like no other time since our founding in 1776." With the caveat that things were more unsettled during the Civil War era, one could hardly argue with the sentiment. Just months before, the president of the United States had refused to concede an election he'd clearly lost, cajoled state election officials to discard lawful Biden ballots and electors, encouraged his motley team of lawyers to file dozens of frivolous lawsuits in the hope that one of the judges he'd appointed would give one a sympathetic hearing, and when all of that failed, fomented a mob to attack the Capitol to stop Congress and Vice President Pence from certifying Biden's victory. But that's not what those generals and admirals were so worked up about. In fact, they believed that by receiving more popular and electoral votes than Trump, Biden had somehow subverted the people's will, and the FBI and Supreme Court had reneged on their duty to set things right. Now that Biden was illegally installed in the White House, they said, "our Country has taken a hard left turn toward Socialism and a Marxist form of tyrannical government."[4]

Marxist? Tyrannical? Joe Biden?

It wasn't just those generals. When a Fox interviewer asked U.S. senator Ron Johnson (R-Wisconsin) for a comment on the Biden administration's decision to stop the Keystone pipeline, he demurred, saying it would be impossible for him to get inside the mind of a "liberal, progressive, socialist, Marxist like President Biden."[5] On his syndicated radio show, in interviews, and in his book *American Marxism,* the former Reagan official Mark Levin also warned that "our institutions are under attack. Our children are now being brainwashed. This isn't the Red Scare or McCarthyism, this is American Marxism."[6]

A latter-day Rip van Winkle who'd slept through the past forty years would be dumbfounded. As a long-serving senator, Biden had been so assiduous about the care and feeding of Delaware's corporations that *National Review* dubbed him "the Senator from MBNA."[7] Biden launched his first presidential bid all the way back in 1987—the same year that Trump floated his first presidential trial balloon. Had things gone differently, the two might have campaigned against each other back then, before Twitter and Facebook were ever thought of, and fax machines and VCRs were still considered high-tech. Instead, Biden spent much of 1988 recovering from a humiliating plagiarism scandal and two brain aneurysms, while Trump had an affair with Marla Maples; bought a $30 million yacht from the arms dealer Adnan Khashoggi; borrowed hundreds of millions of dollars to purchase the Plaza Hotel, the Eastern Air-Shuttle, and the Taj Mahal casino; and launched a luxury helicopter service between New York and Atlantic City.

All of those ventures—including his marriage to Marla Maples—went south within a few years.

What I'm getting at here is that the idea that Biden is a Marxist is as absurd as the notion that Trump is a champion of right-thinking Americanism, whatever that is supposed to be—and everybody knows it, because both have been public personages for a very long time. I was in high school when Biden was first elected to the Senate and I am on Medicare now. Trump's celebrity has forced me to pay attention to him for decades, whether I wanted to or not. The zone has been so "flooded with shit," to paraphrase Steve Bannon, that it's hard to believe anything you read. But it's also important to recognize that none of this is new. Biden is not the first middle-of-the-road politician to be called a communist. And we have seen Trump's like before, though he has gone much further (and very likely sunk much lower) than any of his predecessors.

He wasn't the first celebrity to seek the White House, and he wasn't the first billionaire to style himself a champion of the white working class. He wasn't even the first to use the slogan "America First." The America First Committee, whose most famous spokesman was Charles Lindbergh, lobbied against FDR's efforts to arm the British against Nazi Germany. Trump didn't introduce mudslinging and fearmongering to presidential politics, either. They have played greater and lesser roles in elections going all the way back to 1796, when Jefferson and Adams partisans accused their opposites of being crypto-royalists, Jacobins, and hermaphrodites. John Quincy Adams would call Andrew Jackson a murderer in the 1820s. Jackson partisans fired back with the claim that Adams had been a pimp for the czar of Russia.

The term "the Deep State" may be a relatively new political buzz-phrase (at least in America and on the right), but people on both sides of the political spectrum have worried about the danger of a permanent unelected establishment for as long as this country has existed, whether its members were identified as elite Masons or slaveholders in the first half of the nineteenth century, Caroll Quigley's Round Table in the interwar years, or the "Dark Money" that finances the right and the well-heeled NGOs and foundations (George Soros's Open Society among them) that underwrite the center left today. Extreme ideas and movements have often risen to the fore during times of economic and social change, but with the significant exception of the Civil War, the fever typically broke as the immediate crisis passed. Slow-moving and filled with checks and balances and redundancies as it is, our constitutional system has historically defaulted to a consensual middle, just as its founders intended it to.

But no longer. As a presidential candidate, a president, an ex-president (or president-in-exile, as he all but styled himself), and then a presidential candidate for 2024, Trump has not only inspired conspiracy theories like QAnon but actively promoted them. As late as December 2022, he called for the "termination of all rules, regulations, and articles, even those found in the Constitution" to annul Biden's election and return himself to office. And he's carried millions of Americans along with him. In September 2021, the Chicago Project on Security and Threats found that forty-seven million American adults agreed with the statement that "the 2020 election was stolen from Donald Trump and Joe Biden is an illegitimate president." Twenty-one million agreed that "use of force is justified to restore Donald J. Trump to the presidency."[8]

Back in 1964, William F. Buckley urged Barry Goldwater to put as much light as he could between himself and the John Birch Society, because its founder Robert Welch's claim that Eisenhower was a communist agent was just too nutty. Donald Trump's Republican enablers have been more indulgent, because so many of Trump's strongest supporters are as louche, to use one of Buckley's favorite words, as he is. Candidate Trump not only sat for an interview with Alex Jones in 2015, Jones spoke at President Trump's Stop the Steal rally on January 6, 2021, which he helped to organize—the same Alex Jones who has talked about fantastical military "weather weapons" like steerable tornadoes, and who has repeatedly accused the government of poisoning reservoirs with chemicals that turn children gay in order to reduce the country's population,[9] not to mention faking 9/11 and the Boston Marathon bombing, and who has been ordered to pay nearly $1.5 billion to the families of Newtown victims he defamed as "crisis actors."

In July 2019, Trump hosted a White House summit on big tech's supposed conspiracy to exclude conservative voices from social media. Its participants included Bill Mitchell, an avid QAnon promoter; Tim Pool, who publicized the Seth Rich conspiracy;* James O'Keefe, the political dirty trickster whose Project Veritas ran "stings" against ACORN, Mary Landrieu, NPR, Hillary Clinton, and George Soros (O'Keefe has since been fired by the group's board for financial malfeasance); and a meme maker known as Carpe Donktum. The cartoonist Ben Garrison had been disinvited after the Anti-Defamation League

---

* Rich was a twenty-seven-year-old employee of the Democratic National Committee when he was murdered in the early morning hours of July 10, 2016. Three days later, the website WhatDoesItMean.com claimed he was killed by a hitman that the Clinton campaign hired after they learned he'd been providing information to WikiLeaks, a baseless rumor that the Russian Internet Research Agency retweeted more than two thousand times. Fox News ran and then retracted the story; in 2020 they settled Rich's parents' defamation lawsuit.

complained that his cartoon of George Soros pulling the strings of H. R. McMaster and David Petraeus puppets was anti-Semitic. "The crap you think of is unbelievable," Trump marveled in his opening remarks, adding, "You're very special people, you're very brilliant people, in so many cases."[10] It was high praise, from one professional bullshitter to others.

But like the proverbial stopped clock that is right twice a day, not everything they say is "crap." Hillary Clinton was widely derided in the 1990s when she spoke of a "vast right-wing conspiracy" to destroy her husband's presidency, but after twenty years and more of nonstop demonization, much of it funded by a few deep-pocketed individuals and families like Richard Mellon Scaife, John M. Olin, the Koch brothers, the Mercers, the DeVoses, and the Uihleins, her claim seems a little less fantastical. Trump made enemies in every corner of Washington, including in the clandestine services. Perhaps he really has been targeted by hidden forces. As the saying goes, just because you're paranoid, it doesn't mean someone isn't out to get you.

In her 2009 book *Real Enemies: Conspiracy Theories and American Democracy, World War I to 9/11,* the historian Kathryn Olmsted argued that the U.S. government has brought many of its credibility problems on itself, thanks to its documented record of secrecy, overreach, and excessive deference to wealth and corporate interests. When a government has proven itself to be as untrustworthy as ours has, when, rightly or wrongly, so many of its citizens believe it has betrayed them, it's hardly surprising that demagogues will step in to take advantage. Add to this the human foibles of racism and xenophobia and you have a set of rhetorical levers that can be pulled to produce reliable political effects.

That was the conclusion I reached in *The New Hate: A History of Fear and Loathing on the Populist Right,* the book I published in 2012 about the eerie sameness of conspiracy theories and hate movements throughout American history. In its closing paragraphs, I argued that the not-so-new hate of the Obama era was "at once the expression of a quixotic desire to turn back the clock to a mythical golden age when women and minorities and gays and foreigners were less troublesome than they are today . . . and a cynical ploy to up the turnout of Republican voters." Is that still the case in this Age of Trump and QAnon? Or have Republicans drunk their own Kool-Aid?

Many MAGAs clearly have—and some are well-placed to do serious harm. It's bad enough when an infomercial magnate like Mike Lindell, or a Dartmouth, Cambridge, and Stanford–educated entrepreneur like Patrick Byrne, the former CEO of Overstock.com, squander their dignity and their fortunes to push groundless claims about Biden and the Big Steal. But when Michael Flynn, the former general who was Trump's first national security advisor (and the brother of the current commander of the United States Army Pacific), was caught on tape telling a roomful of Republican faithful that a "Myanmar-style" military coup to remove Biden and restore Trump to power would be a good thing, it was more than a little chilling.[11]

Though Mark Milley, the chairman of the Joint Chiefs of Staff, made it clear that he would not allow troops to be deployed domestically on Trump's behalf[12] ("This is a Reichstag moment," he reportedly told aides on the eve of the January 6 riot),[13] a future president faced with electoral defeat (or Trump himself, should he return to office) may appoint a chairman whose politics are more in line with Flynn's.

Flynn wasn't even an outlier when it came to the Big Steal. After the Capitol building was cleared of rioters and Congress reconvened on the evening of January 6, 147 Republicans—many of them reelected by the same voters whose ballots they proposed to discard—voted not to certify Biden's victory. Americans may never take the peaceful transfer of presidential power for granted again.

How did Trump continue to dominate a party he had led to such ignominious defeats? Republicans lost the House of Representatives in 2018, and the Senate and the White House in 2020. Despite Biden's abysmal approval ratings and Trump's enthusiastic participation in the 2022 midterms, Republicans failed to regain the Senate and barely eked out a majority in Congress. Have Republicans been brainwashed?

There may be something to that. After Steven Hassan joined Sun Myung Moon's Unification Church as a college student in the 1970s, his parents arranged an intervention so he could be deprogrammed; later, he became a psychologist and an expert in thought control. Hassan defines a destructive cult as "an authoritarian pyramid-structured group with someone at the top who claims to know all things and says God is working through him or her" and cult membership as the adoption of a "false self." In his book *The Cult of Trump,* he argues that Trump fits the profile of an abusive cult leader to a T. "Thinking in a cult does not depend on independent verifiable data," Hassan explains. "Information about the world—empirical reality—goes through a filtering system where the default is to support the cult identity and the cult leader and what they tell you to believe."[14]

Something like that seems to be happening with Trumpism. The Big Steal is not just a shibboleth that confirms one's membership in the movement but is increasingly its sole reason for being. Loyalty is all. The GOP didn't even bother to draft a platform for the 2020 election, except to say that it "enthusiastically support[s] the president's America-first agenda."[15] After Trump was indicted in Manhattan for falsifying business records to hide his hush money payoff to the porn star Stormy Daniels in the spring of 2023, most of his presumed rivals for the 2024 Republican nomination lined up to support him. They did the same thing when his two federal indictments were announced, and when he was charged with racketeering in Atlanta.

Some Trump followers are so besotted by Trump's and their own claims of righteous victimization that they lay claim to the same moral high ground that martyrs from the Holocaust and the civil rights movement are now seen to occupy, donning yellow stars to protest vaccine mandates and complaining about the racial discrimination they suffer as white people. The lack of taste may be outrageous, but the hypocrisy is familiar. Nearly sixty years ago, in his infamous "Segregation Now and Forever" speech, George Wallace compared the mandated integration of Alabama schools to the extermination of German Jewry. "As the national racism of Hitler's Germany persecuted a national minority," he said with a poker face, "so the international racism of the liberals seeks to persecute the international white minority to the whim of the international colored majority."[16]

Charles Koch, a lavish funder of right-wing candidates, causes, and strategies over the decades, including racial gerrymandering, has also put himself in the company of civil rights leaders like Martin Luther King Jr., Frederick Douglass, and Susan B. Anthony. "We, too," he told a conservative group in 2015, "are seeking to right injustices that are holding our country back."[17] Josh Mandel, a failed Republican candidate for the Ohio Senate in 2022, went so far as to film a campaign ad on the Edmund Pettus Bridge in Selma, Alabama, claiming that Martin Luther King Jr. would have joined him in his fight against critical race theory.

———

Critical race theory, or CRT, is an academic framework that Kimberlé Williams Crenshaw, a law professor at Columbia and UCLA, and Derrick Bell of Harvard Law School developed in the 1980s to understand the ways that racial biases are institutionalized and perpetuated. Republicans see it as a cruel libel on white people and believe that elementary school teachers are using it to demonize innocent white children, forcing them to bear the burden of guilt for ancient wrongs they had nothing to do with. Senator Ted Cruz declared that it is "every bit as racist as the klansmen in white sheets."[18] Trump agrees. "Critical race theory," he said, "is a Marxist doctrine that rejects the vision of Martin Luther King Jr."[19]

Back in the 1960s, Charles Manson had the twisted idea of murdering innocent people and putting the blame on Blacks to foment an apocalyptic race war. The former Fox News star Tucker Carlson devoted a lot of airtime to the proposition that the war had already begun. In 2021, he pointed to the concept of "white rage," a phrase coined by Emory University professor Carol Anderson to describe the ongoing backlash to civil rights advances.[20] Carlson framed it as another libel against white people that had been concocted out of thin air by angry Black racists. As a picture of a red, white, and blue Democratic donkey flashed on the screen over the words "Anti-White Mania," he posed the questions that, he said, Americans "should be meditating on, day in and day out . . . how do we get out of this vortex, this cycle, before it's too late? How do we save this country before we become Rwanda?"[21]

If you think it's ridiculous that Carlson had anything like a literal bloodletting in mind, the same day he delivered his monologue, Pearson Sharp, a host on the conservative news network OAN, mused that hundreds, thousands, and tens of thousands of American citizens must have conspired to overthrow Trump's presidency. "Any American involved in these efforts—from those who ran the voting machines, to the very highest government officials—is guilty of treason under U.S. Code 2381, which carries with it the penalty of death," he said.[22] Someone was certainly thinking about mass killings.

Whether conscious or unconscious, cynical or sincere, it's classic projection. These MAGA Republicans are inoculating themselves against accusations of racism and election rigging by accusing their adversaries of believing and doing what they seem to believe and do themselves. The rhetorical jujitsu is as distracting as a three-card monte player's patter. And at the end of the day, could that be what lies at the heart of Trumpism? Is it all a big con to extract money from guileless rubes?

It wouldn't be the first time that right-wing populism and blatant hucksterism came together. Consider the second incarnation of the Ku Klux Klan a century ago, which enlisted millions of Americans under the banner of anti-Black, anti-Jewish, anti-Catholic one-hundred-percent Americanism. At its root, the Klan of the late 1910s and 1920s was a multilevel marketing scheme. Its founder, William J. Simmons, and his lieutenants raked in a fortune from sales of Klan regalia, books, and other licensed merchandise, while its members pocketed commissions for all the new dues-paying members they were able to sign up.

As the American historian Rick Perlstein once noted, "Who better suits a marketing strategy than a group that voluntarily organizes itself according to their most passionately shared beliefs?" Stories about Planned Parenthood selling babies' corpses and public-school teachers indoctrinating their students with atheism and critical race theory may not be true, but they can be relied on to raise a lot of money. Build a database of people whose likes and dislikes and fears and resentments are well-known to you, and you can sell them just what they think they need: the miracle cures their doctors and Big Pharma don't want them to know about; gold futures, because the Fed and its fiat money can't be trusted; survival gear and guns and ammo because liberals want to disarm them and leave them vulnerable to the urban gangs that are making inroads into the suburbs.[23]

"It's quite possible to argue that the radical right isn't a political movement financed by quack medicine; it's a political movement *created* to sell quack medicine," Paul Krugman once tweeted.[24] MAGA-supporting doctors like Simone Gold, the founder of America's Frontline Doctors (AFLD), made serious money selling alternative COVID cures. Alex Jones sold his followers products like Superblue toothpaste, "which kills the whole SARS-corona family at point-blank range," and "Super Male Vitality" drops. Steve Bannon, Trump's campaign manager and erstwhile chief strategist, was indicted for diverting $1 million that Trump loyalists donated to We Build the Wall, the ostensibly nonprofit effort to complete Trump's border wall, into his own pockets (and received an unconditional pardon from Trump).

Like cult leaders do with their followers, Trump sells himself to voters as the cure for the country's problems ("I alone can fix it")—and he does so in exactly the same way that a patent medicine huckster sells his elixirs. This shouldn't come as a surprise, as he had already leveraged the Trump brand to sell everything from luxury condos and hotel rooms to greens fees and books, not to mention seats on the Trump Shuttle, mail-order steaks, vodka, business seminars, and TV commercials on *The Apprentice*. Why not the restoration of American greatness too?

Trump's political fundraising never stops; his reelection campaign raked in a quarter of a billion dollars in the first few weeks *after* Election Day—and thanks to pre-checked boxes buried in the fine print, many of his donors' contributions were doubled, tripled, and quadrupled when their credit cards were billed on a monthly basis thereafter. Mar-a-Lago is a private club that his supporters (not to mention favor-seeking businessmen and foreign governments) pay hundreds of thousands of dollars a year to join. But while greed explains a lot, it can't account for everything. Let us not forget that P. T. Barnum, the nineteenth-century master of hype, was a devout Universalist—even he believed in something. At the end of the day, you'd have to be a conspiracy theorist yourself to think that Trump's paranoid style is solely animated by money.

So, what does he really believe? His "only fundamental belief," wrote Adam Serwer in a powerful and much-quoted *Atlantic* essay, is that white men like him should be in charge, and that immigrants, Blacks, feminists, and their traitorous white male allies are stealing white men's birthrights. "His only real, authentic pleasure," Serwer concluded, "is in cruelty."[25]

Trump's white male voters' intuition that their fathers had a better deal than they do is more or less correct, even if the privileges they were born to were utterly undeserved and unjustifiable and MAGA's prescriptions to re-jigger the fix in their favor could not be more dangerous. When a wage earner defaults on a student loan that paid for a worthless certification from a politically connected vocational school, their credit is ruined and they are financially crippled, potentially for the rest of their lives. When a billionaire like Donald Trump defaults on the debts of his public companies, wiping out their shareholders, lenders line up to give him more. The fact that so many economic left-behinds look to Trump as their champion may be perplexing, but no one can doubt that they need one.

Obamacare didn't institute death panels—quite the opposite—but is it altogether crazy to believe the American healthcare system was designed to extract huge sums from the very people who can afford them the least, while delivering suboptimal results? According to a 2019 analysis by the Commonwealth Fund, the United States spent nearly twice as much on healthcare as a share of its economy than any of the other ten richest countries in the Organization for Economic Cooperation and Development. Even so, it had the lowest life expectancy and its chronic disease burden was the highest of all thirty-seven member countries.[26] A follow-up study in 2022 found that the United States has the lowest life expectancy at birth, the highest death rates for avoidable or treatable conditions, the highest maternal and infant mortality rates, and the third-highest suicide rate (after South Korea and Japan).[27]

What's mysterious about populist conspiracy theories is not that they exist; the world we live in is rife with injustices. What's baffling is why the anger those injustices inspire is so often misdirected—and why people who claim to be as vigilant as they are for their rights and liberties cede them so readily to self-serving authoritarians.

But Trumpism isn't about facts or even ideas; it's about feelings. And those feelings are older than Trump or Biden. To get at the roots of America's paranoid style, you have to go all the way back to colonial times. As skeptical as I am of global explanations for complex phenomena, I've come to see that paranoia as the other side of the coin that is the American dream of spiritual and material prosperity and grace.

Most of the white, English-speaking colonists who peopled the New World in the century and a half before the American Revolution were economic refugees and religious pioneers. Most were Protestants, who regarded the Catholic Church and the

Catholic countries as their bitter enemies. The Thirty Years' War, which embroiled Europe between 1618 and 1648, when America began to be colonized in earnest, killed as many as eight million people—60 percent of the population in some parts of Germany. Feudal power structures that had stood for centuries crumbled. By the turn of the eighteenth century, England had changed its state religion multiple times while enduring two full-blown revolutions and a regicide. All of those traumas left their impressions on the American psyche.

So did Protestant doctrine. Justification by faith alone puts a tremendous burden on a believer, especially when it's combined with Puritanism's bleak doctrine of predestination, the belief that no matter how hard you might try to change it, your fate has been sealed since before your birth—and that the success or failure you experience in your life likely foreshadows your eternal destiny. Early Protestants' journals and memoirs are filled with their struggles with faith. *Lord, I believe; help thou mine unbelief.* Catholicism has intercessory rituals, sacraments, saints, and the Virgin Mother that believers can turn to for succor in their moments of weakness and doubt, and the prospect of purgatory if they still don't qualify for heaven. Some of the Puritans' hatred of Catholicism, I suspect, was inspired by a guilty longing for its mercies.

Their anxieties weren't just spiritual. Thanks to the writings of colonial boosters, among them Benjamin Franklin, the myth that poverty was unknown in the New World was widely disseminated. Given the cheapness of land, it was said, any white-skinned immigrant with an ounce of gumption could expect to prosper within a generation. The idea that anyone could own land must have been mind-boggling to seventeenth- and eighteenth-century Europeans, who thought of land ownership as a prerogative of the aristocracy. But subject as the colonists were to the whims of nature and the volatility of markets, the uneven distribution of physical, mental, and material advantages, the perils of credit and the instability of so many of the banks that provided it, not a few of those new land owners struggled and failed. Naturally, they looked for others to blame.

During the second half of the nineteenth century, when the rich were enjoying a Gilded Age but most of the rest of the country was mired in a decades-long depression, Horatio Alger's rags to riches novels, like *Luck and Pluck* and *Ragged Dick,* promoted the myth that hard work and mentorship from a wealthy sponsor—especially one with a marriageable daughter and a fondness for enterprising young lads—provided a sure route to social mobility. Alger, strangely enough, broke into the motivational-book-writing business after he was driven from the ministry for molesting two teenage boys in his Cape Cod parish.[28] Given their horror of pedophilia, you'd think that twenty-first-century Republicans would deplore him as a "groomer," but the myth of bootstrapping lives on.

But what if you do everything you're supposed to and you still don't succeed? White Republicans have no patience for Black people's narratives of victimization—they should just work harder, as Black Republican Horatio Alger Award recipients like Ben Carson, Clarence Thomas, Condoleezza Rice, and Herschel Walker all did. But growing numbers of white Republicans blame their own struggles on affirmative action and anti-white racism. A 2021 poll asked Trump and Biden voters whether they worried that "discrimination against whites will increase significantly in the next few years." Eighty-four percent of Trump voters strongly or somewhat agreed, while only 38 percent of Biden voters did. Ninety-one percent of Biden voters believed that systemic racism is an issue in America, while only 45 percent of Trump voters did. [29]

Like Calvinism, like capitalism, diverse, liberal, small "r" republicanism does not come naturally to most people. Deep down, many Americans in colonial times and many Americans today yearn for the certainties that a heavenly anointed monarch and a universal church provide. Knowing exactly what you must do to be redeemed relieves you of the burdens of introspection and conscience. Being given permission to hate relieves you of the burden of loving your neighbor as yourself, even if he or she is an economic rival. Look closely at the tyrannical New World Order of the conspiracists' nightmares and you'll see a funhouse reflection of the Old World Order that so many of them guiltily pine for—a world without freedom, but also without ambiguity or doubt or mystery.

In chapters to come, I will have more to say about the Protestant/capitalist origins of America's paranoid style, but first, there is more to discover about the political epoch we are living through, which began with Reagan's Morning in America and culminated in MAGA.

3

Through the Looking Glass

I first began to explore the world of conspiracy theory in a systematic way in the mid-aughts when I was researching my book *Cults, Conspiracies, and Secret Societies.* I felt like I had stumbled into an alternate reality. The elementary school I'd attended in the 1960s was a block away from a Masonic lodge, which stood between a candle store and an insurance agency. Suddenly, I had entered a world in which the plumbers, policemen, and traffic court judges I'd seen in its parking lot were sinister actors in league with international Jewish money interests and the globalists at the UN.

As I've written elsewhere, to understand paranoid America without getting swallowed up by it, you have to pick apart the "strands of facticity and factitiousness, of known truths, myths, misunderstandings, and outright lies from which [its] ideologies and doctrines are woven." Documented facts about secret societies like the Knights Templar, the Illuminati, the Knights of Malta, the Ku Klux Klan, and the Masons often stand in sharp contrast to the fanciful and sometimes frightening myths about them that crop up again and again in conspiracist literature. More important still, you have to sift real-life conspiracies from conspiracy theories.

As weird and disturbing and sometimes risible as those conspiracy theories may be, many reflect a healthy skepticism about
the quasi-historical morality tales that most of us were spoon-fed
as children in school. But they go too far in the other direction.
As simplistic as it is to believe that our founding fathers were all
heroes, it's just as specious to assume they were all unalloyed monsters, or more typically, the pawns of other even more powerful
monsters who preferred to lurk in the shadows. The truth is usually somewhere in between.

A few (a very few) conspiracy theorists have been vindicated as
their far-out ideas gained broader acceptance. Commander Edwin
Jenyss Quinby, an avid trolley buff, was dismissed as a crank in
1946 when he wrote and published a pamphlet about "a carefully,
deliberately planned campaign to swindle you out of your most
Important and valuable public utilities—your Electric Railway
system." But it was true. General Motors and a consortium of
other large companies, including Firestone Tire and Rubber, Mack
Manufacturing, and Phillips Petroleum, had been using holding
companies to buy up streetcar companies, tearing up their tracks,
and then locking cities into long-term contracts for buses, spare
parts, and fuel.[1] The second attack in the Gulf of Tonkin did not
happen. The U.S. government did, in fact, carry out experiments
with mind control.

My earliest encounters with fringe thinking were in the mass
market paperbacks about flying saucers and the Bermuda Triangle
I read when I was a teenager in the early 1970s. I watched Erich
von Däniken's *Chariots of the Gods* on TV (which purported to
prove that the Incas and other ancient peoples had been visited by
aliens) and listened to Alex Bennett's conversations with oddball
counterculture types on my transistor radio when I was supposed
to be asleep.

When I was in college, I'd get stoned sometimes and watch Tom Snyder's interviews with proponents of pyramid power and the like on his late-night TV show. I didn't exactly believe them, but some of their claims tickled my fancy and even expanded my thinking. Later still, as a graduate student in literature, and then an editor in commercial book publishing, I came upon Thomas Pynchon's novel *The Crying of Lot 49*, with its secret society of mail carriers, and Robert Anton Wilson's Discordian classic the Illuminatus! trilogy. Don DeLillo's *Libra* is a novel too, but its description of a collision between a false flag and a real assassination plot on November 22, 1963, struck me as a more convincing explanation for what happened in Dallas that day than the Warren Commission's.

But when I at long last turned to the primary literature of conspiracism as a middle-aged writer, it was a lot duller and a lot less anodyne than I'd expected. Nesta Webster, Eustace Mullins, Robert Welch, John A. Stormer, and Lyndon LaRouche, to name just a few representative authors, wrote books that were utterly lacking in the comic-book verve of airport novels like *The Da Vinci Code* or TV's *The X-Files*, never mind the literary craft, Dadaist audacity, and psychological depth that Wilson, Pynchon, and DeLillo brought to the subject. Their endless elucubrations about the New World Order, the Federal Reserve, the Council on Foreign Relations, the UN, the English royal family, and the specter of Luciferian One World government were clearly cut and pasted from a host of earlier books and from one another. Most were crammed to the brim with Red-baiting, anti-Semitism, and gutter racism.

Much the same thing could be said of the smaller number of left-leaning conspiracists. As surely as a voyager who ventures far enough west ends up in the east, political polarities tend to meet at the extremes (a phenomenon that has been dubbed "horseshoe theory"); some writers, like Lyndon LaRouche, migrated over the course of their careers from one end of the political spectrum to the other. That said, my biggest takeaway from my immersion in this world was how very far right the far right turns out to be. I'd thought trickle-down economics, the Kirkpatrick Doctrine, and a tacit tolerance for de facto segregation defined the outermost bounds of modern conservatism. Reading tracts about the "Jew World Order," ZOG (America's Zionist Occupied Government) and its exterminationist designs against white Christians was a chilling experience for me. It was as if I'd opened a Pandora's box of antidemocratic, anti-Semitic, misogynist, white supremacist, and theocratic thinking.

As I became more familiar with the style and contents of conspiracism, I began to hear echoes of it in the outrageous pronouncements of some putatively mainstream politicians like Newt Gingrich, Helen Chenoweth, and Steve King. I also began to see that many of the things the right condemned the left for—wanting to suspend the Constitution, say, unleash an Orwellian thought police on the citizenry, or interfere with families' child-rearing decisions—were things it aspired to do itself, or was already doing.

Before I began my research, I'd presumed that McCarthyism was a phase the country had passed through in the 1950s. The more I learned about America's long history of conspiratorial thinking, the more I realized that McCarthyism was a much older phenomenon, and that it was still going strong. Just as Joe McCarthy claimed to have a list of communists who worked in the State Department, all the way back in 1799 a Massachusetts clergyman named Jedidiah Morse (the father of Samuel Morse) said he had "an official, authenticated list of the names, ages, places of nativity, professions, &c. of the officers and members of a Society of *Illuminati*" in Virginia, and evidence of at least fifteen other cells elsewhere, that were working hand in glove with Thomas Jefferson and the Democratic-Republicans to spread "infidelity, impiety, and immorality" throughout the land.[2] The Illuminati had been a real organization, and Adam Weishaupt, its founder, was a firebrand who hated churches and kings. He was still alive in 1799 (he lived until 1830). But his group had no presence in the United States; it had been discovered and disbanded by the Bavarian government in 1785, just nine years after its founding.

I also came to see how many of the attributes of authoritarian political leadership and cult leadership overlap. As noted in the last chapter, cult leaders and dictators both use programs of cognitive isolation and violence to keep their followers in a state of fearful dependency (cult leaders literally separate recruits from friends and family and force-feed them a diet of lies about their evil intents; dictators control the media so they can amplify a similar message about their enemies).

That enemy, as Richard Hofstadter put it in *The Paranoid Style in American Politics,* is described as "a perfect model of malice, a kind of amoral superman—sinister, ubiquitous, powerful, cruel, sensual, luxury-loving. . . . He makes crises, starts runs on banks, causes depressions, manufactures disasters, and then enjoys and profits from the misery he has produced. . . . He controls the press; he directs the public mind through 'managed news'; he has unlimited funds; he has a new secret for influencing the mind (brainwashing)."[3] He is not just satanic; to many believers, he *is* Satan.

As I read and wrote, I also came to see how many of the historical themes of conspiracy theory had quietly infiltrated the rhetoric and substance of mainstream politics, at times sparking full-blown thought contagions, much as real-life pandemics are set off when a virus "jumps" from one species to another. Eventually, I came to see that I was living through just such a moment myself. Some of the things that catalyzed it were Republicans' adoption of the "Southern Strategy"; the revival of Evangelicalism as a political force; and Newt Gingrich's rise to the House speakership, which he used as a platform to inculcate a new generation of politicians in the use of eliminationist rhetoric. Another seminal event was the fall of the Soviet Union, which temporarily eliminated the need for national solidarity around a common threat.

For decades, Americans had lived under the shadow of an imminent nuclear apocalypse. After the USSR collapsed in 1991, those doomsday fears persisted, but in different forms. Absent the anti-Soviet consensus, the Republican Party was free to fully embrace the revanchist spirit that had buoyed Reagan, ratcheted up to new levels during the Clinton and Obama administrations, and culminated in Trump's presidency and post-presidency.

In a 1989 paper for the University of Chicago Legal Forum, Kimberlé Williams Crenshaw, whose name has already come up in these pages in the context of critical race theory, coined the term "intersectionality" to describe how racism and sexism add up to more than the sum of their parts in the experience of Black women.[4] The more I learned about the world of right-wing conspiracism, the more I began to think of it as a kind of intersectionality in reverse, which united congeries of outsider movements that had little else in common in a shared sense of righteous victimhood that also added up to more than the sum of its parts.

There were survivalists who stockpiled guns and grew their own food to prepare for the coming Hobbesian war of all against all; patriotic militiamen who were avid to water the tree of liberty with other people's blood; Bible-believing fundamentalists who saw Satan as a real and present threat; old-school segregationists; and homophobes who were certain that public-school teachers and Hollywood entertainment executives were not just teaching young people to tolerate same-sex relationships but recruiting them into the lifestyle. There were *Protocols of the Elders of Zion*–style anti-Semites, and Islamophobes, many of them Jewish, who were issuing warnings about the supposed infiltration of sharia law into American institutions, much as Jew haters had raised the alarm about the dangers of so-called Talmudism in the 1920s and '30s.

Republicans opened their arms to all of them. Since the passage of the Civil Rights Act in 1964, the party had been actively recruiting disgruntled southern Democrats, many of them evangelicals. Kevin Phillips explained the party's so-called Southern Strategy to *The New York Times* in 1970: "The more Negroes who register as Democrats in the South, the sooner the Negrophobe whites will quit the Democrats and become Republicans. That's where the votes are."[5]

Pandering to white grievances hadn't exactly been a stretch for Nixon, whose casual racism and anti-Semitism were captured on his Oval Office tapes. In a telephone conversation between him and then–California governor Ronald Reagan in October 1971, he can be heard chortling as Reagan complained about the African UN delegates who voted to recognize the People's Republic of China. "Those monkeys from those African countries—damn them, they're still uncomfortable wearing shoes," Reagan quipped.[6]

Evangelicals had mostly stayed out of American politics as an organized bloc since the Scopes Trial in the 1920s, in which creationism was ridiculed on the national stage. But that began to change after 1954, when the Supreme Court handed down its decision in *Brown v. Board of Education,* which mandated the desegregation of public schools. The televangelist and anti-integration activist Jerry Falwell founded the Lynchburg Christian Academy as a "private school for white students," and also Liberty University, one of the world's largest Christian academic institutions. After the Supreme Court's *Roe v. Wade* decision in 1973, conservative Catholics and evangelical Christians forged alliances that would have been unthinkable just a few years before. In 1979, Falwell and Paul Weyrich launched the Moral Majority, an interfaith federation of groups that campaigned against the Equal Rights Amendment, gay rights, and abortion, and for the restoration of Christian prayer in public schools.

In 1980, shortly after he accepted the Republican nomination for president, Ronald Reagan delivered a speech at the Neshoba County Fair near Philadelphia, Mississippi, where three civil rights workers had been murdered in 1964. The geographic symbolism spoke volumes, and the speech included dog whistles for its "Negrophobe" listeners as well, as it pledged to "restore to the states and local communities those functions which properly belong there."[7]

Newt Gingrich was elected to the House in 1978, the first-ever Republican to represent his district. Over the next decade, he ratcheted up the party's revanchist energies, proclaiming himself to be "the most serious, systematic revolutionary of modern times."[8] In 1990, he prepared a pamphlet called "Language: A Key Mechanism of Control,"[9] which helped systematize both the theory and praxis of his revolution—and not incidentally, turned up the rhetorical heat. It listed "Optimistic Positive Governing words" for Republican candidates to use about themselves and their policies, like "family," "freedom," "truth," "liberty," "legacy," "light," "peace," and "common sense," and contrasting words to describe their Democratic opponents, such as "pathetic," "sick," "bizarre," "betray," "corruption," "intolerant," "status quo," "steal," "permissive," "taxes," "unionized," and "traitors."

More and more, Republicans were characterizing themselves as the champions of a "real America" that is white, Christian, and beleaguered, and their opponents as something altogether other and beyond the pale. Pat Buchanan's speech at the 1992 Republican convention was literally a call to arms: "There is a religious war going on in this country. It is a cultural war, as critical to the kind of nation we shall be as was the Cold War itself, for this war is for the soul of America."[10] Right-wing talk radio reinforced the message: the internal enemy was not just disloyal but sick, perverted, and altogether alien. In fact, it was satanic.

The Exorcist had given me nightmares when I read it in high school, but I hadn't believed its central premise for a moment, which is that demons, imps, and Beelzebub himself are loose in the world. It wasn't until I was writing my book that I understood how many Americans regard the Devil in much the same light that their Puritan forefathers did, or going back even farther, the medieval Catholics who wrote *The Malleus Maleficarum** — as an imminent threat, who is as non-metaphorically present in daily life as he is in global tribulations like wars, famines, and plagues. You could see this vividly in the evangelical comic books Jack Chick published in the 1970s, which purported to reveal the hand of Satan in rock 'n' roll, or the frantic warnings about the spiritual dangers of Ouija boards and Halloween costumes that sometimes spilled out of Christian publications and into the pages of mainstream magazines and newspapers.

None of this was secret; I just hadn't been paying attention. My parents weren't believers themselves, but they'd joined a Reform temple and enrolled my sister and me in its religious school so we'd know who we are (or as I later came to understand it, so we'd

---

* *The Hammer of Witches,* written by Heinrich Kramer in 1486 and published in 1487, the basic handbook on how to identify, prosecute, and kill witches.

understand why so many members of our extended family had
been murdered in Europe, and why not a few of the conspiracy
theorists I would grow up to read and write about either deny that
the Holocaust happened or believe that the Jews brought it on
themselves—or, not uncommonly, both).

But if suburban Reform Jewish kids are raised to believe in
the concepts of good and evil, they don't typically personify them
(with the obvious exceptions of Haman and Hitler). Backward
Jews in the shtetels might have believed in *dybbuks* or demons
but assimilated modern Jews in America only encounter them in
folktales.

I'd noticed the spate of sensational news stories in the 1980s
about the McMartin family in Manhattan Beach, California, and
the Kellers in Oak Hill, Texas, day-care-center operators who'd
been arrested and prosecuted for carrying out sadistic sex rituals with the children in their care. I'd read a lot about Margaret
Kelly Michaels too, a former kindergarten teacher in Maplewood,
New Jersey, who had been tried, convicted, and imprisoned for
child abuse, even though the testimony that condemned her was
as spectral as anything heard in Salem, Massachusetts, in the seventeenth century, and there was a complete lack of forensic evidence to back it up. (The McMartins were acquitted of all charges;
the Kellers were convicted but exonerated after spending twenty-
one years in prison; Michaels' conviction was reversed in 1994
after she'd served seven years of her forty-seven-year sentence.)
But much as a conspiracy theorist might say, I hadn't connected
the dots.

Now that I was writing *Cults, Conspiracies, and Secret Societies*, I
learned that the so-called Satanic Panic had been triggered in part
by *Michelle Remembers*, a best-selling book that was published
in 1980 by a Canadian psychiatrist named Lawrence Pazder and

his wife and former patient Michelle Smith, which purported to document the abuse Smith had suffered when her mother joined a satanic cult. Pazder and Smith not only made numerous television appearances, they ran seminars and workshops for law enforcement officials and mental health professionals and testified as expert witnesses for the prosecution in satanic abuse trials, including the McMartin preschool case.

Millions of evangelicals not only believed that Satan and his minions were terrorizing and abusing preschool children, they were seeing the events foretold in the Book of Revelation playing out on the nightly news. The birthmark on Gorbachev's scalp was the mark of the beast; the Chernobyl meltdown was Wormwood. Saddam Hussein was Apollyon the Destroyer.

Starting in 1995, the best-selling Left Behind series by Tim LaHaye and Jerry B. Jenkins chronicled the adventures of a band of Christian believers during the coming tribulations. The secretary-general of the UN is revealed to be the Antichrist; another villain in the series is the pope, who becomes Pontifex Maximus of the Enigma Babylon One World Faith. But it wasn't just fundamentalist Christians who were pushing globalist conspiracies. The publishing industry had something for every paranoid taste. There were David Icke's tales about the Draco-reptilian conspiracy, in which inter-stellar reptiles disguised as humans, the British royal family and the Bushes among them, play the same role that the Jews did in the *Protocols*. There were equally paranoid (but mostly apolitical) stories about alien rapists in best-selling books like Whitley Strieber's *Communion* and Budd Hopkins's *Missing Time* and *Intruders*. Peering down one rabbit hole after another, I began to discern the "improvisational millennialism" that the political scientist Michael Barkun identified in his book *A Culture of Conspiracy*—a syncretic apocalypticism that mixes and matches all kinds of "stigmatized knowledge" from religious, political, occult, and pseudoscientific sources.[11]

When Bill Clinton was elected in 1992, the anger that had been simmering beneath the surface boiled over. A little over a month after his inauguration, the ATF raided the compound of the Branch Davidians in Waco, Texas, to search for illegal firearms. A splinter of a splinter of Seventh-Day Adventism, the Davidians were led by thirty-four-year-old Vernon Wayne Howell, who had changed his name to David Koresh and declared himself the Messiah. During a two-hour-plus gun battle, four ATF agents and six Davidians died. After a fifty-one-day standoff, the FBI fired tear gas into the compound and attacked it with armored vehicles. The wooden buildings caught fire and at least seventy-six Davidians died, including more than twenty children. Though an independent investigation would exonerate the government for the disaster, it became a casus belli on the far and the not-so-far right.

Inspired by the white supremacist William Luther Pierce's novel *The Turner Diaries,* whose hero blows up the FBI building in Washington, D.C., to jump-start a race war, Timothy McVeigh, a military veteran who was active in the gun show culture and militia movement, organized and carried out a truck bombing of the Alfred P. Murrah Federal Building in Oklahoma City on the second anniversary of the Waco tragedy. One hundred sixty-eight died, many of them children at its on-site day-care center. Unrepentant, McVeigh shared his thinking with Fox News's Rita Cosby from prison while he was awaiting his execution. The bombing, he wrote, was "a retaliatory strike; a counter attack" against a government that "like the Chinese—was deploying tanks against its own citizens." Following the United States' own practices, he continued, "I decided to send a message. . . . Bombing the Murrah Federal Building was morally and strategically equivalent to the U.S.

hitting a government building in Serbia, Iraq, or other nations."[12] McVeigh and his fellow patriotic militants believed the government was fundamentally illegitimate. Some white supremacists called it ZOG, for Zionist Occupied Government. Sovereign citizens, as we saw earlier with Bishop Gaiters and the "Second Constitution," claim that Washington, D.C. was captured by foreign elites a century ago. MAGA Republicans today call it "the administrative state" or the Deep State. Their struggle, as they see it, is to take it back and restore it to the real American people, themselves.

McVeigh's was the deadliest terrorist attack in American history until September 11, 2001, when terrorists associated with the radical Islamic al-Qaeda network hijacked four passenger jets and crashed two of them into the World Trade Center and one into the Pentagon (the fourth crashed in rural Pennsylvania when its passengers resisted). Nearly three thousand died, and for a brief moment, the country came together in a consensus borne of grief, anger, fear, and PTSD. By October, American soldiers were fighting in Afghanistan, whose Taliban had sheltered Osama bin Laden, al-Qaeda's founder and leader. Two years after that, the United States invaded Iraq.

For the first few years of the War on Terror, it seemed as if fear had become the central organizing principle of political life for Democrats as well as Republicans—fear of a hidden enemy that, like the Jews of the *Protocols,* was not a nation-state with a geographical location but a faith whose members could be living and plotting in our midst. As Susan Faludi described it in her brilliant book *The Terror Dream,* op-ed writers and politicians alike compensated for their feelings of helplessness by lionizing masculine first responders and soldiers and sentimentalizing American women as vulnerable maidens. "There is a mystery here," Faludi wrote. "The last remaining superpower, a nation attacked precisely *because* of its imperial preeminence, responded by fixating on its weakness and ineffectuality. . . . What well of insecurity did this mystery unearth?"[13]

The fear of masculine impotence and low sperm counts, of a birth dearth of white babies and an explosion of brown ones animates much of contemporary and historical conspiracism as well. Similar fears of dispossession gave rise to Barruel and Robison's books about the Illuminati as the specter of republican revolutions in the United States and France threatened Europe's kings; to the concoction of the *Protocols* in St. Petersburg in the waning days of the czar; and to the rise of Hitler and the National Socialists in Germany after the humiliations of Versailles and the hyperinflation of the 1920s.

In 2007, when I began writing *Cults, Conspiracies, and Secret Societies,* the hole in the New York skyline where the Twin Towers had stood was still palpable—my Brooklyn apartment looked out at it across the harbor. By then, the triumphant invasions of Afghanistan and Iraq had turned into quagmires and Hurricane Katrina had drowned an American city. By the fall of 2008, as I was putting the finishing touches on the manuscript, America and the world's financial systems were melting down—exactly the kinds of stressors that, as Richard Hofstadter put it in *The Paranoid Style in American Politics,* bring "fundamental fears and hatreds, rather than negotiable interests, into political action."[14] Half of the country was waking up from its fever dream and half was sinking deeper into it. Barack Obama's victory over the war hero John McCain in that November's presidential election might have been even more traumatic for the racist right than 9/11 had been.

As proud as so many Americans were of Obama's "postracial" presidency, the backlash was bigger and louder than anticipated.

Though Tea Partiers, as Obama's fiercest opponents became known, styled themselves as principled believers in small government and balanced budgets, many seemed to be more worried about racial displacement than finance. Internet memes of the Obamas as gorillas abounded, along with jokes about watermelons and fried chicken being served at state dinners. The notion that white people were being systematically persecuted by vengeful Blacks began to take hold. Rush Limbaugh told his vast radio audience that Obama "despised" white people, and that his sole goal was to destroy America. His role model, Limbaugh said, was "Robert Mugabe of Zimbabwe. The next thing to look out for is for Obama to take the farms. . . . That's what Mugabe did, he took the white people's farms."[15] To plumb the depths of Obama's anti-Americanism, Dinesh D'Souza explained, you had to understand his communist father. "Incredibly," he wrote, "the U.S. is being ruled according to the dreams of a Luo tribesman of the 1950s."[16]

As a left-leaning author with an obviously Jewish name who had presumed to write about the irrationality of conspiracy theory, I found myself on the receiving end of some of that same vitriol after *Cults, Conspiracies, and Secret Societies* was published. What struck me over and over again was not just its virulence, but how old the ideas that animated it turned out to be.

Everything old was new again in Paranoid America. Self-styled Austrian School conservatives at the Mises Institute, Congressman Ron Paul prominent among them, were fighting to restore the gold standard, audit the Fed, and relitigate the Civil War. Thanks to Glenn Beck, W. Cleon Skousen's 1981 Mormon revisionist history *The Five Thousand Year Leap* was atop the bestseller list (Skousen had first gained fame in 1958 with *The Naked Communist*). Beck was also using his platform to plug Elizabeth

Dilling's 1934 *The Red Network: A "Who's Who" and Handbook of Radicalism for Patriots,* about the communist infiltration of the FDR administration (he likely didn't know about her book *The Plot Against Christianity,* which drew liberally from *The Protocols of the Elders of Zion*), and Eustace Mullins's writings on the Federal Reserve. (Beck likely didn't know about Mullins's *New History of the Jews* either. Published in 1968, it explained that Jews believe "that by drinking the blood of a Christian victim who was perfect in every way, they could overcome their physical shortcomings and become as powerful as the intelligent civilized beings among whom they had formed their parasitic communities.")[17]

As a popularizer of extreme conspiracist ideas, Beck in his prime was often compared to Father Charles Coughlin, the notoriously anti-Semitic radio priest of the 1930s. Though Beck regarded "social justice" as a great evil (he defined it as "forced redistribution of wealth with a hostility toward individual property rights, under the guise of charity and/or justice")[18] and Father Coughlin named his movement after it, the two did have a lot in common.* Coughlin warned his millions of listeners about the treachery of atheistic Jews ("banksters," he called them), who used their control of the media and commerce to promote communism, and of America's urgent need to form a Christian Front to stop them, like the Nazis were doing in Germany. Beck regularly inveighed against George Soros, the "head of the snake," who was using the Federal Reserve to create a New World Order to replace the capitalist system once it had been destroyed.

Over at Infowars, Alex Jones was channeling Robert Welch's

---

* Coughlin's National Union for Social Justice was inaugurated in 1934; its eponymous newspaper, which reprinted excerpts from *The Protocols of the Elders of Zion,* had a circulation of two hundred thousand.

late writings on the Illuminati. The documentary *Loose Change,* which Jones executive-produced, claimed that 9/11 had been orchestrated by the globalists in the Bush administration, much as John T. Flynn's "The Truth About Pearl Harbor," published in 1944, had accused FDR of intentionally stage-managing the Japanese attack. YouTube documentaries and a host of books were spewing out the same accusations against the Masons that John Quincy Adams had made in the 1820s and '30s.

Though I wrote about all of this and more in my next book, *The New Hate,* which came out in 2012, I struggled to account for it. Mostly, I just wanted to sound the alarm that the shadow side of the American psyche was as active as it was, and that mainstream Republicanism was quietly aligning itself with it.

Then came 2015, and the inexorable ascent of Donald Trump. Though Jeb Bush had been the favorite of the Republican establishment, Trump surged to the top of the polls and stayed there. I published an op-ed in *The New York Times* in which I called Trump "the latest in a long line of demagogues that have appeared throughout American history to point accusing fingers at blacks, foreigners, Masons, Jews, socialists, central bankers and others." White nationalists were energized to see so unapologetically "pro-white" a politician, I wrote, and "would-be Joe-the-Plumbers are inspired to see someone who talks and seemingly thinks just like they do and yet who has so much money." Trump's poisonous message, I concluded, "may carry him to the White House."[19] I believed then, just as I believe now, that Trump's populism was transactional and opportunistic to its core—that if it would have served his purposes to become a champion of Black people and immigrants, he would have done so in a heartbeat, and that if he did win the White House, he would use its power not just to enrich himself and his family, but to purchase the good graces of the same global and corporate elites he claimed to disdain.

I was never so sorry to be right.

Back in 2011, I had covered a sparsely attended meeting of Richard Spencer's National Policy Institute for the Southern Poverty Law Center's *Hatewatch* blog. The NPI carries on the tradition of pseudo-academic "coat-and-tie" racism associated with Sam Francis, William Rusher, and Jared Taylor, the last of whom was a featured speaker at the conference. Race realists, as they call themselves, believe that ethnically and racially homogenous societies are happier and more stable than diverse ones, because, in Taylor's words, "the races are different. Blacks and whites are different. When blacks are left entirely to their own devices, Western Civilization—any kind of civilization—disappears."[20]

The day before the meeting, Spencer trolled establishment Republicans by holding a press conference at the National Press Club, where he announced the release of a white paper entitled "The Majority Strategy: Why the GOP Must Win White America." The gist of it was that the Republican Party is already "effectively the White People's Party," since 90 percent of its votes are cast by whites. Instead of diluting that identity by reaching out to minorities, the GOP should reach in and strengthen its base by demanding restrictions on immigration from nonwhite countries and an end to affirmative action, civil rights, and hate crimes legislation.

Would India allow the Japanese to elect their leaders? Then how can Republicans sit by and allow nonwhite Americans to reelect Barack Obama? If Republicans don't wake up soon, Spencer said, they will "become like the Whigs of old and end up in the ash can of history." Five years later, when Trump was elected, video clips of Spencer leading a packed room in chants of "Hail Trump! Hail our people! Hail victory!" went viral.[21] So many ugly ideas that had been playing at the margins had taken center stage.

One example of this is the normalization of the term "cultural Marxism" in Republican rhetoric. The term was popularized by Michael Minnicino in 1992, when he was a follower of the conspiracy theorist and serial presidential candidate Lyndon LaRouche, to describe the supposed convergence between the critique of capitalism leveled by the Marxist thinkers of the Frankfurt School,* many of them Jewish, and contemporary multiculturalism and feminism. United in their hatred of civilization, Minnicino wrote, all of them promoted a tyrannical "Political Correctness" whose goals are "first, to undermine the Judeo-Christian legacy through an 'abolition of culture' . . . and, second, to determine new cultural forms which would *increase the alienation of the population,* thus creating a 'new barbarism.'"[22]

Adding Islam to the mix (not Islamic extremism, he emphasized, but Islam writ large—a religion practiced by nearly two billion people), the Norwegian mass murderer Anders Behring Breivik cited Minnicino by name in his manifesto and used the term hundreds of times.[23] Minnicino, who had long since cut ties with LaRouche, was rightly horrified and said so.†

Despite its ugly origins and implications, it has since become so normalized that hardly anyone notices when conservative pundits like Jordan Peterson, Tucker Carlson, David Brooks, Ben Shapiro, and Andrew Sullivan drop it. On August 4, 2018, Steve Bannon

---

* The movement was originally centered at the Institute for Social Research at Goethe University in Frankfurt.

† "I do not stand by what I wrote, and I find it unfortunate that it [is] still remembered." (http://www.talk2action.org/story/2011/7/26/161347/099/Front_Page /Author_Cited_by_Anders_Behring_Breivik_Regrets_Original_Essay)

and Brazil's Eduardo Bolsonaro met in New York and pledged to "join forces, especially against cultural marxism."[24] In May 2021, Senator Marco Rubio linked it to Glenn Beck's old bugaboo, social justice. "What [social justice] really is," he explained, "is Cultural Marxism. It is another way to tear apart capitalism and the American way of life."[25] And in June 2023, Florida's governor Ron DeSantis defined his favorite pejorative, "woke," as "a form of Cultural Marxism."[26]

Rubio and DeSantis may not know about the term's sordid associations; they likely regard it as just another one of Newt Gingrich's delegitimizing adjectives. But that's precisely the point: to label someone a Marxist of any kind is to "other" them, even if (especially if) they are the president. For this reason, it is a prime example of the mainstreaming of McCarthyism. But it is also a symptom of what a philosopher would call America's epistemic predicament—the fact that so many of us don't just disagree about politics but inhabit entirely different subjective universes.

We've seen in this chapter how the conspiracist beliefs of the far right influenced and inflected the rhetoric and strategies of Republicanism, priming a large swath of the public to maintain an us-versus-them mentality in regard to large numbers of their fellow Americans. In the next, we'll explore how the susceptibility to conspiracy theory operates at the individual level.

4

Cognitive Dissonance

"The American people are credulous," *The New York Times* despaired on June 26, 1864. "Give them a fact, plain, probable and undisputed, and they readily credit it. Give them a falsehood positively stated, and they believe it with almost equal readiness, even though it bear evidence of falsity upon its face." The occasion for the un-bylined essay was the "great system of lying" that supported the rebellion in the South and the treasonous designs of the Copperheads* in the North.

The avidity to "deceive the popular mind, mislead public sentiment, and falsify upon every conceivable subject," as the *Times's* editorial writer put it more than a century and a half ago, was not a foible that was uniquely of its time. Nor was the corresponding willingness to believe whatever comported most comfortably with one's preexisting beliefs. The capacity to lie to oneself is widely shared. Our beliefs about who we are and who we are not are deeply baked in and thus very difficult to challenge, never mind dispel.

---

* The Copperheads were "Peace Democrats" who advocated for a negotiated settlement to the Civil War.

If you could travel back to 1864 and ask a Copperhead who was lying about the state of the nation, he or she would answer without hesitation that it was *The New York Times,* no matter how many "plain, probable and undisputed" facts to the contrary you might adduce. But you don't have to be a time traveler to see this behavior. Americans live in a country whose political, socio-economic, cultural, geographic, and epistemic divides are as stark as they were back then—and who believe and disbelieve promiscuously, often in spite of clear evidence to the contrary. A Pew study conducted near the end of 2020 found that while 60 percent of the voters it surveyed strongly agreed that "made-up news" had had a major impact on the recent presidential election, precisely what those respondents considered "made up" varied widely—"and often aligned with partisan views."[1]

Americans are not just divided in their presidential preferences, but on the nature of reality itself. In February 2021, almost four months after the polls closed but less than a month after Trump's departure, another set of pollsters asked Republicans and Democrats which statement was closer to their view: "It's a big beautiful world, mostly full of good people, and we must find a way to embrace each other and not allow ourselves to become isolated" or "Our lives are threatened by terrorists, criminals, and illegal immigrants, and our priority should be to protect ourselves."[2] Seventy-five percent of Biden voters opted for the first, while 66 percent of Trump voters chose the second. One America is as vibrantly urban and multicultural as *Sesame Street;* the other looks a lot like *Road Warrior* or *World War Z.*

That same month, *The Washington Post* ran a feature story about a family's struggle to reclaim their mother from the different reality she had taken refuge in since the election, in which "Trump won the legal vote and by a landslide," "paid infiltrators" had "facilitated" the January 6 Capitol riot, and the mainstream media's attacks on Trump and his supporters were redolent of "the war of words against the Jews in the 1930's."[3] Back in the 1970s, the media was filled with stories about heartbroken parents who'd lost their children to cults. Today, some of those same children are trying to reclaim their parents from the alternate realities they choose to live in.

As the psychologist Leon Festinger wrote in 1956, "A man with a conviction is a hard man to change. Tell him you disagree and he turns away. Show him facts or figures and he questions your sources. Appeal to logic and he fails to see your point."[4] Why is that? Because, as Festinger explained in depth in *A Theory of Cognitive Dissonance* and other books, when a deeply held conviction comes into conflict with reality, its holder experiences a "cognitive dissonance" that is so uncomfortable that he or she is driven to reduce or resolve it, either by revising the belief to bring it into consonance with reality, or, if it is too deeply rooted to change, by editing their view of reality to conform with their conviction. Tell a tobacco smoker that their habit causes cancer, for example, and they might quit—but they might also seek out literature about the very few benefits of smoking (it can help in weight loss, they may learn, and smokers are less likely than nonsmokers to get ulcerative colitis). Or they may claim that the experimental evidence about tobacco's dangers is faulty, or that the experimenters were paid by tobacco-hating extremists to lie.

Cognitive dissonance avoidance accounts for why liberals prefer to watch MSNBC and conservatives Fox News, and why we prefer to socialize with people who share our biases. More broadly, it accounts for why some of us stubbornly believe the unbelievable—and disbelieve what we cannot rationally deny.

The kinds of beliefs that are hardest to change and hence

provoke the strongest dissonances are unfalsifiable by definition, meaning our disagreements about them can't be settled by
clicking on Google or Snopes. They are qualitative rather than
quantitative, as they reflect our values. They are issues of faith
(or sometimes bad faith), and as the philosopher Søren Kierke-
gaard famously put it, "faith begins precisely there where thinking
leaves off." Someone who deeply believes that their eternal salvation depends upon their faith that Jesus is the son of God will
likely reject a historical argument about how Jesus was simply a
radical Jew, no matter how cogent and carefully documented it is.

Festinger designed a number of ingenious laboratory experiments to demonstrate cognitive dissonance reduction in action:
for example, giving students a tedious task to do, paying some
of them greater and lesser sums of money to lie to prospective
participants about how interesting the task was, and finally asking them to fill out questionnaires in which they rated the task.
The students who weren't told to lie about the task told the truth
on the questionnaire: that it was boring. Those who were paid
twenty dollars to lie (which was a lot of money in the 1950s—the
equivalent of more than two hundred dollars today) also tended to
answer the questionnaire honestly. But students who were offered
a modest reward to lie to their peers (one dollar) apparently also
lied to themselves, as most said the task was interesting. Festinger
theorized that a twenty-dollar reward was enough to overcome
the participants' guilty consciences; being paid that much money
was a good excuse to lie to strangers. A dollar's payment, though,
wasn't enough of a motivation for them to lie, so the students
changed their opinions to reduce their discomfort.

When the Seekers, a tiny Chicago-based UFO cult, announced
that the world would end on December 21, 1954, Festinger saw
an opportunity to carry out a natural experiment. The Seekers,

he predicted, would handle the inevitable "disconfirmation" of their prophecy in three possible ways. The least committed would either reject the new belief system they'd adopted and return to their lives, or alter it to accommodate its disconfirmation, concluding, perhaps, that they'd misinterpreted the prophecy. Maybe they'd gotten the date wrong, they'd say, or taken literally what they should have construed metaphorically. But the most zealous apostles, the ones who had invested the most in the movement, he speculated, would more than likely take a Kierkegaardian leap into the absurd and redouble their proselytizing in an attempt to create a community of believers that was large enough to cancel out the disconfirmation. Because, as Festinger put it, "if everyone in the whole world believed something there would be no question at all as to the validity of this belief."

Festinger sent some of his graduate students to infiltrate the Seekers and take notes. The result was *When Prophecy Fails,* an ethnographic study that reads at times like the scenario for one of Christopher Guest's deadpan mockumentaries, though its authors (Festinger cowrote it with Henry W. Riecken and Stanley Schachter, two of his colleagues at the Laboratory for Research in Social Relations at the University of Minnesota) never stooped to outright ridicule or condescension. As they noted in the book's opening pages, history is replete with cases of messianic movements that survived the public failures of their prophecies, at least for a time. Montanus, a Christian of the second century, received a revelation that Christ would soon return to the Phrygian town of Pepuza, which would become the New Jerusalem. Though nothing of the sort happened, Pepuza enjoyed a population boom in anticipation of its changed status, and Montanism carried on as a heretical sect there for another four hundred years.

Sabbatai Zevi, a Jewish mystic from Smyrna, declared himself the Messiah in 1648. In 1665, he met the Kabbalist Nathan of Gaza, who declared that Zevi would reveal himself to the world in 1666, kicking off a mass movement of repentance. Within months, Nathan said, Zevi would depose the sultan and make him his servant. When Zevi arrived in Constantinople to do so, he was quickly arrested. Some of his followers fell away, but others reasoned that the fact that the sultan hadn't executed him confirmed he was the Messiah.

But then the sultan made Zevi choose between apostasy and martyrdom, and Zevi agreed to convert to Islam. A contemporary report described the shameful way he groveled, throwing himself "on the ground before the sultan, begging that he might be allowed to take refuge in the sultan's religion. . . . He insulted the Jewish faith and profaned God's name, in full public view."[5] That was a bridge too far for most, but not all, of his followers; the hardest-core of true believers presumed Zevi's conversion had been a part of the plan all along and converted as well. The advent of the Messiah, Nathan said, had turned the world upside down so what was once kosher was now tref. In Cynthia Ozick's words, they developed "a new theology of paradox to account for the apostasy, wherein . . . the 'true' truth is always the concealed truth."[6] A few Dönmeh* communities, as the Turks call these revenant Sabbateans, can be found in Turkey to this day.

Almost two centuries later, in upstate New York, a lay preacher named William Miller closely analyzed the Old Testament Book of Daniel, zeroing in on 8:14 ("And he said to me, 'Unto two thousand three hundred days; then shall the sanctuary be cleansed'"). Substituting years for days, Miller counted forward from 457 BCE,

---

* The word means "transvestite" in Ottoman Turkish; the Sabbateans call themselves "ha-Ma'aminim," Hebrew for "the believers."

when the Persian emperor Artaxerxes issued his decree to rebuild Jerusalem, and surmised that the Apocalypse would occur "sometime between March 21st, 1843, and March 21st, 1844, according to the Jewish mode of computation." As the date neared, Millerism swelled into a mass movement. When March 21, 1844, passed without incident, the Reverend Samuel S. Snow fine-tuned Miller's calculations and set a new target date of October 22, 1844, a day that was destined to go down in history as "the Great Disappointment" when the sun rose and set as it always had.

The Seekers had none of Zevi's or the Millerites' mass appeal; they never numbered more than a few dozen. Their spiritual leader was Dorothy Martin (Festinger and his coauthors called her Mrs. Marian Keech in the book), a fifty-something housewife who'd attended Theosophy lectures, read the literature of the quasi-fascist I AM movement, studied Oahspe, the Faithist Bible that was channeled to the American dentist John Ballou Newbrough in 1882,* and dabbled in the then-freshly minted religion of Scientology. At some point, she'd begun to receive communications from other planes of existence. The first messages she transcribed were from her dead father. Then, spiritual beings from the planets Clarion and Cerus made contact with her. The most important of them, Sananda, told her that he was the latest incarnation of Jesus Christ. In time, he warned her about the tribulations that would usher in the New Age.

Not only would Lake Michigan inundate Chicago, Sananda said, in his quasi-biblical diction, but "the cast of the country of the U.S.A. is that it is to break in twain. In the area of the Mis-

---

* Newbrough founded a Faithist colony in New Jersey, which was relocated first to New York and then to New Mexico. The Land of Shalam, as he called it, was both a religious collective and a refuge for orphaned children.

sissippi, in the region of the Canada, Great Lakes and the Mississippi, to the Gulf of Mexico, into the Central America will be as
changed. The great tilting of the land of the U.S. to the East will
throw up mountains along the Central States. . . . The new mountain range shall be called The Argone Range, which will signify the
ones who have been there are gone."[7] Worldwide, the Egyptian
deserts would bloom, the lost continent of Lemuria would rise
out of the Pacific, and France, England, and Russia would sink
beneath the waves.

As the countdown to December 21, 1954, began, the media
camped out in Martin's neighborhood. Things quickly took a far-
cical turn. When one of Festinger's researchers appeared at her
house, Martin and the Seekers mistook him for a messenger from
Sananda and pressed him to give them a sign. In another episode
of low comedy, one of the members channeled a message that
promised a miracle—Martin's husband would die that same night
and be resurrected. Three times, members checked on Mr. Martin
in his bedroom, and three times they found him peacefully asleep.
After the third time, the messenger lamely explained that the miracle had already happened—he'd died and been resurrected when
no one was watching.

When Sananda told Martin that a flying saucer would pick
them up at four o'clock in the afternoon on December 17 and
transport them to a place of safety, the Seekers stripped all the
metal off their clothes in preparation (for reasons that were not
specified, metal and flying saucers were understood to be a fatal
mix). The saucer didn't come that afternoon, and it didn't come
that night, though they waited in the bitter cold in Martin's back-
yard until early the next morning.

Dr. Charles Laughead (Festinger and company called him Dr.
Armstrong) was a medical doctor and college professor who had

done missionary work in Egypt with his wife, with whom he shared a deep interest in the occult and flying saucers. After they met Martin, Laughead publicized her prophecies. In the early hours of December 21, as the Seekers stood vigil for the last time, Laughead bucked up one of Festinger's secret observers (though it's not unreasonable to surmise that he was shoring up his own faltering faith as well):

> I've given up just about everything. I've cut every tie: I've burned every bridge. I've turned my back on the world. I can't afford to doubt. I have to believe. And there isn't any other truth. . . . I won't doubt even if we have to make an announcement to the press tomorrow and admit we were wrong. You're having your period of doubt now, but hang on, boy, hang on. This is a tough time but we know that the boys upstairs are taking care of us. They've given us their promise.[8]

Martin and the Seekers ultimately rationalized her prophecy's failure as the proof of its success: the announcement they made to the press the next day was not that they had been wrong, but that their steadfastness had been rewarded with the divine decision to postpone the Day of Judgment.

True to Festinger's predictions, while the group's more casual members did drift back into their old lives, its core members doubled down on both their belief and their proselytizing. But only for a time; within a matter of weeks, as Festinger and his coauthors dryly put it, "an unfriendly world finally forced the small band of Lake City believers into diaspora." Still, they concluded, "it is interesting to speculate . . . on what they might have made of their opportunities had they been more effective apostles. . . . Disconfirmation might have portended the beginning, not the end."[9]

That was what had happened with Millerism. If it didn't survive its public comeuppance in its original form, it continued on in others, first as Evangelical Adventism, and then as the Advent Christian Church, which gave birth in turn to Seventh-Day Adventism, the Church of God, and the Jehovah's Witnesses.

In December 1844, two months after the Great Disappointment, seventeen-year-old Ellen White had a vision that showed her that humanity was not yet prepared for the coming of the Lord; instead, she had been "chosen as the instrument by which God would give light to His people." As one modern advocate has put it, while the Adventist Church memorializes October 22, 1844, as the "day of disappointment," it's "far better . . . to remember October 22 as the day of Christ's appointment."[10] Seventh-Day Adventism is still going strong; worldwide, it counts ninety-seven-thousand-plus churches with more than twenty-one million members.

The Jehovah's Witnesses emerged in the 1870s; its leaders would wrongly predict that the world would end in 1914, 1915, 1918, 1920, 1925, 1941, 1975, and 1994. Despite all those disconfirmations, the Witnesses are also flourishing; as of 2020, the church counted over one-hundred-twenty-thousand congregations in nearly two-hundred-fifty countries and had more than eight million missionaries in the field. No new dates have been set for the Apocalypse since 1995.

The Seekers' Dorothy Martin had some of Ellen White's indomitable spirit. While her husband, as Festinger and company observed, was "a man of infinite patience, gentleness, and tolerance amounting almost to self-abasement, he never believed that his wife could communicate with other worlds. . . . He simply went about his ordinary duties in the distributing company where he was a traffic manager, and did not allow the unusual events in his home to disturb in the slightest his daily routine."[11] But the events of 1954 tested the Martins' marriage past its limit. Facing the threat of involuntary psychiatric commitment, Dorothy fled to Arizona under an assumed name. That is where Festinger and his colleagues left her, but her odyssey had just begun.[12]

Within a few years, Sister Thedra, as Martin began to call herself, had opened up new lines of communication with an astral organization at Lake Titicaca in Peru that had been established eons ago by survivors of the destruction of Lemuria. She and some of her new followers moved to Peru for a few unhappy years; eventually she settled near California's Mount Shasta, where she wrote many books (all sixteeen volumes of The Great Awakening series are still in print). Near the end of her long life, she moved to the New Age hotbed of Sedona, Arizona. The last message she received from Sananda arrived in 1992, shortly before she died. It read: "It is now come the time that ye come out of the place wherein ye are. . . . Let it be, for many shall greet thee with glad shouts!"

Cognitive dissonance reduction goes a long way to explain the stickiness of irrational beliefs like Sister Thedra's, but it doesn't begin to explain their contents. The Seekers were only one of a number of millennial UFO cults that sprang up in the 1950s. Other writers were also communicating with alien spirits, among them George Adamski, who wrote about his extraterrestrial travels with the Space Brothers in his best-selling books *The Flying Saucers Have Landed* and *Inside the Space Ships*.* In 1954, the same year that the events described in *When Prophecy Fails* transpired, George King, a London cabdriver and a student of yoga,

* Both Martin and Laughead had met with Adamski before they connected with each other.

was informed via psychic transmission that he had been chosen to become the voice of the "Interplanetary Parliament." He founded the Aetherius Society soon after, which shares the teachings of the Cosmic Masters, whose messages, according to the group's website, reveal "profound, timeless truths about God and the living universe . . . offer[ing] hope to a world living on a knife edge."[13]

Then there was George W. Van Tassel, an airplane mechanic who lived in the shadow of a giant rock in the Mojave Desert. In his pamphlet "I Rode a Flying Saucer," he shared some of the urgent messages he received from alien entities. "I am Ashtar, in the process of attempting to straighten out numerous conditions that affect this planet Shan," read one, dated August 31, 1952. "We are going to give you certain information . . . that will weld together the two great sciences of your people. I refer to all branches of material science and religion. These two are one in truth, separated only by a gap that we shall give you the key to close."[14] Around the same time, in El Cajon, California, an electrical engineer named Ernest L. Norman founded the Unarius Academy with his wife, Ruth, who claimed to be the Archangel Uriel and the reincarnation of Mary Magdalene. Ruth was in telepathic contact with residents of thirty-three planets, including Vixali, Shunan, and Eneshia.[15]

The "clairaudient" communications that William Dudley Pelley received in the early 1950s offered hope to some, but they were filled with dark forebodings too, about the dangers of race mixing and the hidden forces that prevent humanity from achieving its destiny. Pelley had been an award-winning literary writer in the 1910s and '20s before he took a turn into spiritualism and then Hitlerian fascism, organized the paramilitary Silver Legion, ran against Roosevelt for president as the candidate of the Christian Party, and was prosecuted first for mail fraud in the 1930s, and then sedition in 1942. After he was paroled, Pelley devoted the remaining years of his life to expounding and marketing the gnostic philosophy he called Soulcraft.

One part Book of Enoch,* one part Theosophy, with a dash of I AM and British Israelism mixed in, Soulcraft, like L. Ron Hubbard's Scientology, begins with the story of earth's colonization by aliens. They were "denizens of Cosmos, come from distant star worlds mightier than anything we now have in our horizons," as Pelley put it in his 1950 book *Star Guests,* a faux-leather-bound copy of which I found one day in a flea market. Having assumed corporeal forms, the colonists became enslaved by their sensuality and degenerated into wickedness. Then 144,000† Radiant Beings, led by Christ, followed them to Earth to begin the work of salvation, setting humanity on a path of higher evolution. Unfortunately, "a coalition of oriental nations—of which Russia is leader—[gained] such ascendancy that they threaten to overrun and subjugate the globe, reducing its white and Christian peoples to bondage."[16]

Was there something about the United States in the 1950s that made it especially ripe for UFO-flavored apocalypticism? It's a question worth asking, as it could shed light on the rise of apocalyptic Evangelicalism in our own day, not to mention the cultic aspects of Trumpism and QAnon.

Back then, the country had just emerged from a world war that had unleashed carnage on an industrial scale on civilians and soldiers alike, sweeping away the global order and replacing it with

---

* The extracanonical Hebrew text attributed to Noah's great-grandfather.
† The number of members of the tribes of Israel who have the name of God written on their foreheads and survive the tribulation in the Book of Revelation.

a nuclear standoff in which Armageddon was only a button push away. The undeclared war in Korea had brought the world even closer to the brink.

UFOs were objects, to use the Freudian jargon of the time, onto which people's neuroses, fears, and anxieties could be projected and displaced: the Promethean hubris of the Atomic Age, the threats from enemies within and without, the longing for salvation, and in Pelley's case, the racist and anti-Semitic views he could no longer openly espouse. Soulcraft, the Seekers, and the Space Brothers weren't for everyone, of course, but for some they were a rock, a fortress, and a savior. Their teachings were easy to swallow and not at all unfamiliar—in fact they included most of the same soothing bromides about peace and brotherhood that you'd hear in a Sunday sermon in a conventional, mainstream church, but dressed up in a shiny futurism. Even their esoteric teachings were familiar, as they imparted the same quasi-Eastern nostrums about karma and the untapped power of human potential that the books and lectures of Madame Blavatsky, Manly P. Hall, and Edgar Cayce had offered to the last generation.

History was moving so quickly. The mirror America held up to itself had lately reflected a Norman Rockwell tableau of farmland and small towns, drugstores with soda fountains, neat white churches, and Elks lodges. Suddenly it was crowded with cities, each of them surrounded by ring after ring of look-alike suburbs. Your grandparents had ridden to church in a buggy; your parents grew up watching Harold Lloyd, Gloria Swanson, and Charlie Chaplin in the silents. Now there was a television in every home, and squeezed in between the sit-coms, dramas, variety hours, and quiz shows was more unsettling fare—live coverage of grim-faced senators accusing State Department eggheads of treason, and of juvenile delinquents thrusting their hips in time to the primal rhythms of Negro music.

There were Negroes too. Sometimes they were doing the things they were expected to—cleaning white people's houses and taking care of their children, operating elevators and chauffeuring cars—but sometimes they were shown in a completely different light, one that caused no end of painful cognitive dissonance. On September 4, 1957, images of nine terrified Black teenagers flickered across the nation's TV screens. Guarded by soldiers as they waited to register for classes at Central High School in Little Rock, Arkansas, they were beset by a howling mob of white people, whose faces were distorted by animal rage.

I was born in Washington, D.C. in October 1957, a month after the Little Rock crisis and two weeks to the day after the Russians sent Sputnik into orbit, sparking a national panic. ("I'll be damned if I sleep by the light of a Red Moon," then–Senate majority leader Lyndon Baines Johnson declared. "Soon they will be dropping bombs on us from space like kids dropping rocks on the cars from freeway overpasses.")[17] Since my father was a defense worker, he had been instructed to report to a bunker in a hollowed-out mountain in the Virginia countryside in the event of a nuclear attack, but he'd promised my mother that he'd come home to us instead.

It would have never occurred to me at the time that we were any different from our neighbors, but as Jewish transplants from New York, my parents could not have been more alien to some of them if they had come from outer space. My older sister played with a little boy next door whose father was almost never home; my parents had heard he was in the CIA. I sometimes wonder what his mother and her spook husband made of us. Before she met my father, my mother had worked in the U.S. delegation to the UN, where her boss's boss was Alger Hiss. My father's father had been imprisoned by the czar because he was a socialist and an Esperanto activist. My dad was a civilian engineer in the Army

Signal Corps, the rock that McCarthy's anti-communist crusade had foundered on just a few years before.

The pace of change was extraordinary then, and it is moving even faster today. But for many Americans, it is going in the wrong direction. Some of those suburbs that were so new back then have more poverty, crime, and minorities in them today than the big urban centers they were supposed to be refuges from, and a lot of those big cities are nowhere near as big as they were before their factories were relocated to greenfield locations in right-to-work states or offshored to Asia. Drug addiction is no longer just a problem of the inner cities or of the youth culture; many of the opiates that heartland Americans routinely abuse were prescribed for them by their doctors. It wasn't so long ago that brick-sized transistor radios seemed like miracles of miniaturization; nowadays even children carry powerful computers in their pockets that can link them to all the knowledge in the world, but that are programmed to steer them to ad-supported social media sites that feed them a steady diet of rumors, opinions, and lies that are fine-tuned and micro-targeted to arouse their most primitive emotions.

The creeping status anxiety, the semi-hallucinatory fear of dispossession that animated the fringe of radical right-wing Babbittry that Richard Hofstadter wrote about in *The Paranoid Style in American Politics* has become an objective phenomenon, as witnessed by the declining life expectancies of white working-class Americans that Anne Case and Angus Deaton documented in their book *Deaths of Despair and the Future of Capitalism*.

It's not just America that looks different; Americans do too. Non-Hispanic, white, native-born, Christian Americans are on track to become a minority within the next quarter century. Much as Dorothy Martin imagined the great tilting that would give rise to the Argone Range, the ground has shifted beneath the feet of white, rural, male, heterosexual, middle income, Christian Americans. The very idea that you would have to modify the word "American" with "white," "male," "heterosexual," "middle income," "rural," or "Christian" must be disturbing to many of them; it wasn't so long ago that those same things were the default attributes of Americanness.

At a 2008 fundraising event in liberal San Francisco, the then-presidential hopeful Barack Obama made light of those anxieties (at least it seemed like he did if you took his words out of context, as his political adversaries quickly did). "You go into some of these small towns in Pennsylvania and, like a lot of small towns in the Midwest, the jobs have been gone now for twenty-five years," he said. "It's not surprising then that they get bitter, they cling to guns or religion or antipathy toward people who aren't like them or anti-immigrant sentiment or anti-trade sentiment as a way to explain their frustrations."[18] Nine years later, when Hillary Clinton was looking to succeed Obama to the presidency, she added insult to injury when she consigned a lot of those same "racist, sexist, homophobic, xenophobic, [and] Islamophobic" Americans to a "basket of deplorables."[19]*

Those gun- and Bible-loving conservative voters didn't just blame elite Democrats like Barack Obama and Hillary Clinton for turning America into a place where they felt like strangers. Establishment Republicans had presided over the disastrous wars in Iraq and Afghanistan, the rise of the most unequal economy since the 1920s, and its near meltdown in 2008. So, in 2016,

* She also talked about the people "who feel that the government has let them down, the economy has let them down, nobody cares about them, nobody worries about what happens to their lives and their futures, and they're just desperate for change," but those words didn't stick to her the way "deplorable" did.

red America, which is to say rural and exurban white America (funny to think how the connotations of "red" have changed since LBJ's fulminations about the "Red Moon"), rejected both, stacking their chips instead on the presidential candidate who claimed to be so rich that no one could ever buy him (or rather, enough of them did in enough of the right places to give Trump a majority in the Electoral College).

Trump had campaigned as the candidate who would return America to its rightful owners, and his continuing dominance within the overwhelmingly white Republican Party suggests that the sense of cultural, racial, and moral dispossession that he articulates (what political scientists call "dominant group victimhood") was and is widely shared.* But Trump didn't want to risk alienating too many of the "haves" like himself whose votes Republicans historically depended on, so he played both sides against each other. "The rich people actually don't like me . . . Really, the people that like me best are . . . the workers. They're the people I understand the best. Those are the people I grew up with," he said in a speech promoting his tax plan in 2017, which he promised would soak the rich and drive his accountants crazy.[20] Once the plan was signed into law, he addressed a crowd of wealthy admirers at a holiday dinner at Mar-a-Lago. "You all just got a lot richer," he crowed.[21]

Cognitive dissonance reduction helps explain why so many people believe Trump's and their own lies; so does another cognitive quirk called "confirmation bias," which is our tendency, in the words of a famous 1979 psychological study, to "accept

---

* Even by some billionaires, like the late investor Thomas Perkins, who in 2014, in a letter to *The Wall Street Journal,* famously called attention to the supposed parallels between Nazi Germany's war on the Jews and "the progressive war on the American one percent."

'confirming' evidence at face value while subjecting 'disconfirm-ing' evidence to critical evaluation."[22]* Keeping this in mind, an interesting data point from postmortems of the 2016 and 2020 elections is the finding by Tufts political scientist Brian Schaffner and his colleagues that the "single best predictor of who voted for Trump was the belief that systemic racism no longer exists in the U.S.; the second-best predictor was denial that systemic bias exists against women." Nine in ten Republicans reject the idea that structural discrimination against racial minorities exists; three-quarters doubt that women face "entrenched bias." As right as those beliefs may feel emotionally to the aggrieved white males who hold them, they likely engender a certain amount of discomfort as well, as they defy both the canons of acceptable discourse and objective evidence. Trump's campaign gave them permission to own them.[23]

Trump was unique among presidents in that he was not just the subject of a raft of us-against-them conspiracy theories, but a tireless inventor and promoter of them. He explicitly embraced paranoia as a way of life, portraying himself as an alpha predator

* The study took groups of people who self-identified as pro- or anti-capital punishment and measured the strength of their convictions after they were exposed to fictitious evidence that purported to prove or disprove its deterrent effects on crime. When the participants were simply presented with results, they moderated their views somewhat. But when they were told about the methodologies that had produced those results, they went to elaborate lengths to discredit them if they disagreed with them. Another study found that when presented with data that confirmed or disconfirmed politically controversial topics, test subjects who were more mathematically inclined were more likely than others "to use their quantitative-reasoning capacity selectively to conform their interpretation of the data to the result most consistent with their political outlooks." (https://scholarsbank.uoregon.edu/xmlui/handle/1794/22105). The takeaway is that intellectual sophistication alone can't protect you from your biases—in fact, it may fortify them.

Arthur Goldwag

in the Hobbesian wilderness. "Be paranoid," he told participants in one of his motivational seminars back in 2000. "You have to realize that people, sadly, sadly, are very vicious."[24] Be "more paranoid," he admonished the National Republican Congressional Committee in April 2019. "You've got to be a little more paranoid than you are."[25] He didn't hesitate to apply the principle when he was running for reelection.

Biden was so addled, Trump told Fox News's Laura Ingraham, that "he's controlled like a puppet."

"Who do you think is pulling Biden's strings?" she asked. "Is it former Obama people?"

"People that you've never heard of," Trump replied. "People that are in the dark shadows. People that are—"

"What does that mean?" Ingraham interrupted. "That sounds like conspiracy theory. Dark shadows."

"People that you haven't heard of," Trump repeated. "There are people that are on the streets. There are people that are controlling the streets. We had somebody get on a plane from a certain city this weekend and in the plane, it was almost completely loaded with thugs wearing these dark uniforms, black uniforms with gear and this and that. They're on a plane."[26]

Trump needed a counternarrative to explain his scandals, distract from his failures, and most of all, keep his supporters' sense of grievance, anger, and fear at full boil. "Always Remember," he said, "they are coming after ME, because I am fighting for YOU."[27] Antifa and Black Lives Matter had already made America's cities unlivable, Trump said. If Joe Biden was elected, he would unleash them against the suburbs. "The Democrats in D.C. . . . want to . . . abolish our beautiful and successful suburbs."[28]

Like a cult leader, like a beleaguered dictator, Trump insisted to his followers that reality was what he said it was, not what the lying press, the Deep State, the radical left, and Never-Trump Republicans and other RINOs (Republicans in Name Only) claimed. A plague of toxic wokeness was sweeping the land; if the left had its way, it would not only tear down statues of Confederate heroes but raze the Washington Monument and the Jefferson Memorial. Biden will "dissolve your borders, terminate religious liberty, outlaw private health insurance . . . shred your Second Amendment, confiscate your guns and indoctrinate your children with anti-American lies," Trump said.[29] He'll take Christmas "out of the vocabulary."[30]

It was all hyperbole, of course, but it was directed and highly motivated. If a white-coated social scientist sat down a group of suburban Trump voters and administered them a formal true or false test, it's unlikely that most would tick off "true" for statements like "Joseph Biden wants to eliminate the word 'Christmas.'" But Trump's relentless repetition of paranoid themes like that validated his voters' deepest resentments—some of which they had been too ashamed of or afraid of to say out loud. "You don't sell products, benefits, or solutions," the *Trump University Playbook* reminds its instructors. "You sell feelings."[31]

After the election, Trump continued to insist he'd won by a "magnificent landslide," even as the courts rejected his challenges to Pennsylvania's, Georgia's, Michigan's, Nevada's, and Wisconsin's vote counts more than sixty times, and his own attorney general admitted there was no evidence of widespread fraud. Trump and his surrogates blamed all the usual suspects for the Big Steal—immigrants, minorities, big-city Democratic machines, the media. They singled out Ruby Freeman and her daughter Wandrea Moss, two part-time, $16-an-hour election workers in Atlanta, Georgia, as "professional vote scammer[s]" who "stuffed the ballot boxes." At a hearing of the Georgia House Governmental Affairs Committee, Rudy Giuliani described how a video captured the two passing the thumb drives they used to hack into voting machines back and forth between them "as if they're vials of heroin and cocaine. I mean it's obvious to anyone who is a criminal investigator or prosecutor, they're engaged in surreptitious illegal activity."[32] (When they sued him for defamation two years later, he would admit he was lying.)[33]

They blamed some unusual ones too, including rogue Republican state officials; a "radical left" voting machine company that had cooked up a plot to unseat Trump with George Soros, China, and the long-dead Venezuelan dictator Hugo Chávez; and a rogue Italian general, flush with cash from the untraceable $400 million bribe that Obama had given him (taken from the pallets of cash he'd shipped to Iran), who used a military satellite to switch Trump votes to Biden. And of course, there was Trump's own vice president, who "didn't have the courage to do what should have been done to protect our Country and our Constitution," as Trump tweeted on January 6.[34]

Trump's entire public identity was constructed around winning; to preserve it, he needed to challenge whatever facts denied it. UFOs might have been the only conspiracist theme he didn't sound.* Leon Festinger, who died in 1989, would have found a lot of commonalities between the ways that Dorothy Martin and her Seekers dealt with the disconfirmation of her prophecies and the ways that Trump and his MAGA patriots handled the demise of his presidency.

Trump's loss stunned Q believers, especially when Q himself

* "People are saying they're seeing UFOs. Do I believe it? Not particularly," he told George Stephanopoulos in a 2019 interview. (https://thehill.com/homenews/administration/448722-trump-weighs-in-on-ufos-in-stephanopoulos-interview/)

fell ominously silent; after December 8, 2020, he wouldn't be heard from again for a long time.* But as Festinger would have predicted, the disconfirmation of Q's prophecies only strengthened his most ardent followers' faith. "Do not worry. Do not be afraid. THERE IS A PLAN. IT IS A GOOD PLAN," the Q believer Major Patriot tweeted.[35] January 6, 2021, the date that had been set for Congress to certify the election results, was soon widely believed to be the date that "the Show" would finally air— especially when Trump himself invited the faithful to come to Washington for his Stop the Steal rally.

A few minutes before four o'clock in the morning of January 7, after Congress belatedly certified Biden's victory, Trump issued his characteristically graceless "concession" through an aide's Twitter account (his own had been suspended): "Even though I totally disagree with the outcome of the election, and the facts bear me out," it read, "nevertheless there will be an orderly transition on January 20th. I have always said we would continue our fight to ensure that only legal votes were counted. While this represents the end of the greatest first term in presidential history, it's only the beginning of our fight to Make America Great Again."[36]

Unfazed, true believers revised the date of the storm yet again. As the Q exegete noah explained, Trump's deplatforming from Twitter had always been a part of the plan, just as Sabbatai Zevi's

---

* On June 24, 2022, Q returned to 8kun for the first time in over a year. "Shall we play the game again?" his first post asked. When a commenter asked why he had been gone so long, Q replied, "It had to be done this way." Then he posted a third time, saying, "Are you ready to serve your country again? Remember your oath." Writing this footnote, it strikes me that the words "then he posted a third time" have a prophetic ring; it's easy to imagine John Huston reciting them in the same orotund style he used to narrate his 1966 movie *The Bible: In the Beginning*.

apostasy had been a part of his. Q himself predicted it in his ninety-seventh drop, all the way back in November 2017, which read in part: "Paint the picture. Disinformation exists and is necessary. 10 days. Darnkess [sic]. War. Good v. Evil. Roadmap of big picture is here." On December 6, 2017, Q explicitly linked the ten days of "darnkess" to "Shutdown." On June 4, 2020, Q had designated "POTUS twitter removal" as RED1, to be followed by RED2 ("Central communications blackout"), all the way through to RED6 ("SEC OF DEF _instruct1"). Connect the dots, and it was plain to see: the storm would begin on January 18, two days before Biden's inauguration.[37] As another Q interpreter exulted, "Sit back, grab your popcorn and watch the movie. The Patriots are in control. We are in the storm!"[38] But the eighteenth also came and went without incident. Nonetheless, Q believers could see that the military was firmly behind Trump. Just before Biden takes the oath on the twentieth, they said, the TV cameras will be turned off, soldiers will sweep in and take him into custody, and the mass executions will begin.

When Trump skulked off to Mar-a-Lago and Biden was sworn in on January 20, many Q believers did fall away. "I am just performing euthanasia to something I once loved very very much," a site moderator at the 8kun Q Research forum posted heartbrokenly as he deleted its contents (they were restored soon after and he was relieved of his duties).[39]

Ron Watkins, an ardent Q proponent, figuratively broke his sword over his knee. "We need to keep our chins up and go back to our lives as best we are able," he posted. "We have a new president sworn in and it is our responsibility as citizens to respect the Constitution," adding, as if he was signing a classmate's high school yearbook and not surrendering the leadership of the country he loved to a cabal of child rapists, murderers, and cannibals,

"Please remember all the friends and happy memories we made together over the past few years." A few months later, some alleged that Watkins had written most of Q's posts himself to drive traffic to 8kun, which is owned by his father. Watkins denied it, but proposed Steve Bannon and the Q documentarian Cullen Hoback as likelier candidates.[40]

After the inauguration, truer believers than Watkins penciled in a new date on their calendars for Trump's restoration: March 4, the date chosen by the Confederation Congress for presidential inaugurations in 1788 (the Twentieth Amendment changed it to January 20). Still others warned them not to take the bait. "March 4th was set up by Antifa to get everyone to come out! False flag! Stay home," a Telegram user posted.[41] Some looked further ahead to March 20, as that would be the 167th anniversary of the founding of the Republican Party. Still others took refuge in the idea that Trump had never left the White House at all, but that for reasons that would be fully explained when the time was ripe, had allowed himself to go into occultation. In the meantime, he was allowing Biden to carry on a pretend presidency from a Hollywood movie set. Some even convinced themselves that Trump and Biden had exchanged identities, like John Travolta and Nicolas Cage in the movie *Face/Off.*[42] Should Trump be indicted and convicted, the thinking went, it would really be Biden who went to jail. And if Biden had a successful presidency, it would be Trump who deserved the credit for it. It wasn't exactly a ringing endorsement of Republican policies, but the Q movement was never about policy—it had much more in common with early Christian theological controversies, like whether Adam had a navel, or if Jesus was consubstantial with His Father or formed of flesh and blood.

In May 2021, four months after Biden's inauguration, the Public Religion Research Institute, a nonpartisan organization that surveys Americans' religious attitudes, polled the country about QAnon. It found that between 15 and 20 percent of Americans completely or mostly agreed with its three main tenets: that "the government, media, and financial worlds in the U.S. are controlled by a group of Satan-worshipping pedophiles who run a global child sex trafficking operation"; that "there is a storm coming soon that will sweep away the elites in power and restore the rightful leaders"; and that, "because things have gotten so far off track, true American patriots may have to resort to violence in order to save our country."[43] It wasn't surprising, given that Trump himself was telling supporters that he expected to be "reinstated" as president as soon as August 2021.[44]

People who trust far-right media were ten times more likely to believe in QAnon than those who most trust the three major broadcast networks, the PRRI found, while Americans who trust public television were the most likely to be QAnon skeptics. People without college degrees were three times more likely to be believers than college graduates. Twenty-five percent of white evangelicals said they believe in all three tenets of QAnon. Eighty-five percent of Q-believers also believed that COVID-19 was developed intentionally by scientists in a laboratory, and 39 percent believed that the vaccine for COVID-19 contains a "surveillance microchip that is the sign of the beast in biblical prophecy."[45] Interestingly, the group that was least likely to believe in QAnon was Jews.

No matter what Trump's political future looks like, at some point in the near or middle term, we will see his like again. Why am I so sure about this? Because I've spent as much time as I have trying to see the world through conspiracists' eyes. It's taught me to pay as much attention to the negative spaces in the picture that America paints of itself as its positive ones.

Stare at a rendering of a figure-ground vase (also called a Rubin vase), and you'll see either the vase (the positive space) or the silhouetted faces in profile that frame it (its negative space). Stare at America today, and most of us will see the consensual version of reality that our teachers, parents, and the mainstream media conditioned us to see, but some will see a world that is controlled by hidden forces. Gestalt psychologists like Edgar Rubin, who gave the Rubin vase its name, recognized that our brains organize the visual information they receive into patterns, which is why we can look at lines and dots on two-dimensional pieces of paper and see complex, three-dimensional images. But as the Rubin vase demonstrates, our brains can't register two radically different patterns simultaneously if they are contained in the same image. Stare at such a picture long enough and it begins to flash back and forth from one to the other, like an electric advertising sign, a phenomenon known as "multi-stability."

Some of us (all of us, under certain circumstances) may also discern patterns where they don't exist—a man's face in the full moon, the image of the Virgin Mary burnt onto a piece of toast—a phenomenon known as "patternicity."*

It's the same with politics. As we process the streams of information that pour in on us from every direction, we can synthe-

---

* Extreme patternicity or apophenia can be a symptom of a pathological condition such as schizophrenia.

size them and organize them into complex narratives, or we can impose a preexisting template on them.

Patternicity is what's behind the conspiracist obsession with codes—the certainty that the hidden enemy leaves their signatures on their bad acts, much as graffiti artists tag their creations. Q's ingenious decryptions provide one example of this. For another, consider what happened in March 2021, when a Taiwanese container ship got blown sidewise in the Suez Canal, blocking ship traffic in both directions, disrupting global supply chains, and costing the world economy untold billions of dollars. Q followers immediately sussed out the truth: that the ship was filled with sex-trafficked children that were being delivered to Hillary Clinton. How did they know this? Google a picture of the ship. The company that operated it is the Evergreen Marine Corporation, and the word "Evergreen" is spelled out along its hull in gigantic block letters. Hillary Clinton's secret service code name when she was First Lady was Evergreen. Moreover, the ship's call sign was H3RC.

Some conspiracy theorists come by their insights honestly, which is to say, they truly believe that the patterns they discern are real. Others are more creative; the satisfaction they feel when they fit the pieces together is akin to what a novelist feels when a character they've invented displays a mind of their own and the story takes an unanticipated turn. As cynical as the political trolls who exploit the Q believers' credulity, ignorance, and hope may be, many of those believers are people of faith. The narratives they embrace are parables, with beginnings, middles, and ends, rounded off with clear morals. Each is embedded in a larger narrative arc as well, in which the righteous are tested and ultimately rewarded, and the wicked exposed and punished.

As the Never-Trump Republican columnist David Brooks wrote in *The New York Times* some three weeks after the 2020 election, "We live in a country in epistemological crisis, in which much of the Republican Party has become detached from reality."[46] Just as snorers can't hear themselves snore, conspiracy theorists don't see the illogic and the incompatibilities of their competing claims. They saw the fact that Trump received some eleven million more votes in 2020 than he did in 2016 as proof that he was too popular to lose a fair election—even though the same people that counted Trump's eleven-million-plus additional votes counted Biden's votes as well (seven million more than Trump's and fifteen million more than Hillary Clinton received four years before).

If the Deep State really went to all that trouble to steal the election from Trump, then why did it allow so many Republican senators and congressmen to slip through the cracks and win, making it that much harder for Biden to enact his agenda—and so much easier for Trump to gain traction for his next try? If the Deep State is as powerful and ruthless as Trump says, then why doesn't it kill its enemies instead of allowing them to write syndicated newspaper columns, host TV talk shows and podcasts, and run for and win elective office?

In a long piece for *The Atlantic*, Kurt Andersen called America the "global crucible and epicenter" of the "fantasy industrial complex." "Why are we like this?" he asked. "The short answer is because we're Americans—because being American means we can believe anything we want; that our beliefs are equal or superior to anyone else's, experts be damned." Andersen blamed this attitude on everything from post-structuralism and the psychedelic '60s to Ronald Reagan's wishful economic analyses, Christian fundamentalism, the internet, and, preeminently, Donald Trump, whose stroke of political genius, he said, was to wed Americans' "skeptical disillusion with politics" to their "magical thinking about national greatness" while shamelessly pandering to both. What America needs, he concluded, is a national effort to restore reality-based thinking. "If you have children or grandchildren," he pleaded, "teach them to distinguish between true and untrue as fiercely as you do between right and wrong and between wise and foolish."[47]

It's an admirable aspiration, but as partial as I am to sanity and the scientific method, I don't know how useful any such effort could be, given all the things I've been writing about up until now. For one thing, Andersen is preaching to the choir; most of *The Atlantic*'s readers share his empiric biases and they are almost certainly teaching their children and grandchildren to think as they do. As for those incorrigible fantasists, most would insist that if anyone is living in Cloud Cuckoo Land, it is Andersen and his colleagues in the mainstream media. It's not as though every proponent of the Big Steal consciously wants to destroy democracy, or that anti-vaxxers want their elderly parents or themselves to get sick with COVID. They call themselves "truthers" because, as the Dunning-Kruger* effect predicts, they believe they have a handle on the truth.

Back in 2008, in a now infamous paper entitled "Conspiracy Theories," Cass Sunstein and Adrian Vermeule proposed a program of "cognitive infiltration" in which government agents would

---

* A cognitive bias that makes people overestimate their knowledge or expertise. In David Dunning's words (https://www.sciencedirect.com/science/article/abs /pii/B9780123855220000056?via%3Dihub), this "meta-ignorance" leaves its sufferers with a "double burden—not only does their incomplete and misguided knowledge lead them to make mistakes but those exact same deficits also prevent them from recognizing when they are making mistakes and other people choosing more wisely."

join conspiracist chatrooms and introduce viral "truth infections" into their closed-off, self-reinforcing belief systems. "Social cascades," they wrote, "are sometimes quite fragile, precisely because they are based on small slivers of information. Once corrective information is introduced, large numbers of people can be shifted to different views."[48] With its sinister echoes of COINTELPRO's agents provocateurs, the proposal was greeted with horror on both the left and right; moreover, it had the unintended consequence of inflaming the conspiracy world's grandiose sense of persecution.

I don't believe that homeopathically prescribed doses of truth can ablate magical thinking. Reasoning with a true believer is exactly as useful as reasoning with someone who is in love with the wrong person. Cognitive dissonance avoidance, our deep need to deny and distort whatever clashes with what we choose to believe, plays the same outsized role in our national psyche that sexual repression was said to in Freud's fin-de-siècle Vienna. Seen in that light, the paranoid style is, to lift a phrase out of context from William Carlos Williams, a "pure product of America"— one that articulates, to borrow another line from that same poem, "with broken brain the truth about us."

5

The Deepest Bias(es)

If America's paranoid style is homegrown and unique, conspiracy theory is universal. By the early 1920s, *The Protocols of the Elders of Zion* had been translated into German, Polish, French, Italian, and English. Its first Arab translation appeared in 1925, and it was published in Portuguese and Spanish in 1930. Even after some of its German readers acted on its lessons and exterminated millions of Jewish men, women, and children, it continues to be read and studied around the world. It is explicitly cited in Hamas's charter and was the basis of TV miniseries in Egypt and Syria and several documentaries in Iran. It is widely circulated in Japan, where there are almost no Jews.

As deplorable as it is that the *Protocols* would have the propagandistic currency that it does in the Middle East, it's not surprising, as the Arab-Israeli conflict has been inescapable for the past three-quarters of a century and more. It's also understandable that conspiracy theories would be as rife as they are in countries that really are groaning under nonmetaphorical tyrannies, or that did in the not-so-distant past. But the gap between reality and paranoid fantasy is much larger in the United States than it was in Germany and Japan in the 1920s and '30s, and in Russia and much of the Muslim world today. For all of America's long-standing racial, ethnic, and religious enmities, most of its citizens—including many who feel dispossessed—enjoy a relatively high standard of living, and its laws still protect the press from censorship. Unless you are poor, undocumented, incarcerated, or Black, the hand of the government lies much lighter on U.S. citizens than it does in many other countries.

So why here? Exactly what are American conspiracists so afraid of? While the Freemasons—the objects of so much conspiracy theory—really were a revolutionary vanguard in some parts of the world, they were never more than a fraternal society in the United States. Trump's shambolic autogolpe after his loss in 2020 was so unprecedented and ran so counter to American values that many of the people who cheered him on and participated in it deny that that was what he and they intended.

The aspirational ideals of liberty, equality, and freedom of opportunity are as deeply ingrained in our national narrative as the ethos of American exceptionalism. For all their talk of redistribution, even democratic socialists embrace a version of the American Dream. "The American Dream isn't a private club with a cover charge—it's the possibility of remaking your future," as Alexandria Ocasio-Cortez put it when Trump demanded that green cards be withheld from immigrants who use public benefits.[1]

But not everyone. As noted earlier in these pages, I covered a conference of Richard Spencer's alt-right National Policy Institute in 2011. The last speaker I heard was the well-known white nationalist Sam Dickson, David Duke's lawyer and a former candidate for lieutenant governor of Georgia, who described his life's journey from youthful Goldwater activist to a true believer in the ethno-state. His words, spoken in a courtly southern drawl, left an indelible impression on me.[2]

Movement conservatives, the Tea Party, all of them miss the point, he said. While they talk about "taking America back," they forget that the Constitution was poisoned at its inception by "the infection of the French Enlightenment." White people haven't controlled America's government for 150 years. In fact, the constitutional republic is the white race's greatest enemy. "Our government hates us, degrades us, and seeks to destroy us," he said. "We cannot save America. We need to let go and think of something new. America is the God that failed."

Dickson's frankness, of course, is not the norm among conservatives, even if some of his sentiments are more widely shared than most care to acknowledge. Repressed desires, like the forbidden hope that America will end its experiment with democratic republicanism and replace it with an authoritarian Christian regime like Hungary's, give rise to the same kinds of painful dissonances that irrational beliefs do. One way to manage the discomfort is to project those beliefs onto your enemies: *Obama despises America. Biden is a tyrant. Democrats want Republicans dead and they have already started the killings.*

Yet another is to befriend your enemies' enemies. In 1962, Elijah Muhammad, the founder of the Nation of Islam, invited George Lincoln Rockwell, the chief of the American Nazi Party, to address a convention in Chicago. Rockwell did, hailing Elijah Muhammad as "the Adolph Hitler of the Black man."[3] Right-wing Zionists and right-wing authoritarians like Viktor Orbán find common ground in their shared Islamophobia, nationalism, and ethnocentrism.

For a more risible example of this, read one of the impassioned defenses of the House of Windsor that appeared in the wake of Prince Harry and Meghan Markle's televised interview with Oprah Winfrey in March 2021. Markle, an American TV actress whose mother is Black, became the Duchess of Sussex. During the interview, she accused some of her in-laws of harboring racist feelings toward her. Remember, those in-laws are members of the British royal family, an institution whose very existence presumes not just the privilege of its bloodline but its literal, divinely mandated supremacy. No matter what the editors of William F. Buckley's *National Review* might think of Markle, you'd expect them to let America's ancient adversary fight its own battles. Instead, they leapt to the royal family's defense, arguing that an attack on the English Crown is an attack on the values that Americans hold most dear. "The radical Left," it wrote, "has seized upon Oprah Winfrey's televised spectacle . . . in a crusade to invalidate one of the most consequential conservative institutions on the world stage. . . . The aim of modern liberalism," it continued, is "to tear down everything the monarchy represents: tradition, authority, virtue, duty, love of country, and biblical religion."[4]

While it's easy to imagine how dumbfounded and even threatened America's founding fathers might have been by the high status Markle and Winfrey enjoy, as they are both Black women, it's hard to imagine them seconding the *National Review*'s characterization of the royals. "Take any race of animals," Thomas Jefferson famously wrote to a friend on the eve of a royal wedding in 1810, "confine them in idleness and inaction, whether in a sty, a stable, or a state-room, pamper them with high diet, gratify all their sexual appetites, immerse them in sensualities, nourish their passions, let everything bend before them, and banish whatever might lead them to think, and in a few generations they become all body and no mind. . . . Such is the regimen in raising Kings."[5] One can only wonder what the *National Review* makes of the so-called Jefferson Bible, the eighty-six-page bowdlerization of the New Testament from which Jefferson redacted all but its ethical teachings.

As wrong as they are about everything else, the conspiracy theorists seem to be right about one thing. As *National Review* unintentionally demonstrated, a great many of America's problems share a hidden factor. The conspiracy theorists may not identify it correctly—it isn't Jewish chicanery, satanically inspired homosexuals, or space aliens. Nor is it critical race theory or drag queens. It is racism, whether acknowledged or unacknowledged, de jure or de facto, an active principle or a lingering vestige of a willfully misunderstood past.

The conspiracy theorists are right about something else as well: things are not always what our parents and teachers and pastors taught us to believe they are. America has often failed to live up to its exceptionalist ideals. That's not to say that America is exceptionally wicked. As nation-states go, the United States is better than many, and its founders' ideals are mostly admirable, even if they and we have often failed to live up to them.

But like they do in most places, America's financial, political, and social elites really do keep a tight grip on the reins of power—that's why they're called elites—and they work hard to protect their interests. Despite what they tell us, what's good for them is not always what's good for everyone else. While it's true that capitalism has raised living standards across the board, from a child mill worker's perspective one-hundred-fifty years ago or a part-time minimum-wage worker's today, owners continue to enjoy all kinds of unfair advantages. Does the capitalist class routinely hold secret ceremonies in which they ritually rape and murder children? Of course not. Most of their energies go into union busting and political lobbying to keep their taxes low and regulations at a minimum. The owner class constantly tests the limits of what they can get away with, and they get away with a lot.

Our great national myth—that America is a crucible of equal-

ity, tolerance, and boundless entrepreneurial opportunity—has
never been our national reality. Critical race theory doesn't explain
everything (no one theory could), but it surfaces a painful and
undeniable truth: that our liberal humanist traditions were not
only erected on a rickety scaffolding of race supremacism, religious bigotry, land theft, involuntary servitude, and toxic mascu-
linity, but were compromised by them from the very beginning,
as surely as Sam Dickson said they were by the egalitarian values
of the French Enlightenment.

Which isn't to say that things haven't improved—I personally
believe that what Dickson diagnosed as an infectious agent was
the antibody for toxins like himself, and I suspect that he knows
that too. I further suspect that what has driven so many white
American Protestants (Dickson also spoke about his pride in his
Huguenot roots) into right-wing extremism is the realization that
the implicit promise of white, Protestant, male hegemony no longer holds. That's to our credit.

Some of the American dream is real, of course. As a second-
generation Jew, I'm a beneficiary of it, as are the descendants of
many of the other immigrant groups that came here voluntarily.
And while the rules of hypodescent* —the default assignment of
mixed-race children to the race that carries the least status—are
still in effect (cf. Meghan Markle), the stigma of race is losing
much of its force (also cf. Meghan Markle). The so-called race science of the nineteenth and early twentieth centuries, which drew
fine distinctions between a hierarchy of separate European races,
is mostly forgotten. Very few Americans would think of a person

* As Madison Grant wrote in *The Passing of the Great Race* in 1916, "The cross
between a white man and an Indian is an Indian; the cross between a white man
and a Negro is a Negro; the cross between a white man and a Hindu is a Hindu;
and the cross between any of the three European races and a Jew is a Jew."

from a Slavic background, like Melania Trump or Vladimir Putin, as nonwhite today; only a neo-Nazi would describe an Ashkenazi Jew like me as an Asiatic. Most Americans with European roots have long since been melted into the common alloy. Many Americans—including some Black ones, like Oprah Winfrey—really have pulled themselves up by their bootstraps, and for all of its many failures in practice, our system leans toward more rather than less liberty and opportunity. But America's past, like most countries', is not just marred by but defined by force and violence and fear and hate; worse still, as William Faulkner put it in *Requiem for a Nun* (a novel whose plot turned on the legacies of race and rape), "it's not even past."

But the first slave ship didn't arrive in Virginia until 1619, twelve years after Jamestown was founded. America's oldest hatred, I would argue, was not anti-Black but anti-Catholic. The first colonists brought it with them from England. A recent archaeological find sheds new light on this. In 2013, the remains of four men were discovered at the site of a chapel in Jamestown. One of them, Captain Gabriel Archer, had been buried with a silver box that a CT scan showed contained bone fragments and a lead ampulla. It was almost certainly a Catholic reliquary, and it was, in the words of *The Atlantic*'s Adrienne LaFrance, "a bombshell," potential "proof of an underground community of Catholics."[6] * They would have had to have been secret because Catholic worship had been banned in England since 1559, when Queen Elizabeth issued the Act of Uniformity.

We know from the historical record that Archer and John Smith

---

* A less dramatic interpretation is that it was a Catholic reliquary that had been adapted to Anglican use. But the fact that Archer's parents had been fined for their refusal to attend Anglican services suggests otherwise.

were bitter enemies, and that Archer had tried to have Smith removed from the governing council of the colony. "Historians have always considered that [Archer] was trying to elevate his own position," James Horn, the author of *A Kingdom Strange: The Brief and Tragic History of the Lost Colony of Roanoke* and president of the Jamestown Rediscovery Foundation, told LaFrance. "But was there something more going on? . . . Jamestown [was] meant to be the beachhead for an English empire in America that [would] serve as a bulwark against Catholicism. . . . [Archer] could have been the leader of a secret Catholic cell and even possibly a secret Catholic priest." Sounding almost like a conspiracy theorist, Horn asks, "Was he trying to destabilize the colony's leadership from within?"

The English Protestants who colonized the New World feared hunger, illness, and childbirth, which killed one out of eight expectant mothers and a third of their children who were born alive by their fifth birthdays. They feared the raw wilderness and its indigenous inhabitants, who they knew were servants of the Devil, and the witches and other minions of Satan that dwelled among them, disguised as their wives, children, neighbors, servants, and enslaved people. They feared their own sinful natures and Antinomianism or "Free Grace" Protestantism, the radical doctrine that once they were saved, Christians were no longer bound by the moral law, a philosophy, they believed, that could not but lead to licentiousness and attacks on property and the political order. Most of all, they feared Catholicism, which they had been at war with since the time of Henry VIII. The Catholic French had forged alliances with native tribes in the north and west. The Catholic Spaniards controlled the south. The threat of internal subversion was real as well; the Gunpowder Plot conspirators had been executed less than a year before the Jamestown settlers departed England.

The Pilgrims and Puritans who arrived in Massachusetts in 1620 held all those terrors at bay, to quote William Carlos Williams again—this time very much in context, from his fascinating and disturbing book *In the American Grain*—with a program of "merciless whippings, chainings, finings, imprisonments, starvings, burnings in the hands, cuttings off of ears and putting to death."[7] Williams's book is an exploration of the many facets of the American character, assembled collage-like from authentic and imagined testimonies from Eric the Red, Hernán Cortés, Christopher Columbus, Cotton Mather, Daniel Boone, Abraham Lincoln, and others.

Unlike the English Protestants, Williams said, the French Jesuits had taken the strangeness and savagery of the wilderness as they found it, surrendering themselves to its sublime and terrible beauty, living out a creed that avowed that "nothing shall be ignored. All shall be included." As splendidly written as it is, Williams's take on the mystical, life-affirming, sex-positive Jesuits was as romantic as his view of the flesh-hating Puritans was jaundiced; both must be seen as artifacts of his time and place (which was Rutherford, New Jersey, circa 1925, shortly after he'd returned from a visit to bohemian Paris) and clearly colored by his personal prejudices.*

If Williams looked at the Puritans and saw the smug small-mindedness and prudery of his day, many of those Puritans' descendants still see the world much as their ancestors did,

---

* Speaking of prejudices, Williams's tribute to African America—"the colored men and women whom I know intimately add a quality, that is delightful, to the life about me"—is shockingly condescending, even for its day. Though clearly well intended, it's offensive to a modern sensibility, even one that is only moderately woke. I say that not to "cancel" Williams, but to stress how much the canons of acceptable ideas and speech about race and gender change over time, as Williams himself, I suspect, would have been among the first to acknowledge.

though their great enemy is no longer godless papists and savages but depraved liberalism, or at the conspiracist extreme, some differently titled ism that in practice looks and sounds an awful lot like Catholicism.* Illuminism perhaps, or cultural Marxism. Or Zionism, the philosophy, they believe, of an ancient, fabulously wealthy elite whose power transcends national boundaries and whose leaders invisibly bend the world to their wills using the power of propaganda and finance. The Davidic superstate of the *Protocols* is a fantasy, but the Vatican was and is very real.

Most of the Puritans had been raised on *Foxe's Book of Martyrs*, first published in 1563, a compendium of stories about righteous Protestants and their brutally corrupt Roman Catholic tormentors who, try though they might, could not stifle their ardent spirits. "What Christian man would not gladly die against the pope and his adherents?" as one of Foxe's Protestants put it on the eve of his martyrdom. "I know that the papacy is the kingdom of antichrist, altogether full of lies, altogether full of falsehood . . . nothing but idolatry, superstition, errors, hypocrisy, and lies."[8]

"Some Thoughts upon America, and upon the Danger from Roman Catholicks There," an anonymous pamphlet that circulated in London in 1739, noted that Catholics have no compunctions about committing murders and even regicides, thanks to the ease with which they can obtain dispensations, and that they "believe it their Duty to cut [Protestant] Throats," as they deem it "meritous

---

* After I wrote this chapter, I read an excerpt from Michael Wolff's book *The Fall: The End of the Murdoch Empire* in *New York* magazine. A quote from Tucker Carlson leaped out at me: "'You know, I am not antisemitic, and I am not anti-Black; that's a complete misunderstanding of what I am. . . . I am anti-Catholic.' . . . That was the retro message of the pale face, tousled hair, and prep-school uniform: Wasp. In this, his atavism was a purer kind than that of Fox or Trump. His reached back further, recalling an earlier America."

[*sic*] . . . Honour and Service to the All-merciful God."⁹ As the historian and priest John Tracy Ellis put it in his book *American Catholicism,* "A universal anti-Catholic bias was brought to Jamestown in 1607 and vigilantly cultivated in all the thirteen colonies from Massachusetts to Georgia." Ellis also quotes a remark made to him by Arthur Schlesinger Sr., which has been cited in virtually every subsequent book and article about anti-Catholicism in America: "I regard the prejudice against your Church as the deepest bias in the history of the American people."¹⁰

The Pilgrims and Puritans that settled Massachusetts were seekers of religious freedom, but only for themselves—their goal was a theocracy that would suppress all but their own true religion. Though other colonies were more tolerant of dissenting Protestants and even Catholics than Massachusetts, the principle that religion and state are separate spheres is a legacy of the Enlightenment, not the Reformation—and though it is enshrined in the Constitution, it is far from universally accepted.*

Practicing Catholics were explicitly banned from Massachusetts, Connecticut, and New Hampshire. Roger Williams founded Rhode Island as a refuge for religious dissenters in 1636, but virtually no Catholics lived there to enjoy the privilege of freedom of worship at the time. Pennsylvania and Delaware also tolerated Catholics, but few lived in either colony until much later. Virginia expelled priests from its territory in 1641. Georgia offered freedom of worship to all "except papists." New York banned Catholi-

---

* In May 2022, Kandiss Taylor, a failed Republican candidate for Georgia's governorship, explained the First Amendment thusly: "The First Amendment right, which is our right to worship Jesus freely—that's why we have a country. That's why we have Georgia. That's why we had our Founding Fathers come over here and destroy American Indians' homes and their land." (https://www.newsweek.com/native-americans-made-sacrifice-our-right-worship-jesus-taylor-1708855)

cism in 1688; New Jersey passed its first formal anti-Catholic law in 1691; in 1701, it granted liberty of conscience to all "except papists." South Carolina enacted similar legislation in 1697 but dropped its religious test in 1790; Catholics were not allowed to hold public office in Massachusetts until 1833, in North Carolina until 1835, and in New Jersey until 1844.

Maryland's chief sponsor, Lord Baltimore, had envisioned the colony as a refuge for Catholics like himself, but it didn't go as planned. Though the Maryland Toleration Act, which became law in 1649, granted the right of free worship for any "professing to believe in Jesus Christ," it was overturned in the early 1650s when Puritans briefly seized control of its government. It was restored a few years later, only to be overturned again in 1692, when Catholicism was formally banned in the colony.

As Robert Emmett Curran wrote in his book *Papist Devils: Catholics in British America, 1574–1783,* anti-Catholicism was "an effective unifying force, both in England and in British America, in defining a society by an 'other' that contradicted all that that society stood for and whose very survival the 'other,' by its very presence, threatened."[11]

When the War of the Austrian Succession heated up in late 1740, rumors ran rampant in the colonies that the Catholic Hapsburgs had organized an army of Iroquois led by priests, who were also organizing slave revolts. James Oglethorpe dispatched a warning from Georgia that Spain was infiltrating its agents into cities throughout the colonies, with instructions to set them to the torch. In 1755, British soldiers expelled the Catholic Acadians from Nova Scotia, costing at least five thousand of them their lives as they were transported into exile. "We are now upon a great and noble Scheme of sending the neutral French out of this Province, who have always been secret Enemies, and have encouraged our Savages to cut our Throats. If we effect their Expulsion, it will be one of the greatest things that ever the English did in America," a contemporary newspaper editorialized. A year later, the British and the French were at war. Colonial ministers described the conflict in apocalyptic terms: "The French now adhere and belong to Antichrist," declared the New Jersey minister Theodorus Frelinghuysen.[12]

Every November 5, New York and Massachusetts held parades and ritual burnings in effigy of the pope, Satan, and Guy Fawkes to commemorate the failure of the 1605 Gunpowder Plot. One of the five so-called Intolerable Acts that inspired colonists to write the Declaration of Independence was England's Quebec Act of 1774, which granted freedom of worship and the right to hold office to Roman Catholics. But once the American Revolution began, those same intolerably Catholic French Canadians—not to mention France itself—became key allies. General George Washington deplored the "ridiculous and childish custom" of Pope's Day and demanded that the celebrations be stopped, lest they offend America's new allies.

In 1790, when Washington had become America's first president, he addressed an open letter to "Roman Catholics in America" (as he would also do for the Jews of Newport, Rhode Island), acknowledging their patriotism, specifying the full rights (as opposed to mere toleration) they enjoyed as citizens, and pledging that their fellow Americans "will not forget . . . the important assistance which they received from a nation in which the Roman Catholic faith is professed."[13]

In 1765, John Adams famously quipped that Catholics were as uncommon in the colonies as comets or earthquakes. By 1790, when the population of the newly independent United States had reached about three million, its total number of Catholics was still just twenty thousand or so. But after the Louisiana Purchase in 1803, America's Catholic population swelled to about seventy-five

thousand; by 1820, it was more than two hundred thousand—
and that was before the first great waves of immigration from
Ireland and Germany. Now Catholics were not just spiritual enemies but economic competitors. In 1834, the Ursuline convent
in Charlestown, Boston, was put to the torch by a mob when
rumors circulated that the Protestant girls that attended its school
were being forced to convert. That same year, Jedidiah Morse's
son Samuel, a portrait painter who would go on to invent the
telegraph, circulated rumors that the Hapsburgs, working hand
in glove with the Vatican, were infiltrating an army of conquest
into the United States:

> The conspirators against our liberties, who have been admitted
> from abroad through the liberality of our institutions, are now
> *organized* in every part of the country; they are all subordinates,
> standing in regular steps of slave and master, from the most abject
> dolt that obeys the commands of his priest, up to the great master-
> slave Metternich, who commands and obeys his illustrious Mas-
> ter, the Emperor. . . . There is a similar organization among the
> Catholics of other countries.[14]

Around the same time, *The Awful Disclosures of Maria Monk;
or, The Hidden Secrets of a Nun's Life in a Convent Exposed,* the
ghostwritten memoirs of a woman who claimed to have been
held as a sex slave in a Montreal convent, became America's all-
time best seller. Maria Monk's real-life story was as squalid and
filled with unlikely twists and turns as anything you'd see on an
afternoon tabloid TV show. After she became famous, her mother
emerged from the woodwork to expose her as a congenital liar
who'd become incorrigible after a pencil was stuck in her ear,
damaging her brain. Her book was thoroughly debunked by a

Protestant journalist named William Leete Stone; the only misadventure she hadn't endured, it seems, was being held as a sex slave in a Canadian convent. Maria's illegitimate daughter would embrace Catholicism and attempt to start a publishing career of her own; Maria herself died in jail in 1849 after being convicted of robbing a john.

The same year *The Awful Disclosures* was published, Lyman Beecher, a Presbyterian minister, co-founder of the American Temperance Society, and father of Harriet Beecher Stowe, whose *Uncle Tom's Cabin* would displace Maria Monk's book as America's all-time best seller in the 1850s, published his *A Plea for the West,* which warned that the Catholic powers of Europe were extending their influence into the American West via mass immigration. Given the total control the church exercised over its priests and that its priests held over their congregations, he said, the subversion of democracy could be the only result. "The opinions of the Protestant clergy are congenial with liberty," he concluded, while Catholicism "is adverse to liberty."[15]

By the late 1840s, at the height of the potato famine, Irish Catholic immigration had risen to a flood tide; at least one and a half million Irish emigrated between 1846 and 1855, most to the United States. When Catholic parents complained that their children were forced to read from Protestant Bibles and recite Protestant prayers in America's public schools, angry Protestants in Philadelphia rioted. Though lawmakers considered funding both Catholic and Protestant public schools for a time, the Solomonic solution they ultimately settled on was to simply secularize the curriculum and teach the Bible as literature—a decision that satisfied neither side and ultimately led America's Catholics to build a separate system of parochial schools. At the height of the controversy, the up-and-coming New York journalist Walt Whitman editorialized in *The New York Aurora* about the "gang of false and villainous priests, whose despicable souls never generate any aspiration beyond their own narrow and horrible and beastly superstition . . . dregs of foreign filth—refuse of convents."[16]

A number of anti-Catholic secret societies arose. The American Brotherhood (which quickly changed its name to the Order of United Americans) was founded in New York City in 1844 with a mission "to release our country from the thralldom of foreign domination." The Order of United American Mechanics began in Philadelphia a year later, and in 1850, the Order of the Star Spangled Banner was founded in New York with the explicit goal of driving Catholic immigrants from public office and organizing boycotts against their businesses. The *New-York Tribune's* Horace Greeley dubbed the groups "Know Nothings" because of their oaths of secrecy, but also because of their ignorant narrowmindedness.[17] The name caught on, and like so many other pejoratives, was adopted as an honorific by their members.

While the Know Nothings opposed so-called papism on moral grounds, they were pragmatic in practice; their chief aims were to reverse the downward pressure on wages caused by immigration and the rising corruption of the Catholic-dominated urban political machines. The owner class was more ambivalent. While they were happy to replace American workers with hungry immigrants who would work harder for less, they worried about the revolutionary spirit of 1848 sweeping Italy, Germany, and Ireland, among other countries, which some of those immigrants carried with them from abroad. By 1855, the Know Nothings had coalesced into a full-blown political party, the American Party, which filled some of the void left by the collapse of the Whigs. "As a nation," the former Whig Abraham Lincoln wrote to his friend Joshua Speed at the time, "we began by declaring that '*all men are created equal.'* . . . When the Know-Nothings get control, it will read 'all men are created equal, except negroes, *and foreigners, and catholics.'* "[18] Nonetheless, eight governors, more than one hundred U.S. congressmen, and the mayors of three major cities had been elected on American Party tickets by the end of the decade.

Compared to the monstrous injustice of slavery, the decades of sectional strife it caused, and the cataclysmic disasters of secession, the war, Reconstruction, and the Jim Crow era that followed, the clamor over Catholic immigration was little more than background noise. That said, the American Party provided a rare opportunity for the fraying republic to come together around a different shared hatred during the decade of Bleeding Kansas, as John Higham, author of the seminal study *Strangers in the Land: Patterns of American Nativism, 1860–1925,* put it.

Slavery, of course, generated its own conspiracy theories. Between the Know Nothings and the pro- and anti-slavery movements, the United States in the 1850s was as rife with hateful theorizing as it is today. Some abolitionists recast the entire history of the United States until then as the unfolding of an explicit plot, masterminded by the southern Slave Power in collusion with the northern Money Power, to not just perpetuate and expand the enslavement of Negroes, but, in the words of the abolitionist William Goodell, to enslave "the laboring white population" of the North. "We speak not now of latent *tendencies,*" he wrote, in the familiar cadences of conspiracy theorists. "We inquire after the *objects* and the actual *operations* of the slaveholding statesmen. . . . A child can put the two facts together and understand their import."[19]

Southern politicians had goaded the United States into the War of 1812 to bankrupt New England and weaken the North, the story went. The war with Mexico was fought solely to add another slave state to the republic. In his *History of the Plots and Crimes of the Great Conspiracy to Overthrow Liberty in America,* John Smith Dye further accused operatives from the Slave Power faction of orchestrating a failed assassination attempt on Andrew Jackson in 1835, and of poisoning William Henry Harrison with arsenic to ensure that Texas would be annexed. Zachary Taylor was murdered, he said, after he opposed the extension of slavery into California. The railroad accident that killed Franklin Pierce's son was no accident, and it ensured Pierce's pliancy thereafter. James Buchanan narrowly escaped death when operatives from the Slave Power faction sprinkled arsenic on the lump sugar at Washington's National Hotel, killing dozens of northern politicians who were dining there, and causing Buchanan to fall critically ill. No southerners were harmed, he said, because southerners only use ground sugar to sweeten their coffee.*

Once the Civil War began, the tide of nativism ebbed—how could it not, when so many Catholic immigrants fought and died to preserve the Union? But it soon rose again. The cartoonist Thomas Nast was born a Catholic but became an Episcopalian as a young man. An abolitionist and a witness to the draft riots in New York City, the editorial cartoons he published in the 1860s and 1870s were virulently anti-Irish and anti-Catholic. Nast was not alone; a number of those anti-Catholic fraternal orders would revive during the Long Depression of the 1870s, and some new ones were established, most notably the American Protective Association in 1887. The recent rash of bank runs had been orchestrated by the Vatican to soften up America for attack, the APA

---

* There was in fact a rash of mysterious deaths at the National Hotel, but most medical experts now believe the cause was dysentery (there was a leak in the hotel's sewage system). (https://history.house.gov/Historical-Highlights/1851 -1900/The-Mysterious-National-Hotel-Disease/)

declared. A document called "Instructions to Catholics," which it claimed was written by the pope, was "discovered" and widely distributed. "In order to find employment for the many thousands of the faithful who are coming daily to swell the ranks of our catholic army, which will in due time possess this land," it read in part, "we must secure control of . . . every enterprise requiring labor . . . this will render it necessary to remove or crowd out the American heretics who are now employed."[20]

In 1893, *The Detroit Patriotic American* published another obvious forgery, this one purported to be an encyclical written by Pope Leo XIII, absolving American Catholics from any oaths of loyalty they might have sworn to the United States and commanding them to prepare to "exterminate all heretics" as soon as that coming September. The resulting hysteria, mostly in rural places where actual Catholics were few and far between, was reminiscent of the panic that swept the United States in the days, weeks, and months after 9/11, when people in midwestern farm communities were reporting sightings of al-Qaeda operatives.

By the turn of the twentieth century, a couple of new hatreds were on the rise. Scientific racism and eugenics were gaining broad acceptance, and Jim Crow laws were being formalized in the South, sealing the utter failure of Reconstruction. Political (as opposed to religious and cultural) anti-Semitism was also gaining traction. The agrarian populism that arose in the last third of the nineteenth century had a lot of progressive, anti-corporate features, but it was also rife with theories about the Rothschilds' control of finance. Populists like Georgia's Tom Watson simply stacked those newer hatreds on top of the old.

Watson's eponymous magazine and *The Menace,* an anti-Catholic weekly published in Aurora, Missouri, publicized the bogus fourth-degree Knights of Columbus oath, which was adapted from the equally fraudulent Extreme Oath of the Jesuits, which had first surfaced in Robert Ware and John Nalson's 1682 *Foxes and Firebrands.* It was even read into the *Congressional Record,* as *The Protocols of the Elders of Zion* would be in 1938. Knights of Columbus members, it was said, swore an oath to the pope in which they promised to "make and wage relentless war, secretly and openly, against all heretics, Protestants and Masons . . . to extirpate them from the face of the whole earth."[21] Anti-Catholicism was a prominent feature of the burgeoning Christian fundamentalist movement (the first edition of *The Fundamentals,* the multivolume collection of essays that lays out its basic doctrines, was published in 1910).

Anti-Catholicism also figured largely in the temperance movement, as it had since the days of Lyman Beecher (Democrats had been decried as the party of "rum, Romanism, and rebellion" since 1884). When the United States entered World War I in 1917, Sidney Johnston Catts, the Prohibition Party's newly elected governor of Florida, served up a ragout of anti-Black and anti-Catholic hatreds, accusing the monks of Saint Leo Abbey outside Tampa of plotting to arm local Blacks so they could assist in the kaiser's supposedly imminent invasion. Once Florida was in the kaiser's hands, he said, the Vatican would be relocated to Florida.

Anti-Catholicism was also a major component of the revived Ku Klux Klan, which, starting in 1915, organized boycotts against Catholic businesses and campaigned against Catholic politicians in addition to its racist and anti-Semitic activities. Thanks in large part to its efforts, Alfred Smith's quest for the Democratic presidential nomination was defeated in 1924. When Smith secured the nomination in 1928, he came under attack not just from the troglodytes in the KKK, but Yankee intellectuals. In an open letter to *The Atlantic,* he was challenged to answer abstruse questions about Pope Leo XIII's 1885 encyclical "Immortale Dei"— specifically, whether he would defer to his church or his country in the event of a conflict between the two. "By what right," Smith replied, in a letter that the renowned priest, teacher, and army chaplain Father Francis P. Duffy helped him write, "do you ask me to assume responsibility for every statement that may be made in any encyclical letter? . . . So little are these matters of the essence of my faith that I, a devout Catholic since childhood, never heard of them until I read your letter."[22] In his autobiography, Smith said he was also dogged by rumors that New York's freshly dug Holland Tunnel led directly to the Vatican. A much-reproduced cartoon with the caption "Cabinet Meeting—If Al Were President" depicted Smith dressed in a bellhop's uniform, serving whiskey to a cabinet that was made up entirely of priests and bishops.[23]

Three decades later, in 1960, one-hundred and fifty prominent Protestant clergy and laymen convened at the Mayflower Hotel in Washington, D.C., for a meeting of an ad hoc organization that called itself Citizens for Religious Freedom. Norman Vincent Peale, whose Marble Collegiate Church in Manhattan Donald Trump attended as a child (and who officiated at Trump's first wedding),[24] served as its spokesman, declaring that Kennedy's candidacy had put "our American culture . . . at stake. . . . I don't say it won't survive, but it won't be what it was." The group issued a formal statement that declared it was "inconceivable that a Roman Catholic President would not be under extreme pressure by the hierarchy of his church to accede to its policies with respect to foreign relations . . . and otherwise breach the wall of separation of church and state." The evangelist Billy Graham sent a letter to the two million names on his mailing list, urging them to organize for Nixon via their Sunday schools and churches. O. K. Armstrong,

a Missouri congressman, organized speeches and other activities
through such organizations as Protestants and Other Americans
United for Separation of Church and State.

Kennedy felt compelled to respond. In a speech at the Greater
Houston Ministerial Association, he affirmed that "I am not the
Catholic candidate for president, I am the Democratic Party's
candidate for president, who happens also to be a Catholic. I do
not speak for my church on public matters, and the church does
not speak for me."[25]

The point I have been trying to make with these examples
of America's oldest bias is not that our country is still as anti-
Catholic as it was in the days of the Puritans, the Know Nothings,
the APA, Tom Watson, or even JFK, because that's not remotely
the case. More than a fifth of Americans are Catholic, making
Catholicism America's largest religious denomination by far. But
it's not the size of the Catholic population that is significant, it's
how assimilated its members are, how indistinguishable in most
respects from other Christian Americans. One sign of that is how
much like America they look politically: as of 2020, 48 percent of
American Catholics identified as Republicans, and 47 percent as
Democrats, according to Pew Research, and when it came to hot-
button issues like abortion, they aligned with their parties rather
than their church. Seventy-seven percent of Democratic Catholics
were pro-choice, while 63 percent of Republican Catholics were
pro-life.[26]

As noted earlier, conservative evangelicals and Catholics found
common cause in the so-called pro-life movement. But the thaw
had set in long before *Roe v. Wade,* driven by Catholicism's sheer
numbers and I suspect also by white flight. For most of their history, Catholic immigrants, like Jews, had crowded into cities.
In Boston and New York, Catholics became political bosses and

fonts of patronage; as a result, Catholics came to dominate urban public services like the police and firefighters.

But starting in the 1930s, and accelerating rapidly after World War II, white urbanites, including Catholics, began moving from cities to the newly built suburbs. My borough of Brooklyn, New York, is filled with evidence of this diaspora, in the form of abandoned, underutilized, or repurposed parochial schools, churches, monasteries, and convents. There were parochial schools in the suburbs too, but plenty of Catholic parents sent their kids to public schools, where they easily blended in. After Vatican II, Catholics didn't even eat fish on Fridays or conduct their religious rituals in a strange language. More and more, Roman Catholicism was accepted as another Christian denomination rather than a separate and hostile religion and culture.

Though advocacy groups like the Catholic League may characterize critiques of the church's stance on abortion and its protection of pedophile priests as "Catholic-bashing," they are nothing of the sort, any more than criticism of Israel's treatment of Palestinians is definitionally anti-Semitic. As I write these words, six of the nine justices on the Supreme Court are Catholics, and Joe Biden, another Catholic, occupies the White House. It's hard to make a case that Catholics are actively persecuted in the United States, even if their religion is not universally respected.

Not that Republicans haven't tried to use the specter of anti-papism to their advantage—or that Democrats haven't sometimes made it easier for them to do so. When Amy Coney Barrett was nominated for a judgeship on the U.S. Court of Appeals for the Seventh Circuit in 2017, some of the questions Democratic senators put to her during her confirmation hearing were reminiscent of those that Al Smith and JFK had been compelled to answer. In a 1998 article in the *Marquette Law Review,* Barrett,

4042422224421

then a law professor at Notre Dame, had argued that Catholic judges who follow the church's teachings on capital punishment should recuse themselves when the alternative is to enforce the death penalty. "Judges cannot—nor should they try to—align our legal system with the Church's moral teaching whenever the two diverge," she wrote. "They should, however, conform their own behavior to the Church's standard." At the same time, she wrote, "mere identification of a judge as Catholic is not a sufficient reason [to demand recusal]. Indeed, it is constitutionally insufficient."[27] Did the same reasoning apply to *Roe v. Wade* and abortion?* Democrats asked her to elaborate, reminding her that she'd delivered a commencement address at Notre Dame's law school in which she'd said that "your legal career is but a means to an end, and . . . that end is building the kingdom of God." California's Democratic senator Dianne Feinstein remarked, "I think whatever a religion is, it has its own dogma. The law is totally different. And I think in your case, professor, when you read your speeches, the conclusion one draws is that the dogma lives loudly within you, and that's of concern."[28]

When Trump tapped Barrett to replace the liberal justice Ruth Bader Ginsburg on the Supreme Court in the fall of 2020, Republicans prepared to defend her nomination on the high ground of religious liberty, hoping that liberals' attacks would serve to energize evangelical and conservative Catholic voters to turn out for Trump in the presidential election that was just weeks away. But Democrats steered clear of that whole line of questioning, forcing conservative partisans to deliver the outraged speeches they'd prepared in a vacuum. As Linda Greenhouse described it in *The New York Review of Books,* Senator Josh Hawley of Missouri posed a

---

* Barrett did not recuse herself from *Dobbs v. Jackson* in 2022, in which the court held that abortion is not a constitutional right, effectively reversing *Roe v. Wade.*

rhetorical question to the nominee that "deserved the grandstanding award, a competitive category in any confirmation hearing. 'I'm not aware of any law or provision of the Constitution,' he began, 'that says if you are a member of the Catholic church and adhere to the teachings of the Catholic church or you have religious convictions in line with those of your church teaching, that you're therefore barred from office. Are you aware of any constitutional provision to that effect?' "[29]

Some Republican scourges of left-wing Catholic-bashing bash Catholicism themselves when it comes to the Vatican's views on capital punishment, guns, poverty, the environment, refugees, and human rights. As a commenter at one right-wing website complained, Pope Francis has expressed suspiciously liberal, even socialist, opinions about some of those issues. "Many believe," he insinuated, "that Francis' friendship with radical leftist, multi-billionaire George Soros has influenced [him] to minimize his talk about opposing abortion and homosexuality and maximize his role in protecting the environment, supporting gun control, and opening the Vatican to representatives of other religions, cults and quasi-religious groups."[30] Some far-right evangelicals never did accept the idea that Catholics could be their allies. The internet is still rife with anti-Catholic conspiracy theories that seemingly haven't been updated in a century or more.

Back in 2011, a website called Vatican Assassins identified me as a "Papal Court Jew" after I wrote a post for the Southern Poverty Law Center's *Hatewatch* blog that disputed its contention that the Jesuits had murdered JFK. "The wicked Southern Poverty Law Center is funded by the Vatican . . . ," it declared, and "is one of the pope's tools in continuing to foster the pro-Black/anti-White agenda here in Rome's Fourteenth Amendment American Empire."[31] There are many similar sites.

One claims that "the papacy is the most deadly enemy the

United States will ever have to face" and that Jesuits are not only "entrenched at the highest levels of all branches and departments of the U.S. Government," but control American Airlines, TWA, Anheuser-Busch, AT&T, Coca-Cola, UPS, Walt Disney, and Wells Fargo, to name just a few corporations.[32] Its assertions are backed up with quotes from a variety of published sources, for example, "The American people must be very blind indeed, if they do not see that if they do nothing to prevent it, the day is very near when the Jesuits will rule their country, from the magnificent White House at Washington, to the humblest civil and military department of this vast Republic." Its author is Charles Chiniquy, a former priest and the author of *Fifty Years in the Church of Rome,* published in 1885 and available in its entirety at the Bible Believers website.

Chiniquy claimed to be friendly with Abraham Lincoln, whose assassination, he said, was orchestrated by the Vatican. But that's not all. The first shot at Fort Sumter was fired by a Catholic; the bishop of New York organized the draft riots; and General George Meade, a Catholic, allowed Lee's army to escape and regroup after Gettysburg. The Vatican was the only foreign power to recognize the Confederacy, as evidenced by Pius IX's letter to Jefferson Davis, which was addressed to the "Illustrious and Honorable President." John Wilkes Booth was a secret Catholic, Chiniquy said—and some of the guests in Mrs. Surratt's boardinghouse, where the plot to assassinate Lincoln was hatched, were priests. And as if all that wasn't damning enough, Chiniquy had met a minister in Chicago who told him (and later swore in an affidavit) that on April 14, 1865, "he was in the Roman Catholic village of St. Joseph, Minnesota State, when, at about six o'clock in the afternoon, he was told by a Roman Catholic of the place . . . that the State Secretary Seward and President Lincoln had just been killed." The next Sunday, "a friend gave me a copy of a telegram sent to him on the Saturday, reporting that Abraham Lincoln and Secretary Seward had been assassinated the very day before, which was Friday, the 14th, at 10 p.m. But how could the Roman Catholic purveyor of the priests of St. Joseph have told me the same thing, before several witnesses, just four hours before its occurrence?"[33] The conspiracy was so vast that even the Catholics in St. Joseph were in on it.

Another far-right site describes "Crowngate," the British-Vatican-Israeli war against the American people and Russia that has raged since the thirteen colonies "appeared to gain their independence"[34] in 1776—this despite the fact that Israel didn't come into being until the 1940s.

And finally, there's Congresswoman Marjorie Taylor Greene, who was born a Catholic but left the church, she says, when "I became a mother, because I realized that I could not trust the Church leadership to protect my children from pedophiles, and that they harbored monsters even in their own ranks."[35] The church's bishops, she said, are not only controlled by Satan, but are Democrats. They use "taxpayer money to advocate for the illegal invasion across our borders. . . . What more can we expect from criminals and abusers living unaccountable lives of luxury funded by the rest of us, draped in fine linens while choirboys are raped?"[36]

Greene began her political career by promoting QAnon on Facebook, a movement that is obsessed with pedophilia. Given the revelations about priestly abuse over the past decades, it's reasonable to wonder if the conspiracist preoccupation with pedophilia isn't somehow connected. An opinion column by the historian Karen Liebreich, published in *The Washington Post* in February 2019, suggests that the church has been covering up priestly pedophilia since as early as the seventeenth century.

Historians believed that the Pious Schools, an order of priests founded by Joseph Calasanz, was suppressed in 1646 because of its association with Galileo. But when Liebreich examined the Inquisition's records, which were opened to researchers for the first time in 1998, she discovered that complaints about priests' "impure friendships with schoolboys" at the Pious Schools had begun to circulate in 1629. When Calasanz sent an investigator to look into the rumors about Father Stefano Cherubini, he reminded him that "Your Reverence's sole aim is to cover up this great shame in order that it does not come to the notice of our superiors." Instead of being defrocked, Cherubini was promoted and transferred to a different school. Cherubini ended up succeeding Calasanz as the head of the order, which was suppressed not because of Galileo or Cherubini's abuses, but solely because of Cherubini's bureaucratic incompetence. As for Calasanz, he was canonized in 1767; in 1948 he was named the "Universal Patron of all the Christian popular schools in the world." "There is of course," Liebreich notes, "an unmissable, grim irony in the elevation of someone who was complicit in the sexual abuse of children as the patron saint of Catholic education."[37]

Picture this classic conspiracist tableau: in a dungeon beneath a gloomy mansion, a group of immensely rich and powerful men, draped in silk robes, utter incantations in a strange tongue while sipping libations of human blood. Clouds of incense hang in the air.

Whether those celebrants are believed to be Elders of Zion, Illuminated Masons, billionaire apparatchiks of the New World Order, the elites of the QAnon believers' imagination, or all of them working together, the image's ur-source is Roman Catholic priests celebrating the Mass, as refracted through the distorting lenses of biblical End Times prophecies, the geopolitics of the Reformation, middle-class Americans' resentments of the opaque and sometimes questionable practices of bankers and financiers, and, ironically, Catholicism's own long-standing fears of Illuminism and Freemasonry.

For the Puritans, Catholics were the Romans, the ancient enemy the early Christians defined themselves in opposition to (along with the pharisaical Jews). For the Catholics, the enemy was not just the Jews who rejected Christ, but the heterodox Christians who denied that the Catholic Church is the body of Christ, and the forces of Marxism, scientism, nihilism, atheism, secularism, and all of the other isms that have been eating away at the one true church's authority and power.

Of course, real Jews and Masons, as opposed to the Jews and Masons of the conspiracist imagination, don't practice magic or worship Satan, because most Jews don't believe in the literal Devil, and while many Masons are Christians, few are superstitious.* Neither drinks blood—figurative, real, or transubstantiated—in their ceremonials. But conspiracists nonetheless imagine that their enemies celebrate Black Masses, because they think in Manichaean binaries—good versus evil, Christian versus Jew, Protestant versus Catholic, American versus non-American, civilization versus barbarism—and perhaps because they guiltily project the aspects of themselves that they are ashamed of onto their enemies. The Christian blood that Jews were accused of mixing into their Passover matzos, the adrenochrome that Q believers say the elites extract from children, is the Eucharist defiled.

---

* Some Masons are drawn to the arcana of Jewish mysticism and modern mystery cults like Rosicrucianism, but out of a spirit of intellectual adventurousness rather than simple faith.

Protestant conspiracy theorists look at their enemies and see
Catholics. So do Catholic conspiracy theorists, at least when they
are looking at the Masons. And it's no wonder, because so many
of the Masons' secret rituals evoke their society's fanciful connections with medieval Catholicism.

Beyond the Masons' specific references to the Knights Templar and Jacques de Molay, the Templars' last grand master (he
was burned at the stake in 1314), the Gothic cosplay that figures
in so many of their rituals is also characteristic of a lot of the
Romantic art, architecture, landscape design, and literature of the
late eighteenth and early nineteenth centuries. The Ku Klux Klan,
which recruited many of its members from Masonic lodges, also
adapted Catholic ritual and robes. The capirote, the pointed hood
that Spanish and Italian penitents have worn since the Inquisition, was the likely source for the headpieces the Klan riders wore
in D. W. Griffith's *Birth of a Nation,* and that the revived KKK
then adopted (the regalia of Reconstruction-era Klansmen was
less formalized).[38*]

Unlike the Klan, the Freemasons were never organized around
exclusion and hatred; their ideal was and is enlightenment.
According to their founding myth, Hiram Abiff, the chief archi-
tect of the Temple of Solomon, was martyred when he refused to
reveal the stonecutters guild's occult secrets. In truth, Freemasonry
is only a few centuries old, and like the American Constitution,
is very much a product of the Enlightenment. The first Masonic

* The second KKK sold the costumes to their millions of members via mail
order. Made by the Gates City Manufacturing Company in Atlanta, the standard
Klansman hood and robe in white cotton denim was for rank-and-file members;
the "Terror" (also white cotton, but with a red waist cord) was for higher-ranked
members; and the "Special Terror" (white satin hood, plus three red silk tassels)
was for grand dragons, titans, giants, cyclops, and magis.

Grand Lodge was founded in England in 1717; the first American lodge opened in Philadelphia in 1731 with Benjamin Franklin as a charter member. There are numerous varieties of Masonry (the York Rite, the Ancient and Accepted Scottish Rite, the Knights Templar, the Order of the Eastern Star, Royal Arch Masonry, and more). Some, like the Knights Templar, are explicitly Christian, but the ethos that most subscribe to is best described as humanistic deism. And if the Masons have a consistent class identity, it is bourgeois.

It's not surprising that George Washington and Benjamin Franklin were Masons. Both were non-churchgoing men of affairs, devout republicans who were good with money and conversant with science (especially Franklin, though Washington studied and applied the agronomy of his day, experimenting widely with new techniques in planting, plowing, manuring, and crop rotation). Other prominent American Masons of the period were Paul Revere, John Marshall, John Hancock, and James Monroe. Among Europe's well-known eighteenth-century Masons were the Marquis de Lafayette (an aristocrat to be sure, but something of a class traitor), and Goethe, Mozart, and Voltaire. In South and Central America, Simón Bolívar, El Libertador, was a Mason. There have been very conservative and racist Masons too. Albert Pike, for example, was a leader and major theorist of the Scottish Rite, one of the most speculative and esoteric varieties of Freemasonry; he was also a Confederate general, an avowed white supremacist, and active in the early KKK. But most were progressive-minded representatives of the rising Protestant middle class.

Esoteric Masons' engagement with arcana like Greco-Egyptian hermeticism, Gnosticism, Kabbalah, the Koran, and alchemy came from the same place as their interest in science—a wide-ranging curiosity unfettered by religious dogma, and the confidence that human beings are inherently perfectible, that anyone can work and study their way toward wisdom, happiness, and spiritual integration as they ascend through the degrees of the Craft. This is a very different view of the human condition than Catholicism's or Calvinism's, which maintain that mankind is inherently depraved and cannot earn grace, but only be granted it by Christ, either directly or via the church's intercession. That is why the pope condemned Masonry in 1738, a ban that was reaffirmed as recently as 1983 by Cardinal Ratzinger when he was prefect of the Congregation for the Doctrine of the Faith, formerly known as the Roman Inquisition (in 2005, he would become Pope Benedict XVI).

Freemasonry came under fire in the United States in the 1820s, after William Morgan, a former brewery owner and veteran of the War of 1812, disappeared after he'd written an exposé of Masonry and sold it to a publisher. If the Masons murdered him to protect their secrets, as was widely supposed, their plan backfired spectacularly. Morgan's book was published posthumously as *The Mysteries of Freemasonry, Containing All the Degrees of the Order Conferred in a Master's Lodge.* The controversy surrounding the dissappearance snowballed into a full-blown national political movement with the formation of the Anti-Masonic Party, whose bête noire was Andrew Jackson, the former grand master of Tennessee.

Jackson is remembered today as a populist and an avowed enemy of the permanent Washington establishment. Donald Trump declared himself a Jacksonian during his first presidential campaign in 2016; after he was elected, he hung Jackson's portrait in the Oval Office and visited his grave.* But in Jackson's

* Trump's vague public pronouncements about his illustrious predecessor, conveyed through a spokesperson ("an amazing figure in American history—very unique in so many ways") are so generic that it's likely that Steve Bannon, his chief strategist at the time, was the real Jacksonian. (https://www.nytimes.com/2017/01/20/us/politics/donald-trump-andrew-jackson.html?mtrref=thehill.com)

own day, his enemies castigated him as an elitist and would-be despot. Some of that animus was likely personal. John Quincy Adams had eked out a win against Jackson in 1824, but lost the presidency to him in 1828 after an especially vicious campaign.* Though Adams enjoyed a long and consequential ex-presidency as a lawyer, abolitionist, and member of Congress, he devoted a surprising amount of his energies in the 1830s to anti-Masonry, even writing a book, *Letters on Freemasonry,* in which he attacked the Masons as "a conspiracy of the few against the equal rights of the many" and "a seed of evil, which can never produce any good." Freemasons take oaths binding them to their order instead of to the republic, Adams said—so how patriotic could they be?[39]

His book exhaustively cataloged the ghoulish tortures that Masons supposedly visited on disloyal members like Morgan, lovingly detailing the cuttings of throats, tearing out of hearts, and "smiting off the skull to serve as a cup for the fifth libation" that were the penalties for disloyalty. And he called explicit attention to Masonry's resemblance to Catholicism, which was also accused of torturing its apostates and putting loyalty to the pope before loyalty to the nation (much as Jews are accused of doing with Israel today).

Alexis de Tocqueville was in the United States when the Anti-Mason movement was at full boil, but what made a stronger impression on him was Americans' irrepressible "associationism." "Americans of all ages," he wrote in *Democracy in America,* "all conditions, and all dispositions, constantly form associations. They have not only commercial and manufacturing companies, in which all take part, but associations of a thousand other kinds—religious, moral, serious, futile, extensive, or restricted, enormous

---

* Jackson had won pluralities of the popular vote and the Electoral College, but Adams prevailed when the election was thrown into the House.

or diminutive."[40] That associationism proved itself to be much stronger than anti-Masonry; by the late 1830s, the Foresters, the Good Fellows, the Odd Fellows, the Druids, the Improved Order of Red Men, the Heptasophs, and many more such groups—including all those anti-Catholic secret societies I wrote about earlier—were all thriving. Not to mention the Masons themselves, who emerged from their years in the wilderness unscathed.

The strongest and most lasting impetus for anti-Masonry wasn't political but religious. It was no coincidence that Batavia, New York, where William Morgan lived and died, was in the heart of the "Burned-Over District" that was the seat of the Second Great Awakening, the surge of revivalism in the first half of the nineteenth century that gave birth to Millerism, Adventism, the Jehovah's Witnesses, and the Church of Jesus Christ of Latter-Day Saints (whose founder, Joseph Smith, adapted some of its iconography from Masonic lore). Like Catholics, Protestants recognized the threat the Masons' "religious indifferentism" (the heretical idea that people of any religion can be redeemed, so long as they follow that religion's teachings sincerely) posed to their one true religion.

In 1868, Protestant evangelists formed an organization called the National Christian Association Opposed to Secret Societies; in 1883, it published *The Anti-Masonic Scrap Book,* which argued that the Freemasons belonged "to the same family with Jesuitism, the Commune, spirit circle, free-love, and Mormonism" and preyed "like night vampires upon the vitals of the Republic."[41]

The Masons evoked the same horror in Catholics that the Jesuits did for Protestants. In 1884, Pope Leo XIII issued his encyclical on Freemasonry, which attacked it for its sympathies for "the monstrous doctrines of the socialists and communists" and declared it incompatible with "the ideal of political government conformed to the principles of Christian wisdom." If the

Jesuits had been the shock troops for the Counter-Reformation, the Masons were seen as the advance guard of deism and scientific secularism. "No man," the encyclical concluded, "for any reason whatsoever" should "join the Masonic sect, if he values his Catholic name and his eternal salvation . . . as the whole principle and object of the sect lies in what is vicious and criminal."[42]

If I seem to be downplaying the potency of anti-Black racism and anti-Semitism in this chapter, I'm not. Remember, my topic is not prejudice per se, but paranoid conspiracism. For much of American history, racism has been openly acknowledged and supported by the force of law. As such, Blacks themselves weren't so much the objects of conspiracist thinking as their non-Black allies in the Abolition and the civil rights movements were.

As for anti-Semitism, once *The Protocols of the Elders of Zion* began to be widely translated after the turn of the twentieth century, conspiracists of every stripe* off-loaded the wicked attributes of Catholics, Masons, Illuminists, anarchists, robber barons, bankers, and revolutionaries onto Jews. Judaism was said to have co-opted the Masons, just as it had labor unions and other progressive movements, to undermine the power of the state. "Gentile masonry blindly serves as a screen for us and our objects," says Protocol 4. "Until we come into our kingdom . . . ," Protocol 15 adds, "we shall create and multiply free masonic lodges in all the countries of the world, absorb into them all who may become or who are prominent in public activity, for these lodges we shall find our principal intelligence office and means of influence."[43]

The Holocaust was the culmination of two thousand years of successionist theology, the belief that Christianity completed and

---

* Among them Black nationalists like the Nation of Islam and the Black Hebrew Israelites.

nullified both the Judaic law and Judaism itself, and of a century of political and social resentment as Jews throughout western Europe were finally made citizens of their countries. But Jews were relative latecomers to the global conspiracy theories that formed the basis of Nazism, and that they still feature in so largely today.

The person who gave American anti-Semitism its biggest platform ever was the industrialist Henry Ford.* "There is a race, a part of humanity," he wrote of the Jews in *The Dearborn Independent*, the newspaper he purchased in 1918 and mostly used to promote *The Protocols of the Elders of Zion*,† "which has never yet been received as a welcome part, and which has succeeded in raising itself to a power that the proudest Gentile race has never claimed, not even Rome in the days of her proudest power." Though the Jews were still nationless, Ford and his White Russian ghostwriters cast them as the world's most rapacious imperialists. Though most of the Jews who had begun pouring into America from eastern Europe toward the end of the nineteenth century were penniless, they were presumed to be fabulously wealthy.

"*The Protocols* do not regard the dispersal of the Jews abroad upon the face of the earth as a calamity, but as a providential arrangement by which the World Plan can be the more certainly executed,"[44] Ford wrote. The Diaspora was a punishment the Jews not only deserved but had freely chosen; as such, they should not be pitied but despised and feared. Ford's anti-Semitism was monstrous, but you can at least understand where it came from. He

* As it happens, Ford was a Freemason. He achieved the third degree in Palestine Lodge No. 357 in Detroit, Michigan in 1894, and the thirty-third degree in 1940.

† One can only wonder whether historians will regard Elon Musk's purchase of Twitter, which soon after became a platform for anti-Semitic conspiracy theories, as a similar gambit by a captain of industry with strong opinions.

had heard it proclaimed from the pulpit by Protestant ministers as a child, and he read it in the Silverite tracts of the agrarian populists (which I will have more to say about in the next chapter).

Ford had a sentimental attachment to the rural America that formed him, which caused him no end of cognitive dissonance, because if he couldn't find someone else to blame for its decline, he might have had to take a critical look at himself. Economists still use the term "Fordism" to describe the standardized, mass-production consumer economy that transformed small-town America into a patchwork of look-alike cities and suburbs. Mass-produced automobiles literally and figuratively released rural people from their ties to the land. Underemployed farm laborers moved to Detroit to work in Ford's factories, and the cars Americans bought on credit not only made them mobile but provided young people and adulterous marrieds with trysting places.

Ford's anti-Semitism exonerated him not just for the ruination of the wholesome way of life that he remembered, but the ruthlessness of the capitalism that he practiced. That which we call capitalism, he explained in *The International Jew,* is an illusion, because "the manufacturer, the manager of work, the provider of tools and jobs—we refer to him as the 'capitalist' . . . himself must go to capitalists for the money with which to finance his plans." The common enemy of both labor and capital, he wrote, is "super-capitalism . . . a super-government which is allied to no government, which is free from them all, and yet which has its hand in them all." To save America, to save the world, those super-capitalists must be crushed. "If the Jew is in control," Ford asked, "how did it happen? This is a free country. The Jew comprises only about three per cent of the population. . . . Is it because of his superior ability, or is it because of the inferiority and don't-care attitude of the Gentiles? . . . Unless the Jews are super-men," Ford concluded, "the Gentiles will have themselves to blame for what has transpired." *Where is the modern Haman who will do what must be done?* he might as well have asked.

Even after spending years parsing the paranoid style, the geno-cidal implications of Ford's logic stuns me—as does the fact that he continues to be held up to schoolchildren as a model American entrepreneur. It really is no wonder that Germany's rising fascists looked on "Ford as the leader of the growing Fascisti movement in America," as a reporter from the *Chicago Tribune* put it in 1923. "We admire particularly his anti-Jewish policy which is the Bavar-ian Fascisti platform. We have just had his anti-Jewish articles translated and published," Hitler told him. "The book is being circulated to millions throughout Germany." The article goes on to note that Ford's "picture occupies the place of honor in Herr Hittler's [*sic*] sanctum."[45]

If you are seeking the origins of the American Paranoid, there are many places to look. For Protestants in the colonial era, the great historical adversary was Satan, as embodied in the Catho-lic Church. The dread this transnational superstate inspired was virtually hardwired into their psyches, like the fear of snakes. At the same time, I suspect, they felt an unconscious, largely unac-knowledged nostalgia for its certainties. The lineaments of that primal hatred live on in contemporary conspiracists' fever dreams about the all-powerful Illuminati and the Elders of Zion, whose members feed themselves with children's blood and injections of adrenochrome and interfere with the sovereignty of nations.

Both Catholic and Protestant doctrine demand that its believ-ers repudiate Freemasonry's values, but few Americans do, because our political institutions grew out of the same soil that Freema-sonry did, which is the practical, empiricist, tolerant, and secular ethos of the Enlightenment that Sam Dickson believes poisoned the American experiment at its birth.

Religious tolerance, if not indifferentism, is what underlies Madison's and Jefferson's wall of separation between church and state. "It does me no injury for my neighbor to say there are twenty gods, or no god," Jefferson famously wrote.[46] But despite the mountains of evidence that show that religious pluralism encourages rather than harms religious belief (56 percent of Americans say they believe in God as described in the Bible, as opposed to just 27 percent of western Europeans),[47] an influential minority of religious Americans would just as soon tear it down. Many have their doubts about democratic republicanism as well. The only sure guarantor of their freedom, they say, is power—specifically, the ability to wield power against religions, ideas, and people they don't like.

If anti-Catholicism and anti-Masonry no longer play explicit roles in U.S. politics, the subject of the next chapter—the ideological and geographic fault lines between farm and city and church and state—illuminates another continuity between colonial times and the present.

6

Farm and City, Church and State

When it came to the Jews, Henry Ford was one of the most florid haters America has ever known. But when it came to his own rural heritage, he was awash in sentimentality. In 1919, when a road improvement project threatened his childhood home, he saw to it that it was picked up off its foundations, moved out of the way, and lovingly restored. It would become the nucleus of Greenfield Village, his tribute to his own and his country's imagined childhood innocence.

Going all the way back to classical Greece, urbanites have idealized the simple pursuits of farmers and herders as a prelapsarian paradise that they could never return to. America's pastoral past was neither simple nor innocent, but for a time it offered a way of life that was more equitable than what most Europeans had experienced. As that changed, rural America would become a hotbed of conspiracist discontent.

J. Hector St. John de Crèvecoeur was a cartographer in the French Colonial Militia during the French and Indian War. After the peace, he married the daughter of a New York merchant and moved to the Hudson Valley, where he ran a family farm in the

1760s and '70s. Here there "are no aristocratical families," he wrote in his book *Letters from an American Farmer,* "no courts, no kings, no bishops, no ecclesiastical dominion, no invisible power giving to a few a very visible one; no great manufacturers employing thousands, no great refinements of luxury." Though he romanticized the English colonies as a classless and slaveless Arcadia ("We have no princes, for whom we toil, starve, and bleed: we are the most perfect society now existing in the world"), Crèvecoeur's reports from the New World were not altogether fanciful when it came to freeborn white people. "The rich and the poor are not so far removed from each other as they are in Europe," he correctly noted. "Some few towns excepted, we are all tillers of the earth, from Nova Scotia to West Florida. . . . We are all animated with the spirit of an industry which is unfettered and unrestrained, because each person works for himself."[1]

Whether they were native-born or newly emigrated, even rich Americans had nowhere near the sort of wealth that Europe's landowning aristocrats did. Few white Americans were as poor as Europe's peasantry either, except perhaps some of the "bad" sorts who lived in the backwoods, civilizational throwbacks who eked out a marginal subsistence by hunting and occasional theft ("Want stimulates that propensity to rapacity and injustice, too natural to needy men," as Crèvecoeur noted). Even in the South, where slave labor enabled much larger agricultural enterprises that produced tobacco and cotton for export, preindustrial English America was much more equal economically than it would become. According to recent research by Peter Lindert and Jeffrey Williamson, the richest 1 percent in the colonies accounted for just 8.5 percent of the total national income in 1774. Compare that to the more than 20 percent of income that the 1 percent control today (plus more than a third of wealth).[2]

The notion that democracy and agrarianism went together (and that slavery was in no way undemocratic) defined the thinking of as sophisticated and cosmopolitan a figure as Thomas Jefferson, who wrote in a letter to John Jay in 1785 that "cultivators of the earth are the most valuable citizens. They are the most vigorous, the most independent, the most virtuous, & they are tied to their country & wedded to it's [*sic*] liberty & interests by the most lasting bonds." A few years later, in a letter to James Madison, Jefferson tied the fate of the republic to its rural character: "I think our governments will remain virtuous for many centuries," he wrote, "as long as they are chiefly agricultural; and this will be as long as there shall be vacant lands in any part of America. When they get piled upon one another in large cities, as in Europe, they will become corrupt as in Europe."[3]

All of that would change within a decade or so. As textile mills and other great manufactories came into being, North American cities became centers of production as well as trade and rapidly expanded. Simple tillers of the earth were not immune to the lure of cash and rapid economic growth either. As homesteaders pushed west in search of opportunity, many seized it by flipping the undeveloped land they'd been granted by the government or stolen from its aboriginal inhabitants. The most enterprising pioneers indebted themselves so they could buy out their neighbors and capture the greater returns that accrue to scale. But the country was growing so quickly that it made as much economic sense to simply hold on to the acreage for a few years and then sell it at a premium when the line of development moved closer, than to sink money and labor into digging irrigation trenches, cutting terraces into hillsides, rotating crops so as not to wear out the soil (as tobacco notoriously does), and so on.

By the mid-nineteenth century, American agricultural products were global commodities. A thunderstorm in Egypt, a drought in Ukraine, a hurricane in Central America could affect prices for years to come. Small-scale farmers could still scrape a modest living off the land, but it was no way to get rich. Railroads and grain elevators charged exorbitant rates, eating into profits before harvests reached their markets. Banks held liens not just on farmers' land but the very seeds they needed to plant the following season—and as loosely regulated and poorly run as those banks often were, they frequently failed, taking whatever savings their depositors had managed to accumulate with them. Once in debt, it was impossible for an honest farmer to climb out of it, as the value of the dollars that those debts were denominated in was constantly rising because it was pegged to scarce gold. As critical as agriculture was to the health and welfare of the country, most family farms provided their owners with only a bare subsistence. If southern plantation owners thought of themselves as landed gentry, the Civil War put an end to that.

But as Richard Hofstadter wrote in *The Age of Reform,* the more commercial and urban America became, the more tightly Americans clung to their imagined Edenic past. "The American mind," he wrote, was wedded to an "agrarian myth [that] represents a kind of homage that Americans have paid to the fancied innocence of their origins."[4] Agrarian populism was the inevitable result—a movement that pitted frustrated farmers against the urban financial elites that increasingly controlled their destinies.

The populists divided the world into two kinds of people: makers (or producers) and takers. As they saw it, farmers and artisans and even factory workers produced things of value, while landlords, rent-seeking middlemen, capitalist financiers, and the poor simply took. Cities were the domains of takers, rich and poor alike. "The agrarian myth," in Hofstadter's words, "encouraged farmers to believe that they were not themselves an organic part of the whole order of business enterprise and speculation that flourished in the city, partaking of its character and sharing in its risks, but rather the innocent pastoral victims of a conspiracy hatched in the distance." By the turn of the twentieth century, agrarian populists had come to believe "that the city was a parasitical growth on the country."[5] "Burn down your cities and leave our farms," as William Jennings Bryan put it, "and your cities will spring up again as if by magic; but destroy our farms, and the grass will grow in the streets of every city in the country."[6]

If populists decried the winner-take-all inequities of the Gilded Age, others celebrated them. A body of aspirational literature, both religious and secular, showed the ambitious how they could work the system to earn an earthly reward. A century before, Benjamin Franklin's autobiography had described a program of self-improvement that, in the Masonic spirit, anyone could follow to achieve moral perfection and material success. The eponymous hero of Horatio Alger's *Ragged Dick,* published in 1868, rose from bootblack to businessman. Of course, there were powerful critiques of Gilded Age capitalism too. The works of Mark Twain, Stephen Crane, Frank Norris, Theodore Dreiser, Sinclair Lewis, and Upton Sinclair have entered the canon, but some of their now-forgotten peers were even more influential in their lifetimes.

When the Long Depression began in the 1870s, business barons made the most of the opportunity to buy up distressed companies on the cheap and consolidate their monopoly power over markets. As unemployment rose and Marxist and anarchist ideas spread in the cities, rural Americans were drawn to a different kind of radicalism. Mrs. Sarah E. V. Emery's *Seven Financial Conspiracies Which Have Enslaved the American People,* published in 1887, identified the class of "roving bandits" who had preyed since antiquity on the hardworking producers who live by "tilling the soil, raising flocks and herds, delving in mines, working in wood, brass, and iron, or deriving their subsistence from the waters over which God has given them dominion." Today, she wrote, those bandits carry out their brigandage under "more euphonious titles, and new methods of robbery are employed. Instead of 'robber king' and 'brigand chief' we have today the money king, the coal king, the cattle king, the railroad magnate, the telegraph monopolist and the lumber baron. Instead of spoils and plunders, we have interests, dividends, revenues, and rents."[7]

The first of their seven conspiracies was to ensnare the country in a ruinous civil war, which provided the bandits with the opportunity to lend money to the government at usurious rates. Lincoln held them off at first by printing paper money. The resulting inflation cheapened the dollar for a time, but the Shylocks worked assiduously to restore the power of coin. Their culminating conspiracy was the great "Crime of 1873," when Congress demonetized silver. Silver was more plentiful than gold, and hence cheaper; once the gold standard was restored, the resulting deflation made life much harder for debtors. The writer and politician Ignatius Donnelly similarly identified an Anglo-American gold trust that had been pulling strings since the Civil War, enacting "a vast conspiracy against mankind" that was "rapidly taking possession of the world." If it was not overthrown, he wrote in the preamble to the agrarian populist People's Party platform of 1892, "it forebodes terrible social convulsions, the destruction of civilization, or the establishment of absolute despotism."[8]

William Hope "Coin" Harvey, author of the best-selling *Coin's Financial School* (1894), wrote a novel, *A Tale of Two Nations,*[9] that recast the conspiracy into a melodrama that any reader could relate to and understand. Over in London, Baron Rothe, a sinister Jewish banker, dispatches his deputy to the United States to "bury the knife deep into the heart of this nation." America's ancient enemy England was working hand in glove with Christendom's oldest enemy, the Jew. And their victims were virtuous family farmers.

General Grant's General Orders No. 11, which had expelled "the Jews as a class" from Tennessee, Mississippi, and Kentucky—and which was immediately countermanded by Lincoln—had been (and still is) the sole instance of European-style state-sponsored anti-Semitism in American history. Anti-Jewish sentiment was rife in nineteenth-century America, of course, but it had been rooted in religious and social differences rather than politics and economics.

Suddenly the Jews were looming larger than the hated Jesuits in the rural conspiracist imagination. As William Faulkner's bilious Jason Compson sputtered in his novel *The Sound and the Fury,* " 'You think the farmer gets anything out of [cotton] except a red neck and a hump in his back? . . . Let him make a big crop and it wont be worth picking; let him make a small crop and he wont have enough to gin. And what for? so a bunch of damn eastern jews . . . I have nothing against jews as an individual,' I says. 'It's just the race. You'll admit that they produce nothing.' "[10]

Establishment Republicans are as pro-Israel in principle as American evangelicals are. Until recently, the GOP's economic policies were shaped by prominent Jewish monetarists like Milton Friedman, and its foreign policy by Jewish neoconservatives like Henry Kissinger and Elliott Abrams. But since the rise of Trump, epithets like "globalist," "neoconservative," "Soros," and "cultural Marxist" have become dog whistles that Republican politicians frequently sound and that the anti-Semitic far right clearly understands. Paranoids see matrices of connection everywhere, and in their fantasies, it is usually a Jew who sits at the center of the elaborate clockwork. As it is with those populist Republicans today, so it was with populists then.

By 1896, when the populist William Jennings Bryan became the Democratic Party's dark horse nominee for the presidency, those money theories had moved to the center of political discourse. Not just farmers, but laborers of all stripes had been nailed to a cross of gold, as he put it in the famous speech that won him the nomination. The Romans and the Jews* of the day were not just the financiers of Wall Street and the City of London, but every speculator who made money from money. "When you come before us and tell us that we shall disturb your business interests," Bryan thundered, "we reply that you have disturbed our business interests by your action. We say to you that you have made too limited in its application the definition of a businessman." He continued:

The man who is employed for wages is as much a businessman as his employer. The attorney in a country town is as much a businessman as the corporation counsel in a great metropolis. The merchant at the crossroads store is as much a businessman as the merchant of New York. The farmer who goes forth in the morning and toils all day . . . is as much a businessman as the man who goes upon the Board of Trade and bets upon the price of grain. The miners who go 1,000 feet into the earth or climb 2,000 feet

* Like today's Soros-hating Republicans, many populists denied that they hated Jews as a people. Some of them were undoubtedly sincere. "We are not attacking a race, we are attacking greed and avarice," Bryan told a Jewish audience in Chicago. "I do not know of any class of our people who, by reason of their history, can better sympathize with the struggling masses in this campaign than can the Hebrew race."

upon the cliffs and bring forth from their hiding places the precious metals to be poured in the channels of trade are as much businessmen as the few financial magnates who in a backroom corner the money of the world.[11]

It was a remarkable repositioning of the Democratic Party, from defenders of the slave interests to the champions of producers of all kinds—from manual laborers to small business proprietors—as opposed to rent-seeking landowners and financiers. The speech also included as sharp a repudiation of trickle-down economics as was ever articulated before (or arguably since) the Reagan era:

> There are two ideas of government. There are those who believe that if you just legislate to make the well-to-do prosperous, that their prosperity will leak through on those below. The Democratic idea has been that if you legislate to make the masses prosperous their prosperity will find its way up and through every class that rests upon it.[12]

But while the Democratic Party was transformed for the better by the forces that created Silverism, it was debased by the crude hatreds that lay at the root of its economic analysis.

The genteel progressivism of the early twentieth century suffered from a similar flaw. Though many of the reforms it enacted were positive, a good many of progressivism's leaders—like so many of the rural populists—were xenophobes and racists. It wasn't as if they started out progressive and then traded their forward-looking ideas for backward racist ones. They held both; in fact, they considered their theories about eugenics to be as progressive as their zeal for food inspections and trust-busting. As Ta-Nehisi Coates put it, "If the New Deal is ours"—meaning the Democrats'—"so is Theodore Bilbo,"[13] the Mississippi senator who was a Roosevelt and New Deal supporter, but who also said the United States is "strictly a white man's country, with a white man's civilization."*

One hundred years later, Trump would also channel the forms if not the substance of populist redistributionism,† with promises of government largess for "real" Americans and punishments for immigrants and foreign takers (his "China replacement" program,[14] for example, subsidized the soybean farmers who were hurt by the retaliatory tariffs China levied on American agricultural products). Though he was born and raised in New York City and owned some of its iconic skyscrapers, Trump ingratiated himself with his rural and suburban supporters by demonizing "Democrat-run" cities as centers of crime, corruption, immigration, and Black people. "All Democrat-run cities, in every case, they're going to hell," he said in July 2020.[15]

Silverism occupies a similar niche in America's history as Luddism‡ does in Great Britain's; both were ultimately futile attempts

---

* Bilbo's opinions about the Jews were equally jaundiced. In 1945, while speechifying against a proposal to make Roosevelt's wartime antidiscrimination orders permanent, he noted that while some of his best friends were Jewish (he actually said that), "there is a certain class of 'Kike' Jews in New York, organized with the CIO and the Negroes, who are trying to force through this fanatical legislation." (https://www.jta.org/archive/bilbo-denounces-kike-jews-from-new-york-in-attack-on-fepc-in-senate)

† In 2019, *Forbes* noted that the combined net worth of Trump's cabinet was $3.2 billion. Its members at the time included the billionaire Betsy DeVos; the investment banker Wilbur Ross (who had worked at the Rothschild bank); the investor Steven Mnuchin, whose father was a Goldman Sachs director; and Elaine Chao, whose family owns a shipping company (and who is married to the Republican senator Mitch McConnell).

‡ The revolutionary movement among skilled weavers in northern England in the early years of the nineteenth century, who correctly feared that machines would replace them and tried to save their livelihoods by sabotaging them.

to stop a tectonic economic transformation. Even as advances in agronomy, chemical fertilizers, and pesticides massively increased agricultural yields, mechanization reduced the need for labor. Farmers and farm workers began to abandon the land. The Great Migration of African American laborers to northern cities in the interwar years, the Dust Bowl crisis of the 1930s, the rash of repossessions that inspired the Farm Aid concerts of the 1980s (and arguably the Satanic Panics and UFO abduction flaps that roiled rural America during the same decade) were all part and parcel of a global shift in the means of agricultural production.

In 1900, 41 percent of the U.S. workforce was employed in agriculture. By 1930, around the time that Henry Ford opened Greenfield Village, the share had been virtually halved to 21.5 percent; by 2002, it was less than 2 percent (1.9 percent). At the same time, corporate agriculture has done fantastically well as an industry. Between 1948 and 1999, agricultural productivity grew at a rate of 1.9 percent per year.[16]

A similarly traumatic upheaval occurred in manufacturing and lower-level white collar work during the second half of the twentieth century. Between automation and offshoring, the share of the American workforce involved in direct production of manufactured goods fell from more than a third in the 1970s to less than 10 percent today.[17] Thanks to new technologies, deregulation, and globalization, American firms no longer had to pay high wages; unionized workers could be replaced by either robots or people in the comparatively undeveloped world, who are content to work for what they can get (and can be easily replaced if they're not). With the advent of desktop computing in the 1980s, huge numbers of administrative and clerical jobs were eliminated as well. People who would have once been proud producers were demoted to low-end jobs in the burgeoning service economy.

It wasn't just the occupational composition of the American workforce that was changing—so was its ethnicity. The Hart-Celler Act, also known as the Immigration and Nationality Act of 1965, repealed the quotas that had been set in 1924 to preserve America's "European" character.* Those quotas had had catastrophic consequences for would-be Jewish refugees from Nazi Germany in the 1930s. Though the Hart-Celler Act included caps, immediate relatives of immigrants were exempted, and those caps were raised several times over the next fifty years. As a result, the foreign-born population of the United States rose from 9.6 million in 1965 to 45 million in 2015, 14 percent of the population as compared to just 5 percent. More than half of those new immigrants were Latin American, and a quarter of them were Asian.[18] By 2015, Mexican, Indian, Filipino, Chinese, Vietnamese, Salvadoran, Cuban, South Korean, Dominican, and Guatemalan immigrants accounted for nearly 60 percent of America's foreign-born population. In 1965, 84 percent of the U.S. population claimed European descent; by 2015 the percentage had fallen to 62 percent.

The 2020 census captured the first-ever recorded decline in the nation's white population. White shares fell in all fifty states, 358 out of the U.S.'s 364 metropolitan regions, and 3,012 of its 3,141 counties. Twenty-seven of its one hundred largest metropolitan regions, including New York, Los Angeles, Washington, D.C., Miami, Dallas, and Atlanta, had minority white populations. The Latino share of the population increased by 18.5 percent and the

---

* The rates were pegged at 2 percent of the numbers of foreign-born residents from allowed countries as of the 1890 census, before the massive spikes of immigration from eastern Europe and Italy had occurred. Chinese immigration had already been banned by the Chinese Exclusion Act in 1882; the ban was extended to the rest of Asia in 1917 and 1924.

Asian share by nearly 6 percent over the decade.[19] More than half of Americans under age sixteen are already nonwhite; if trends continue, whites will become an absolute minority by 2045.[20] Given this background, it's not surprising that there has been a resurgence of white nationalism.

Drill down further, and there's still more bad news for white American hegemony. The places that have maintained their majority white character, and that tend to vote Republican, are growing neither their populations nor their economies. According to an analysis of the 2020 census by Mark Muro of the Brookings Institution's Metropolitan Policy Program, "Republican counties represent a waning, traditional economic base, situated in struggling small towns and rural areas . . . growth, in the most literal sense, is somewhere else. Prosperity is out of reach."[21]

Trump enjoyed showing visitors the map that shaded all the counties he'd won in red, and no wonder, because he won five times as many as Hillary Clinton (2,626 to 487). But that sea of red was deceiving. Fully half of the people in the United States live in just 143 counties, and most of them voted for Clinton. Clinton counties were not just more populous than the ones that voted for Trump, they were more prosperous by far, accounting for 64 percent of the nation's economic output.[22] Almost half of Trump's counties had seen their growth rates decline. As extensive as it was, Trump's geography was a geography of decline.[23]

Those statistics are dry, but they help explain why so many white nationalist tropes have worked their way into the mainstream since the turn of the millennium. Back in 1994, while serving a 190-year prison sentence for murder, bank robbery, and more, David Lane, a member of the white nationalist group the Order and the

coiner of its two fourteen-word slogans,* published the "White
Genocide Manifesto," which famously declared that " 'racial integration' is only a euphemism for genocide."[24] A few years later, the
white nationalist Robert Whitaker coined what became known in
the white nationalist movement as "the Mantra": "They say they
are anti-racist. What they are is anti-white. Anti-racist is a code
word for anti-white."[25]

By the mid-2000s, Republicans were adapting that mantra to
their own purposes. Though few shared Lane's open detestation
of the U.S. government ("America is the murderer of the White
Race," he wrote in his essay "Tri-Colored Treason." "I wouldn't
contaminate my toilet with your red, white and blue rag"),[26]
many Republicans who call themselves patriots leveraged those
same fears of racial replacement as they worked to end the supposed indoctrination of schoolchildren into the tenets of critical
race theory.

Their expectation is that the next generation of minority teachers and historians will will be as racist as they were—that just as
their own white-centered histories sanitized the destruction of the
Americas' indigenous cultures, replaced the brute facts of slavery
with parables about Black uplift and Christianization, recast the
Constitution as a divinely inspired document based on Christian scripture, and the Civil War as a glorious Lost Cause that
had nothing to do with race, the majority's new woke texts will
demonize or, worse still, erase white people.

Watch any news channel except Fox, Newsmax, or OAN,
MAGA Republicans complain, scan the headlines in *The New
York Times* and *The Washington Post,* and all you'll see are stories

* "We must secure the existence of our people and a future for white children" and
"Because the beauty of the White Aryan woman must not perish from the Earth."

about structural racism, police brutality, and violence against women, Blacks, Asians, gays, and trans people. What about middle-aged white men? Has anyone noticed that they are an endangered species?

They're not, obviously. There will be white men and white women in the world for a long time to come, though the definition of whiteness will likely broaden to accommodate new entrants, just as it did over the past century, when the Irish, Slavs, southern Italians, and even Jews were more or less welcomed to the race. I write "more or less," because the whiteness of Jews is still a matter of debate in some quarters.* But if the notion of white genocide is hyperbolic, a subset of white Americans is in fact struggling according to almost every measure—men between the ages of twenty-five and sixty-four who have not earned four-year college degrees.

The Princeton economist Anne Case and her husband, Angus Deaton, who was awarded the Nobel Prize in economics in 2015, wrote about this in a much-talked-about academic paper and then a 2020 book entitled *Deaths of Despair and the Future of Capitalism.*

* David Duke shattered the peace of one of Jared Taylor's American Renaissance conferences back in 2006, when he darkly alluded to "a power in the world that dominates our media, influences our government and that has led to the internal destruction of our will and spirit," causing a Jewish white nationalist to storm out of the room. Taylor's openness to Jewish participation in white nationalism makes me think of the Groucho Marx quip—"I refuse to join any club that would have me as a member." Most Jews, even those whose politics are much more to the right than mine, are rightly skeptical of groups like American Renaissance. But there is considerable contention within Israel and throughout the Diaspora about whether the Ashkenazim grant themselves privileges they deny to Sephardic, Mizrahi, and Black Jews. Christians of European descent don't have a monopoly on racial animus and anxiety. (https://www.splcenter .org/fighting-hate/intelligence-report/2006/schism-over-anti-semitism-divides -key-white-nationalist-group-american-renaissance)

While Black Americans still have vastly less wealth, higher rates of poverty and incarceration, and shorter life expectancies than whites on average, they noted, trends for Black educational attainment, wages, and income are rising, and Black mortality rates have steadily improved. But starting in the second decade of the twenty-first century, death rates among white working-class men spiked so sharply that they brought down the average life expectancy of the entire U.S. population, something that statisticians hadn't seen since the First World War and the great flu pandemic of 1918. Those excess deaths were attributable to suicides, drug overdoses, and alcoholic liver disease. This is strictly an American issue; while blue-collar workers in other advanced economies face significant structural challenges, their average life spans are still increasing.

The crux of the issue was not simply that blue-collar work was being automated and offshored and that wages for the remaining low-skill jobs were stagnant.* The two most critical contributors to the crisis were status issues and medical care. The service jobs that have replaced unionized manufacturing jobs are not only low paying and insecure; they provide virtually no potential for growth or personal initiative. Cleaners, security guards, food-service workers, drivers, and warehouse pickers are typically employed by subcontractors; workers in those jobs are made to feel like temporary stand-ins for the robots that will eventually replace them. Where manual workers once shared a sense of solidarity with their white-collar colleagues and some were able to climb the ladder, now "there is a world of the more educated, and a world of the less educated; no one in the latter has hope of joining the former," write Case and Deaton.[27] Low-education workers' social capital has declined along with their earning power, with the consequence that there

---

* Actually worse than stagnant. Between 1979 and 2017, the growth rate for median wages for white men without college degrees was -0.2 percent per year.

are more broken marriages, more single-parent households, lower church attendance, and more chronic disease and addiction.

When they seek medical care for these conditions, they find that America's for-profit system is not only hit or miss when it comes to outcomes, but wildly expensive. It absorbs 18 percent of the U.S. GDP—four times what the country pays for defense and about three times what it pays for education. Those costs, Case and Deaton write, are "like a tribute that Americans have to pay to a foreign power."[28] About half of Americans get their insurance through their jobs, but nonunion service jobs are often classed as temporary work, meaning they provide no benefits. Though Obamacare has made insurance more affordable for those who don't have jobs or don't qualify for Medicare or Medicaid, it's still a big expense, and some states refuse to use the Medicaid subsidies that the system makes available to them.

Depressed and often in pain, large numbers of under- and unemployed white working-class men avoid going to doctors until their chronic conditions force them to. Those conditions—obesity, type 2 diabetes, heart disease, high blood pressure—are the same ones that afflict poor minorities. Many self-medicate with alcohol, become addicted to prescription painkillers, and then resort to illegal drugs when their prescriptions run out or they can no longer afford to get them filled. The United States' gun culture— America literally has more guns than people—ensures that many have an easy means at hand for taking their lives when the psychic and physical costs of existence become unbearable.* Case and

---

* As of 2018, America had 120.5 firearms per 100 residents. 45,222 gun deaths were reported in 2020, 19,384 of them intentional and unintentional homicides and police shootings, and 24,292 of them suicides (https://www.bbc.com/news/world-us-canada-41488081). Among the latter was one of my oldest and dearest friends, the writer and illustrator Richard Torregrossa, who killed himself on February 18 of that same year.

Deaton mapped out the geography of those white working-class deaths of despair, and not surprisingly, there was considerable overlap with Trump's geography of decline.

One part of the picture Case and Deaton paint is ambiguous. While white American working-class men are less religious than they once were as measured by the traditional metric of regular church attendance, a 2021 Pew survey found that the number of white Americans identifying as evangelicals had actually grown during Trump's presidency—and that those evangelicals supported Trump by an astonishing 75 to 85 percent.[29] The reason for this, Ryan Burge speculated in a *New York Times* op-ed, is not because of faith per se, but Republicanism. "For many Americans," he wrote, "to be a conservative Republican is to be an evangelical Christian, regardless of whether they ever attend a Sunday service."[30] Two strains of Evangelicalism have been particularly influential in the MAGA world—the so-called prosperity gospel, and that associated with white Christian nationalism. Trump was personally inspired by the first. An understanding of the second may help resolve some of Trumpism's apparent contradictions.

Trump and the televangelist Paula White-Cain, have known each other since 2002; she owned an apartment in one of his buildings and was an invited guest at the taping of the first season finale of *The Apprentice*.[31] After he was elected, she became one of his spiritual advisors. One of her most-quoted mots is "If you really want to do something you will find a way; if you don't, you will find an excuse"; another is "If you believe God, you can create anything in your life."

As already mentioned in these pages, Trump attended the Marble Collegiate Church as a child and young man. "Norman Vincent Peale, the great Norman Vincent Peale, was my pastor," Trump recalled in 2015. "He was so great . . . you could listen to him all day long."[32] The author of the mega–best seller *The Power of Positive Thinking*, Peale famously preached that if you "promise yourself success at the beginning of each day . . . you'll be surprised how often things will turn out that way."

Jeff Sharlet, the author of *The Family: The Secret Fundamentalism at the Heart of American Power*, covered a number of Trump rallies in 2016 for *Vanity Fair*. "Back then," he wrote, "the candidate was taken as living proof of what's known as the Prosperity Gospel, a kind of country cousin to establishment Christian conservatism, not so much about saving society as it is about getting right with God by getting rich. Show your faith in his blessings, as revealed in the opulent lives of his anointed preachers, and good fortune will trickle down. Like Trump, the Prosperity Gospel is transactional. . . . Quid pro quo, a deal with God."[33]

But what if the deal goes bad? What if you believe as hard as you can, and success still eludes you? What if, like those white working-class men without college degrees, you wake up each morning, only to find your prospects getting worse? As inspiring as the prosperity gospel is for people who have already tasted some success and want more; as reassuring as it is for people who have a lot already and don't want to feel guilty about getting more, it can't but leave a taste of ashes in the mouths of those who find themselves having less and less. Like the Puritan doctrine of predestination, it adds insult to injury by telling you that your failure is your own fault, that you lack faith and are a bad Christian.

Unless, of course, you choose a different narrative, one that's more like one of those Mel Gibson movies in which first the hero's family and then the hero himself is victimized by bad people, over and over again and more horribly each time, until he finally strikes back in righteous anger. Which brings us to white Christian nationalism.

In their book *The Flag and the Cross: White Christian Nation-*

alism and the Threat to American Democracy, the sociologists
Samuel L. Perry and Philip S. Gorski identify white Christian
nationalism as the key to understanding the weird juxtapositions
of gallows and crosses, and American and Confederate flags that
were on display at the U.S. Capitol on January 6. Neither a creed
nor an explicit political movement, they write, it is more of a
shared narrative or myth about America's founding and history,
in which white Christians established a nation on a foundation of
biblical law, earning God's blessing and becoming the city upon a
hill, just as John Winthrop said they would in his *Arbella* sermon.

White Christian nationalists believe that this divine plan for
America has been put into jeopardy by un-American unbelievers,
who must be violently resisted and purged. They understand freedom "in a libertarian way, as freedom from restrictions, especially
by the government," Perry and Gorski write. "Order is understood in a hierarchical way, with white Christian men at the top.
And violence is seen as a righteous means of defending freedom
and restoring order, means that are reserved to Christian men."[34]

Though "this 'us vs. them' tribalism may seem un-Christian,"
they continue, and "the glorification of violence even more so,"
the contradictions resolve when you look at them through the lens
of End Times theology. Society is as unsettled as it is because the
End Times have begun. White Christian nationalists don't want
to repair the world; they want to get on God's right side so they
can survive the global bloodletting that has already started and live
in the heavenly kingdom that will follow. This shared catastroph-
ism helps explain why there is so much affinity between Christian
nationalism and MAGA. "Premillennialists," Perry and Gorski
write, "believe that there will be a final battle between good and
evil, a life-and-death struggle between natural and supernatural
forces . . . [and] Trump's worldview is similar. 'Disaster' is one of

his favorite words. He sees life as an endless battle between us and them. He sees hidden conspiracies everywhere."[35]

Since white Christian nationalists are a minority, they see no virtue in the principle of majority rule. If anything, they regard it as a recipe for their own extinction. The relationship between white Christian nationalism and the belief that anti-white discrimination is a real and present danger is linear and direct. When Perry and Gorski surveyed Black and white Americans, they found that the higher white Americans scored on the attributes of Christian nationalism, the more they believed they were discriminated against and the less they believed that Blacks faced much discrimination at all.

Like QAnon, the white Christian nationalist narrative evokes the conspiracist ur-story in which the world is ruled by an impostor god. As in a classic Western movie, the duly appointed authorities are not just weak and corrupt, they are wicked. The vaccines they want you to take are poisonous; the lessons they teach your children are propagandistic lies, designed to stifle their spirits. The hero must arm himself to protect his family, or, if he is bold enough, to strike a blow against the tyrants. Resistance is all.

When the Capitol rioters entered the Senate chamber on January 6, 2021, Jacob Chansley, the tattooed and horned Q Shaman, climbed atop the dais and intoned a prayer, thanking the "divine, omniscient, omnipotent creator God" for allowing him and his companions to "exercise our rights, to allow us to send a message to all the tyrants, the communists and the globalists that this is our nation, not theirs."[36]

Our nation, not theirs.

Chansley fancied himself a warrior, doing battle with an army of demons. In one of the many interviews he gave before his arrest (he pleaded guilty to a variety of federal charges and was sentenced to forty-one months in prison), he explained:

In order to beat this evil occultic force, you need . . . an occultic
force that is (on) the side of God, of love, almost like on the side
of the angels as opposed to the demons. As a shaman I am like a
multidimensional or hyperdimensional being . . . I am able to per-
ceive multiple different frequencies of light beyond my five senses,
and it allows me to see into these other, higher dimensions [where]
these entities—these pedophiles, these rapists, these murderers,
these really high up people—that they almost like hide in the shadows. Nobody can see that because their third eye ain't open. And
that's where things like fluoride and stuff like that comes in.[37]

Fluoride and stuff like that. "The most monstrously conceived
and dangerous Communist plot we have ever had to face," is
how *Dr. Strangelove*'s General Jack D. Ripper characterized the
fluoridation of municipal drinking water supplies, a public health
initiative that began in the 1940s to strengthen children's teeth.
Though the scientific consensus on its safety and effectiveness
remains intact, there were and are some nontrivial reasons for
concern; in 2015, the U.S. Department of Health and Human
Services recommended that fluoride levels in reservoirs be significantly decreased because of an increase in fluorosis, tooth staining
caused by an excess of the mineral. But the conspiracy theories
promoted by the John Birch Society and others in the 1950s and
'60s, like so many Americans' fears of COVID-19 vaccines today,
came from a more primal place.

Christian nationalism isn't the sole source of conspiracy theory,
as the "Trumpian ecumenicism" of the Capitol rioters proves (the
phrase comes from a headline over a Religion News Service story).
Though it's far from a big tent, MAGA is more diverse than it may
appear at first glance, and includes a small but growing number of
people of color, some right-wing Zionists and Muslims, as well as

non-believing Libertarians from the tech world. But as Perry and Gorski noted in an interview, what all these groups' different narratives have in common is their placement of "the American story at the center of the cosmic drama":

> America is the exceptional nation, the chosen nation that is playing a special role in the battle between good and evil. The endtimes, etc. So who doesn't want to be at the center of the cosmic drama? It's why we get drawn into thriller novels or the Harry Potter books, right? Because it's the same sense of, you know, There's all this secret stuff that's actually going on, and there are a few people who know, and they are going to defend freedom or the good and fight against evil.[38]

In late 2012, after Obama won his second term, Republican pundits on the Sunday morning political shows and op-ed pages acknowledged the changing fundamentals of America's demography, and how poorly they seemed to bode for Republicans' ability to win national elections going forward. "Public opinion is obviously evolving," Alan Charles Raul, a former figure in the Reagan administration wrote in *The Washington Post*. "Drinking too much tea has left us jittery."[39]

Leaders listened, and in March 2013, the Republican National Committee released a hundred-page postmortem of the election, underlining the need for further outreach to women, African Americans, Asians, Hispanics, and gays. The GOP has been "continually marginalizing itself," commented Sally Bradshaw, a GOP strategist and co-chair of the study. Reince Priebus, then the new chairman of the RNC (and later Trump's chief of staff), explicitly appealed to straying Republicans and potential new ones who had their doubts: "Let me say this: we want to earn your trust again;

to those who have yet to trust us, we welcome you with open arms."[40]

Still others agreed with Richard Spencer and the National Policy Institute's premortem of the same election, that the GOP needed to stop reaching out and reach in instead, to strengthen its white base. What was needed, they said, was a meaner, louder candidate from outside the political establishment.

But perhaps the most interesting analysis of the 2012 election was in a blog post written by a Baltimore-based software entrepreneur named Dave Troy, who focused not so much on policy or communications strategies as population densities. "Studying election results county by county," he wrote on November 19, "a stunning pattern emerges. . . . 98% of the 50 most dense counties voted Obama. 98% of the 50 least dense counties voted for Romney."[41]

When he graphed the data, you could see a clear break point: where population densities were less than eight hundred people per square mile, there was a 66 percent chance that a voter would cast his or her ballot for a Republican. But once population density passed that threshold, the chances were 66 percent that a voter would choose a Democrat. With a few exceptions, like Salt Lake City and Oklahoma City (neither of which are particularly dense), cities in red states mostly trended blue, while low-density jurisdictions in otherwise blue states trended red.

During the summer of 2022, I shared an early manuscript of this book with a friend who is well-connected in the technology world. He mentioned that he is friends with Dave Troy and sent me a piece he'd just published in *The Washington Spectator,* entitled "Paranoia on Parade: How Goldbugs, Libertarians, and Religious Extremists Brought America to the Brink."[42] I read it with interest, asked my friend for an introduction, and in due course we spoke on the phone.

Troy told me he is less concerned about right-wing zealots' magical thinking than he is about the real-world activities that some of the wealthiest and most powerful of them have been involved in since at least the 1930s. I mentioned the "Business Plot" to take down FDR in chapter 1. Troy talked about the Council for National Policy, a group founded by the evangelical leader Tim LaHaye, the billionaire Nelson Bunker Hunt, and the conservative activists Paul Weyrich and Richard Viguerie in 1981 as an anti-communist counterbalance to the Council on Foreign Relations, and the pre- and post-Trump shenanigans of Putin-friendly rightists like Mike Flynn and Steve Bannon. When I told him I remembered reading his post about population densities in 2012, he said that it was completely germane to his thinking about the right.

People in low-density and high-density places tend to have different lifestyles and different values, he said; they also have very little direct contact with each other, so their views are self-reinforcing. People in urban cores tend to vote Democratic while rural people vote Republican. People in mixed-density suburbs have more contact with their opposites, so their allegiances are more malleable, which is why such places are often swing districts. Troy called this a "networked model." Our political beliefs are shaped primarily by the people in our networks, he said. We support the candidates and platforms that our families and the members of our social networks support.

As we were winding up our call, he suggested I read a book about the Salem witch trials, which used a networked model to explain the madness that overtook that community three and a half centuries ago. I downloaded it on Kindle that same day. Paul Boyer and Stephen Nissenbaum, both professors at the University of Massachusetts Amherst, published *Salem Possessed: The Social Origins of Witchcraft* in 1974. Drawing on archival sources, including public records of town meetings, tax assessments, legal petitions, trial transcripts, wills, deeds, estate inventories, and manuscript volumes of sermons, they placed the familiar events in a radically different context than what is usually described.

In most narratives of the events, and especially latter-day dramatizations of them, the witch-hunters are cast as the dominant group and their victims as weak and marginalized outsiders. Some of the accused witches, like Mary Black and Tituba, fit that description. But they were exceptions that proved an opposite rule. In fact, most of the accusers were from families with less money and status than the people they accused. Like the Germans in the Battle of the Bulge, wrote Boyer and Nissenbaum, their attacks were launched "in the midst of a general and sustained retreat."[43]

The accusers were denizens of Salem Village (now called Danvers, Massachusetts), which at the time was a rural outpost of Salem Town. As a port and mercantile center, Salem Town was one of the wealthiest and most urbanized cities in seventeenth-century Massachusetts. Salem Village was miles inland. Nonetheless, it was not allowed to have an independent church, its men were required to travel to the city for militia and guard duty, and its taxes were mostly spent on the upkeep of the city. The village's farmers had been fighting for greater political and religious autonomy for years, and many of the accusers' families had been involved in acrimonious litigation over estates with their wealthier relatives in town. The witches' first supposed victims were the daughters of Salem Village's Reverend Parris, who was locked in a bitter struggle with the powers in Salem Town to keep his job.

When the accusations began in early 1692, Massachusetts had been without a governor or a fully functioning court system since the revolution of 1688. The trials began soon after William Phips, the new governor, arrived in Massachusetts from England, and they ended when Phips's wife was accused of witchcraft. One of Phips's shipmates was Increase Mather, Massachusetts's most prominent Puritan minister and the father of Cotton Mather. The two Mathers would argue against the use of spectral evidence in court, which was testimony about how a witch had appeared to an accuser in a dream or vision and harassed or even bit and choked them.

Boyer and Nissenbaum noted that there had been other accusations of witchcraft in New England and a handful of executions, but they had not metastasized as they did in Salem. And they pointed out that the bewitched young girls who made the accusations might have just as easily been accused of witchcraft themselves. Why were their accusations believed? For that matter, why weren't they celebrated? One of the supposed signs of the girls' enchantment was their glossolalia, or babbling, which could have just as easily been interpreted as religious ecstasies of the sort that you see at Pentecostal meetings today.

When Mercy Short, a servant girl in Boston, was said to have been hexed by one of the Salem witches, Cotton Mather took a special interest in her case and used it "as an opportunity for the religious edification of the community." Instead of isolating her, Mather encouraged young people to gather in Mercy's "Haunted Chamber" for prayer meetings. Mercy participated in them and sometimes spoke with a wisdom and sophistication that seemed to have been channeled from a higher power, Mather said, as did some of the other worshippers. Those gatherings, Boyer and Nissenbaum observe, suggest "nothing so much as the early stages of what would become, a generation later, a looming feature of the American social landscape: a religious revival."

The "Little Awakening" of 1734 began in Northampton, Massachusetts, in almost exactly the same way that the Salem witchcraft outbreak had, with people experiencing "great terrors" and "distresses" which brought them to "the borders of despair," culminating in the suicide of a man named Joseph Hawley. Afterward, other townspeople reported hearing voices urging them to harm themselves. But the local minister Jonathan Edwards, the renowned theologian and author of the famous sermon "Sinners in the Hands of an Angry God," interpreted the episode as a "remarkable pouring out of the spirit of God," preached on it, and as a result, brought several hundred new converts to his church. There were two critical differences between the events in Northampton and Salem, Boyer and Nissenbaum write: context and who was stirring the pot. "In each of these communities . . . the behavior of groups of young people . . . served as a kind of Rorschach test into which adults read their own concerns and expectations."[44] In Salem, there was the ongoing conflict between urban haves and rural left-behinds, a central government that was temporarily absent, and a minister fanning the flames. In Northampton, the minister was the prodigy (he was leading a congregation in New York when he was only eighteen) who would become America's first great revivalist.

Think back to 1954 and the tribulations that Dorothy Martin predicted. What was the context? Senator Joseph McCarthy was censured that year, bringing America's latter-day witch trials to an end, but there was still an awful lot of grist for people's apocalyptic mills to grind. Mass polio vaccinations began that year, and the Supreme Court delivered its unanimous decision in *Brown v. Board of Education*. The words "under God" were added to the Pledge of Allegiance, and in Akron, Ohio, Oral Roberts was filming the first televised revivals. The French suffered a crushing defeat in the Battle of Dien Bien Phu in Vietnam and a hydrogen bomb was tested on the Bikini Atoll. Eisenhower coined the phrase "domino effect" to describe the spread of communism and signed the Communist Control Act, outlawing the Communist Party in the United States. Hurricanes Alice, Carol, and Hazel, among others, caused massive losses of life and property.

And now zoom ahead to our own divisive epoch. Just as in Salem and Northampton, the same events can spark wildly different reactions, depending on the geographic, demographic, economic, and cultural networks in which they are experienced and interpreted. In the introduction to this book, I mentioned the conspiracist concern with weather-altering technologies. Lest you think I was exaggerating, in the fall of 2022, when Hurricane Ian devastated parts of Florida, the far-right propagandist and failed congressional candidate DeAnna Lorraine, host of the podcast *Winning the Culture War,* talked about its suspicious timing and location. "We understand that the 'Deep State,' they have weather manipulation technology," she said. "These huge hurricanes always seem to target red states, red districts, and always at a convenient time—typically right before elections."[45] Because who ever heard of a hurricane happening in the fall, and in Florida, Louisiana, or Texas? The irony, of course, is that while many of those far-right theorists deny the existence of anthropogenic climate change out of one side of their mouths, they accuse the government of weaponizing the weather out of the other.

As for "who's stirring the pot," look at Florida's governor Ron DeSantis, who while he almost certainly doesn't believe in weather weapons, nonetheless weaponized the storm politically himself, complaining that the "national regime media" had hoped that Tampa would bear the brunt of it, "because they thought that would be worse for Florida. That's how these people think. I mean, they don't care about the people of this state. . . . They want to use storms and destruction from storms as a way to advance their agenda."[46] DeSantis knew whereof he spoke. In 2013, when he was a freshman congressman, he voted against providing federal aid to victims of Hurricane Sandy in the Northeast. You might have thought he cared more about advancing his own political career in Florida than helping the people of New York and New Jersey.

But we've traveled a long way from the city/rural divide that I began this chapter with. In the next chapter, I want to look a little deeper into that looming feature of the American social landscape, the religious revival. For what is a Trump rally, after all, but a tent meeting for Trumpolotrists?

7

Into the Fire

On August 8, 2022, the FBI executed a search warrant at Donald Trump's Mar-a-Lago residence so agents could retrieve documents that had been improperly removed from the White House and that Trump's lawyers had sworn had already been returned. They found a lot of them, some in boxes in a storage room near the swimming pool where cleaning supplies, beach chairs, and umbrellas were also kept, others in Trump's desk. At least a dozen of them, a *Washington Post* story noted a few weeks later, detailed "top-secret U.S. operations so closely guarded that many senior national security officials are kept in the dark about them." Such documents, the article continued, would normally be kept under lock and key in secure government facilities, with control officers on duty around the clock to keep tabs on them.[1] Though pundits confidently (and rightly) predicted that Trump's loyalists would stick with him through this scandal as they had through all the ones before, it seemed likely that he—or someone close to him at the very least—would be prosecuted (he and two co-conspirators would be indicted in the spring and summer of 2023).*

---

* The political implications became a little murkier in January 2023, when con-

Biden had begun his presidency by studiously ignoring Trump
and Trumpism, refusing, for a time, to even speak his name out
loud. But as the midterms grew nearer, he went on the offense. In
one speech, he labeled extreme Trump supporters "semi-fascists."
Despite the predictable howls of outrage from the usual sources,
he doubled down a few days later, delivering a speech outside
Philadelphia's Independence Hall in which he said that "Donald
Trump and the MAGA Republicans represent an extremism that
threatens the very foundations of our republic." They "do not
respect the Constitution," he said. "They do not believe in the
rule of law. They do not recognize the will of the people. . . . They
spread fear and lies—lies told for profit and power."[2]

Trump and his handpicked candidates had turned the midterms into a referendum on Biden's legitimacy and Trump's inevitable candidacy in 2024. Biden was gambling that the sword could
cut both ways—that if Trump could energize his base by making
the midterms about him, Biden could rouse the much larger set
of voters who had not cast their ballots for Trump by turning the
midterms into a referendum on democracy itself.

So, when I read that Trump would appear at a "Save America" rally in Wilkes-Barre, Pennsylvania, to lend support to Doug
Mastriano and Mehmet Oz, the GOP's candidates for Pennsylvania's gubernatorial and senate races, but even more important,
to respond to the "raid" on Mar-a-Lago and Joe Biden's subsequent attacks, I figured that news would be made. More than that,
it would be an opportunity to get out of my Brooklyn bubble
and experience MAGA America for myself. Who knew? Maybe

fidential documents were also discovered in an office Joe Biden used in the years
between his vice presidency and presidency, as well as in his garage, and a special
prosecutor was appointed to look into the matter. Days later, confidential documents also turned up at former vice president Mike Pence's residence.

Trump's charisma would bowl me over, as it had so many others, and change my whole way of thinking. Stranger things have happened.

When I told my friends that I was going to a Trump rally, almost all of them warned me to be careful, as if I would be putting myself in physical jeopardy. I found their concern ironic, the MAGAs of north-central Pennsylvania would likely be even more nervous about venturing into our corner of the world, where gangs of gun-wielding Antifa and BLM activists roam the streets, and everyone who isn't mis-spending their welfare checks is mainlining critical race theory. My friend Scott, a professor of East Asian studies, offered to join me, so I reserved seats for both of us.

My phone buzzed several times while we were driving to the rally; they were messages from Trump's son Don Jr., urging us to hurry lest we be turned away. Crowds had been pouring in since early that morning, he said; the parking lot was nearly full. We arrived at the Mohegan Sun Arena at two thirty in the afternoon, an hour and a half before the event's scheduled starting time, driving past a tractor-trailer rig covered with fading signage about Benghazi and Hillary Clinton and up to a security gate whose guard waved us through without looking at our tickets. There were plenty of places to park, but the line to get inside was epic, snaking up and down the rows of cars, all the way from the makeshift enclosure where the Bikers for Trump had parked their Harley-Davidsons to the cluster of food trucks and portable toilets outside the entrance.

The air was thick with humidity and the sun was hot. I was glad I'd remembered to bring a hat, but if I hadn't, there were plenty of vendors selling red MAGA caps out of the backs of their vans, not to mention Blue Lives Matter flags and "Proud to

Be Deplorable," "Fauci Lies," and "Let's Go Brandon" T-shirts. An ambulance rolled past, its lights flashing, bringing aid, I presumed, to a heat-dazed senior. The line had barely moved after an hour, but the mood around us was resolutely upbeat. My friend engaged the two women ahead of us in conversation. Both lived in the area and had seen Trump speak many times. One was married to a marine, and as much as he loved Trump he hated waiting on lines, so she had agreed to represent him, she said. Biden had visited Wilkes-Barre earlier that week, her friend told us, and less than a hundred people showed up to see him. Even so, the Secret Service had tied up traffic downtown for hours.

At four o'clock, the jumbotron outside the arena lit up; Marjorie Taylor Greene was warming up the crowd inside. "Joe Biden has declared all of you are extremists," she said. "Joe Biden has declared that half of this country are enemies of the state!" Then Mehmet Oz took her place, talking about how his immigrant parents had come to America legally. A little later, someone whose name I didn't catch bore witness to the horrific conditions in the Washington gulag where the political prisoners from the January insurrection were being held.

For all the "White Lives Matter" T-shirts I saw, I didn't hear anyone say the N-word. There was even a modicum of ethnic diversity. A Black man ahead of us was wearing a T-shirt that said "I'm Black and I Love Trump." Up on the jumbotron, a Newsmax reporter was interviewing a pair of *shtreimel*-wearing Hasids. A gaggle of Asian women marched by, carrying "Make America Great Again" signs. "We are from China," one of them intoned sadly. "We came to America to be free. Please bring back Trump so we can keep America free." No one was talking about critical race theory, cultural Marxism, or Soros either, though I'm sure if I had asked anyone about those topics, I would have gotten some interesting responses.

I don't mean to imply that 99 percent of the attendees weren't white or that there weren't any semi- or 100-percent fascists in the crowd. More than likely there were—just as there would have been at any of the hockey games that are played in the arena (it's the home of the Wilkes-Barre/Scranton Penguins, the Pittsburgh Penguins' farm team). But it seemed to me that it wasn't politics per se that had drawn most of the people to Wilkes-Barre that day. It was the opportunity to spend time with one another, celebrating their shared identity as people who love Trump in defiance of all the people who don't. Just by being there, they were owning the libs. When you get up close to it, Trumpolotry looks a lot more like it's about identity than ideas. The world may look down on us, they seemed to be saying, but here we are.

As we drew closer to the entrance, a startlingly beautiful, blissfully stoned young Black man with shoulder-length dreadlocks pulled a wagon heaped with Trump-themed regalia past us, laughing softly to himself, as if at some private joke. The "Ultra-Maga" T-shirt he was wearing was fresh out of the package; you could still see the creases in it. "Look at him," my friend said under his breath. "If this was a religious festival in ancient China you would have seen his like—descendants of war captives, freed slaves, refugees from rural famines—selling fake relics to the pilgrims."

An elderly lady stood next to a white SUV with a metal "Trump Edition" badge glued to its tailgate, smiling distractedly and holding a pair of sneakers in her hands. Her thick white socks were grass stained. "Do you need help getting your shoes back on?" my friend asked. She thanked him and explained that her feet had swelled up so she'd been sitting in her car with the air conditioner on while her husband waited on the line. It was worth all the trouble to see Trump, she told us. She'd waited longer to see him before.

A helicopter hovered over the parking lot for a while; later, we spotted a drone. I wondered if they weren't beaming aerial photos of the crowd to Trump's airplane, so he could build up a head of steam for his speech. I looked at the clock on my phone as we passed through a gate and into a canvas-covered enclosure where the metal detectors were—it was 5:45. To the strains of "Yankee Doodle," scratched out on an electric guitar by a man in a MAGA cap while a man dressed like a Minute Man beat out time on a snare drum, we finally entered the arena's concession area, where new lines were forming in front of the food stands.

The sound system blasted Rick Derringer's "I Am a Real American" as we looked for seats inside. Despite our long wait, we had no trouble finding a pair with decent sight lines. Down in the rink, a speakers' dais had been set up at one of the goal lines. Behind a bank of TV cameras was a closed-off area for the press. Some of the reporters inside it were tapping on their laptops; others eyed the crowd warily. Googling the arena's capacity on my phone, I learned it was eight thousand three hundred. With the extra seats on the floor and the risers behind the dais, I guessed it could hold nine or ten thousand people.

And then another long wait began. Thanks to the song selections, the vibe was more like a high school reunion than *Triumph of the Will*. Down in the rink, a group of heavily made-up women in red-white-and-blue costumes and Uncle Sam hats were bopping to Elton John's "Goodbye Yellow Brick Road." Some very small children played tag. Most of the attendees were older, but there was a sprinkling of young families, some couples who looked like they were on dates, and groups of teenagers who had likely come in with their parents. A lady in the row ahead of us had brought her cat with her; it sat peacefully on her lap, seemingly unfazed by the noise and spectacle. When the Village People's "Y.M.C.A." began to play, people around us stood up and did the hand motions together.

An hour crawled by, then another. To my surprise, there were no speeches from the floor; just a steady stream of golden old-ies and Andrew Lloyd Webber show tunes. A synth-heavy ballad that I didn't recognize, I learned later, was likely LaLa Deaton's "WWG1WGA" (which stands for QAnon's motto, "Where we go one, we go all"). At one point, I could have sworn I heard the crowd singing along with something in German, but I might have dozed off. It had been a long day.

As the minutes and hours ticked by, the counter on the score-board clocked the contributions flowing into Trump's Save America PAC in real time: $25 from Joe in Altoona, $50 from Cindy from Scranton, $150 from Jesse from Harrisburg, and on and on. It was as if they'd lifted up MAGA's hood, so we could see how smoothly its big V-12 engine was running.

By eight p.m., most of the seats in the arena were full. The houselights dimmed, and a gaggle of VIPs emerged and walked the floor. Spotlights gleamed off Doug Mastriano's bald head and illuminated Marjorie Taylor Greene's mane of yellow hair. Mehmet Oz was taller than I expected. Someone behind me was telling his companions that Trump's plane had landed, and his motorcade had left the airport. "I just want to see him for a min-ute, and then I'm going home," one replied. The music stopped and the scoreboard went black. Then it lit up again, playing a montage of heavily edited news clips in which a confused and disoriented Biden stuttered and stumbled and walked into walls. "If he can't talk," the announcer gravely asked at the end, "how can he possibly lead?"

Suddenly the arena erupted in cheers. At long last, Donald Trump was making his entrance. He stood at the dais in silence for a long time, larger than life in his loose-fitting blue suit, long red tie, and that amazing orange comb-over, soaking in the crowd's applause. "Our country is going to hell!" he said at last. Declaring that the coming election will be a referendum on the "corruption and extremism of Joe Biden and the radical Democrat Party," he characterized Biden's recent speech as "the most vicious, hateful and divisive . . . ever delivered by an American president, vilifying seventy-five million citizens, plus another probably seventy-five to one-fifty." That was a pretty startling number, given that only 159 million ballots had been cast in 2020. If as many as 225 million Americans are hard-core MAGA supporters, then how did Biden and the Democrats manage to get even one vote? Trump answered my question within seconds: "They cheat like hell!"

"There's only one party that's waging war in American democracy by censoring free speech, criminalizing dissent, disarming law-abiding citizens, issuing lawless mandates and unconstitutional orders, imprisoning political protesters . . . rigging elections, weaponizing the Justice Department and the FBI," he continued, with his familiar Queens intonations. "The FBI and the Justice Department have become vicious monsters, controlled by radical left scoundrels, lawyers, and the media who tell them what to do . . . they're trying to silence me and more importantly, they are trying to silence you."

The crowd roared its approval. "Save us, save us, save us!" a woman sitting a few rows ahead of us shrieked hysterically. It was like a scene from a religious revival, but instead of rushing up the aisle to bear witness and be saved, she allowed herself to be comforted by her neighbors.

"The MAGA movement is the greatest in the history of our country," Trump proclaimed. "And maybe in the history of the world. . . . We are trying to save our country because such bad things are happening to our beautiful, beloved America. We will make America great again. I will never turn my back on you. And you will never turn your back on me because we love our nation. . . . It was not just my home that was raided last month. It was the hopes and dreams of every citizen who I've been fighting for since the moment I came down the golden escalator in 2015, wanting to represent the people."

The applause was deafening, as it was whenever he remembered to say "you" and "we." But as his speech continued, most of it turned out to be about "I" and "me"—Trump's magnificence, and even more so, his grievances. And it felt . . . old, as most of those grievances harkened back not just to 2020, but to 2015 and 2016. There was a long riff about Hillary Clinton's emails—what was she thinking, taking such terrible risks with our national secrets? He talked about Russia Russia Russia, and how it was all a big hoax and he was 100 percent exonerated. No collusion! Adam Schiff, whose head looks just like a big watermelon, made it all up.

Speaking of Russia, there would have never been a war in Ukraine if he were still president. "Putin really wouldn't have done it. I would have said, 'Vladimir, you're not gonna do that, Vladimir.' He knew that. He knew it. He knew it. But he did it as soon as the election was rigged and it was considered over." Trump literally couldn't bring himself to say that Biden had won—or harder still, that he had lost.

He talked about the venue we were sitting in and the size of the crowd. "You know this place? I think it holds twelve thousand people. So, we sold out in about fifteen seconds and I said what are we going to do for the people that can't get in? That's why a lot of times, I like fields because fields, you could just keep having them. In Alabama, we had sixty-six thousand people. Figure this: Outside of Houston, Texas, we had eighty-nine thousand people show up." Back when he was president, Trump said, gas was $1.87 a gallon, actually $1.42, but he allowed the price to go up so the oil companies wouldn't go broke. Now it's $8.00, and the electric cars they want to make you buy are terrible because they take so long to recharge. Trump finished building the wall on the southern border, and it was beautiful and it worked but Biden tore it down, inviting the hordes of invaders to come in and do their worst. You could "take the five worst presidents in American history and put them together, and they would not have done the damage Joe Biden has done to our country in less than two years." But what can you expect? "He's cognitively impaired."

"You know, they don't want you to have guns but it's okay for the IRS," Trump said. Biden wants to arm eighty-seven thousand new agents and send them after you. China is bad, the worst, but Trump had a great relationship with Xi, who "rules with an iron fist one point five billion people. Yeah, I'd say he's smart, wouldn't you say he's smart?" Xi executes drug dealers the same day they're arrested, just like Trump will do when he returns to the White House.

By this point, the crowd was starting to get a little restless. It wasn't that they didn't love their president-in-exile. It was just that, after waiting so long in the hot sun, after sitting for so long in the air-conditioning grooving to the sounds of the '70s, it was a little hard to get excited about the same stories about America's decline and humiliation that he'd been telling five and six years ago. A certain languor descended over the arena. The applause lines drew a little less applause, the cheers were a little less raucous. It felt a bit like it does during the eighth inning of a ball game late in the season, when the home team is already out of the playoffs and they're three runs down.

Looking around me, I saw one of those women in Uncle Sam hats heading for the exit. The family in front of us got up and sidled toward the aisle on our right. I looked to my left, and nearly every seat in the row was empty. Around nine thirty, Trump finally remembered that he was there to support Mehmet Oz and Doug Mastriano, and started talking about how terrible their opponents were. John Fetterman, Oz's rival for the Senate, dresses like a bum, he said, and uses illegal drugs. He wears a hoodie, can you imagine? I could, because a lot of the men in the audience were dressed the same way. When Oz himself finally started to speak, we figured the event had run its course and joined the stream of people who were leaving. But when we emerged in the parking lot just a few minutes later, there was Trump on the jumbotron, talking. We just looked at each other and shook our heads. Neither of us could summon the strength to go back inside.

Newsweek posted a transcript; when I read it the next day, I saw that we'd missed his rants about critical race theory (Trump purged it from schools, the military, and the government but Biden put it right back in) and trans women in sports ("You have this swimmer. . . . She's worked all her life. . . . She looks to the right, and she sees this massive human being . . . what is he, like six-six or something? He's got a wingspan bigger than Wilt Chamberlain"). He talked about energy: just two years ago, he said, we had been so energy dominant that we could have "been bigger than Russia and Saudi Arabia combined times two." He talked about abortion. "I believe in the exceptions," he said, while Democrats just like ripping babies out of women's wombs—or better yet, murdering them after they're born. As for what those exceptions might be, Trump threaded the needle: "The states will make the decision and in Pennsylvania, I have a feeling that decision will be an interesting decision, but it's up to the states and that's the way it was always supposed to be."

"Despite great outside dangers, our greatest threat remains the sick, sinister and evil people from within our own country," Trump said in his peroration.[3]

All that left me with one question: If a feeble old man like Biden can steal the presidency from a latter-day Caesar like Trump, undoing all his mighty works in a matter of months, then why should I bother to vote in the midterms? Trump said it himself: If the Republican Party is run by RINOs, then why elect more of them? They'll only betray us like they betrayed Trump. And for that matter, why return him to office in 2024?

The whole point of a rally is to motivate your supporters. Sure, you have to wave the bloody shirt and lead them through Orwell's Two Minutes Hate to get them in the mood, but then you need to lift their spirits. You tell them they are not forgotten, that you see them and value them for who they are, and you tantalize them with a vision of hope and possibility—*I have been to the mountaintop,* and all that. Trump promises retribution, but all the good things he evokes—$1.42 gasoline, low taxes, high employment, the respect of Xi, Putin, and Kim Jong Un, an America protected by impregnable walls and punitive tariffs—are seemingly in the irrecoverable past.

End Times evangelicals and revolutionaries of all stripes don't want the world as they know it to end simply so they can watch it burn—they want to live in the paradise that comes after all the tribulations. At one point, Trump asked the crowd if they wanted him to throw his hat in the ring for 2024, as if there was any possibility that he wouldn't. He got all the applause he asked for and more, but it felt a bit as if he was taunting them. I mean, if things were even half as dire as he said they were and only he could fix them, then why hadn't he fixed them for good when he had the chance, given that he had enjoyed the most successful presidency in history?

Why hadn't we seen Democrats' heads on pikes, like Q prophesied and Steve Bannon promised?[4] It was the populist paradox. When your electability depends on your voters' conviction that the country is systemically corrupt and broken, then what advantage is there to incumbency or, in Trump's case, ex-incumbency? It seemed to me that what was driving Trump wasn't the desire to be president, but to squeeze as much juice as he could out of what was left of his brand. And, of course, to protect himself from prosecution.

Like Biden said, when you get down to it, MAGA is all about "lies told for profit and power." Trump had learned the hard way that exercising legitimate power via legislation is hard work that often yields mixed results. So, why not just grab your supporters by their ankles, turn them upside down, and shake out their pockets?

Trump may have the temperament of a dictator but he lacks the instincts. Political power, as Mao said, grows out of the barrel of a gun, and neither Trump nor his followers have the courage, the discipline, or the will to fight and win a revolution, never mind build a new political and social order. Trump would have to be less of a crybaby and more of a killer to do that, like his frenemies Putin, Xi, and Kim Jong Un.

When put to the test, even the ultra-MAGAs that raided the Capitol turned out to be more like rowdy soccer hooligans than a revolutionary cadre. Fire them up with rhetorical reminders of what they were and what they have become, and they turn into a mob, with all the transient and destructive enthusiasms of a mob. But when the Deep State struck back, Trump didn't take to the hills like Mao or Castro did and move among the people with his guerilla armies like a fish swims in the sea. Instead, he had an endless pity party, cashing in with podcasts, books, and radio shows.

The Trump rally evoked the tent revivals that have been so much a part of American rural culture since colonial days. But at the same time, it was a reminder of what was missing. Sure, his followers enjoyed hearing about the hellfire and damnation and ruin and destruction that he would rain down on their enemies. But they came there for grace, for him to figuratively lay his hands on them and heal them. Like Sabbatai Zevi's Jewish followers in the seventeenth century, the Millerites and the Mormons in the nineteenth century, or QAnon true believers today, Trump's followers are desperate for meaning, and more than that, redemption. But Trump was winding them up, only to send them on their way unsatisfied. It was coitus interruptus on an industrial scale.

Like so many modern dictators, Trump has a messiah complex that his followers are only too happy to indulge. Though he had maintained a cautious distance from QAnon during the 2020 election, now he was openly aligning himself with the movement. That seemed like a dangerous gambit. Since QAnon and the white Christian nationalists see him as at least a divine instrument and possibly even a divinity, he may be raising the bar higher than he can reach. Once you declare yourself to be God, your disciples expect you to heal the sick and multiply loaves and fishes, or at the very least, put Hillary Clinton in jail. They may even want you to be martyred, so they can have the satisfaction of seeing you rise from the dead.

Just as *Roe v. Wade* brought Bible-believing Protestants and conservative Catholics together in the pro-life movement, Trumpism has catalyzed new alliances between Catholic integralists* and Dominionist Protestants, who, despite their many doctrinal differences, both believe that the founders intended the United States to be a theocracy, governed by biblical law. The Seven

---

* The Josias, an integralist website, defines Catholic integralism as a "tradition of thought that, rejecting the liberal separation of politics from concern with the end of human life, holds that. . . . the temporal power must be subordinated to the spiritual power." (https://thejosias.com/2016/10/17/integralism-in-three-sentences/)

Mountain Mandate,* which gave rise to the New Apostolic Reformation (the evangelical movement that Trump's spiritual advisor Paula White-Cain is associated with), dates back to a vision shared by Loren Cunningham, Bill Bright, and Francis Schaeffer in 1975, in which they were told that Christ will not return until his servants secure each of the seven major spheres of influence in the world: education, religion, family, business, government/military, arts and entertainment, and the media. The irony is that the movement has a deeper appeal without Trump than with him. President Trump is just another politician. An ex-President Trump who was unfairly driven from office and hounded by liberal prosecutors is a martyr.

On December 12, 2020, the Jericho March, a hastily organized movement to overturn Biden's election, held a rally in Washington, D.C. Among the prominent conservatives and evangelicals who spoke was General Mike Flynn, Trump's former national security advisor, who assured the crowd that an attack on Trump was an attack on them. In the middle of his speech, Marine One, with Trump aboard, appeared, hovering over the crowd like the spirit of God. Raising his voice over the sound of its rotors, Flynn shouted a story about the "Israeli-ites [*sic*]" and their victory over the city of Jericho. "Nothing can resist the power of prayer," he concluded. "These Jericho walls we are standing inside of, this Deep State . . . is evil and there is corruption and there is light and truth. We're going to get to the light and we're going to get to the truth. And us inside, we're going to knock those walls down. We're going to knock those walls down."[5]

---

* After Isaiah 2:2: "In the last days the mountain of the Lord's temple will be established as the highest of the mountains; it will be exalted above the hills, and all nations will stream to it."

Also among the speakers was Infowars' Alex Jones, who rallied the crowd with the cry, "We will never bow down to the Satanic pedophile New World Order! Joe Biden is a globalist, and Joe Biden will be removed, one way or another!"[6] Partnering with the Oklahoma entrepreneur Clay Clark, Flynn later put together a traveling extravaganza, the ReAwaken America Tour, that visited dozens of cities in 2021 and 2022, offering ticket holders the opportunity to buy books and tchotchkes, listen to MAGA celebrities like Mike Lindell, Roger Stone, and Trump's sons Don Jr. and Eric rail about the horrors of unisex bathrooms and minority voting, and then take a plunge in a baptismal font.

Do mountebanks like Trump and Alex Jones and zealots like Mike Flynn and Mike Lindell experience paranoia themselves or simply package it for others so they can harness it to their own purposes? It's one of those unanswerable chicken/egg questions, but for whatever it's worth, I still tend to believe the latter. You can't have winners without losers, and America has more than its share of both. The paranoid style has something for everyone who feels looked down upon or marginalized or cheated out of what they believe should be theirs by right—or who has figured out a way to make money from people who think and feel that way.

Paranoids who are unhappy in matters of money see central bankers as the personification of evil. Paranoids who are unhappy in love become men's rightists and theorize about the malevolent principles of misandry and gynocentrism. Paranoids who are worried about the waning of white privilege and the dilution of white sperm may become white nationalists. Paranoids who secretly fear that God hates them can look for new targets for His wrath. Most conspiracists assume their opponents are as dogmatic and literal-minded as they are themselves, only in reverse—that they figuratively (or not so figuratively) hang their crucifixes upside down and say the Lord's Prayer backward.

All of this helps explain Trump's staying power. He makes no bones about whom he hates and why, whether it's a woman accusing him of sexual assault, a business rival who bested him in a deal, a political ally who flaked when the chips were down, or an egghead who forgot that Trump also attended an Ivy League school, and that he is not just smart but a genius. Trump is all about himself, but at the same time, he is a mirror for every other disappointed person who once believed they stood at the center of the universe but learned otherwise to their sorrow. *Look at me,* Trump says. *I am everything you envy—rich, powerful, loved by beautiful women. And see how badly I'm treated.*

Trump's followers have another reason to stick with him too, one that anyone who has been betrayed by someone they loved can easily understand, which is the sunk cost fallacy. It's easier to throw good money after bad than admit you've been had. "The Emperor's New Clothes" provides as good an explanation as any for the incredibly destructive epoch we are living through. In their desperate need to deny that they've been had, all but a handful of Republicans have bound themselves to a messiah that in their heart of hearts, they know is false.

Being played for a sucker, being laughed at, as Trump would put it, is incredibly painful. *If Trump isn't who he says he is,* they have to wonder, *then what does that say about me?*

Afterword

When my book *The New Hate: Fear and Loathing on the Populist Right* came out, my publisher arranged some bookstore events to promote it. After I spoke at Powell's Books in Portland, Oregon, a prospective reader confronted me with a question. "What about the left? And if you feel so oppressed in America," he added, with a distinctly hostile edge to his voice, "why don't you move to North Korea?"

"I wouldn't want to live in North Korea," I admitted. But while I didn't exempt the left from irrational thinking and hate, I said, I didn't buy the Tea Party's lies about Democratic extremism either. "You won't find many extremists on the Democratic side of the aisle in statehouses and Congress," I continued. "Nor will you find many programmatic racists. But as moderate as most elected Democrats are, as moderate as many Republicans may be, an awful lot of Republicans who know better have been weaponizing tropes from the racist and rightist fringe to gain partisan advantage." My fear, I concluded, paraphrasing the closing passages of *The New Hate*, is that if they do get elected, they won't be able to put that genie back in the bottle.

It was 2012, the last year of Obama's first term, and the Republican primaries had already begun. Left-wing hate had emerged as a major theme in the candidates' stump speeches. Rick Santorum inveighed against "the intolerance of the left," borne of its contempt, he said, for "folks who use reason, common sense, and divine revelation."[1] Former House Speaker Newt Gingrich—who'd dubbed Obama "the most successful food stamp president in American history"[2]—had scored an upset victory over Mitt Romney in South Carolina. "The founding fathers of America are the source from which we draw our understanding of America," he declared in his victory speech, drawing a sharp contrast with Obama, who "draws his from . . . radical left wingers and people who don't like the classical America."[3]

Race, class, and religious hatreds were potent weapons in a contest against a Black, Harvard-educated president with an Arab-sounding name, but most Republicans deployed them via indirection and innuendo lest they muddy themselves. "If you're looking for free stuff you don't have to pay for," Romney said, "vote for the other guy. That's what he's all about."[4] Better to imply that Obama has contempt for Bible-believing Christians than to lie that he is a Muslim (something nearly one in five Americans and one in three Republicans wrongly believed at the time);[5] better to turn the tables and expose him as an inveterate persecutor of white people than admit that you're a racist yourself.

Had it been possible for us to look ahead ten years and see what the Party of Lincoln has become, most of us, I suspect—even people like me, who made their bread and butter exposing the right's fear and loathing—would have been flabbergasted to discover how much more blatant the "othering" of their opponents has become, not to mention the disdain they display for the institutions of "classical America," the military and law enforcement not excepted. The FBI, America's "Gestapo," is filled with "Trump Hating Marxist Thugs," the Republican front-runner for the 2024 presidential nomination raged in January 2023.[6] The American military isn't "learning to fight and protect us from some very bad people, they want to go woke, they want to go woke—that's all they talk about now," he said at a Fox News town hall six months later.[7] As I write these words in August 2023, that same front-runner is still bragging about his epistolary love affair with North Korea's Kim Jong Un. That front-runner, of course, is Donald J. Trump, who still insists he won reelection by a landslide in 2020.

"For seven years," Trump told an enthusiastic crowd at a CPAC convention in early 2023, "you and I have been engaged in an epic struggle to rescue our country from the people who hate it and want to absolutely destroy it. We are going to finish what we started. We will demolish the deep state. We will expel the war mongers. . . . We will drive out the globalists. We will cast out the communists. We . . . will liberate America from those villains and scoundrels once and for all."

Those villains and scoundrels, to be sure, are not just Democrats but Republicanism's old guard. "We had a Republican party that was ruled by freaks, neocons, globalists, open border zealots and fools but we are never going back," he vowed.[8] Many of them had served in his own administration. His former attorney general Bill Barr is "a coward who didn't do his job."[9] His former chief of staff General John Kelly "pretended to be a 'tough guy,' but was actually weak and ineffective, born with a VERY small 'brain.'" Kelly's successor Mick Mulvaney was "perhaps the dumbest person" at the White House and a "born loser." His former national security advisor John Bolton is a "moron."[10]

To ensure that he can make good on his promises, Trump's strategists have proposed to concentrate much more power in the White House than in his first term and use it to purge the government of anyone insufficiently MAGA. "Our current executive branch," declared John McEntee, Trump's former White House personnel chief and one of the key leaders of Project 25, a Heritage Foundation–sponsored program to prepare for Trump's restoration, "was conceived of by liberals for the purpose of promulgating liberal policies. There is no way to make the existing structure function in a conservative manner. . . . What's necessary is a complete system overhaul."

It isn't just Trump that's running. A dozen or so other Republican hopefuls are seeking the 2024 presidential nomination, but their campaigns all appear to be doomed to failure, in most cases because of their reluctance to risk alienating Trump voters (not to mention Trump himself) by criticizing him.

Trump's former vice president Mike Pence—who Trump said deserved to be hanged on January 6—claims to be the true heir to MAGA, but hardly any voters are buying; to them he is a traitor. Florida governor Ron DeSantis, who read passages from *The Art of the Deal* to his children in a 2018 campaign commercial, has attacked Trump from the right as overly gay- and vaccine-friendly, but mostly he's put himself forward as a more competent version of Trump with none of his baggage. "If you want to slay this administrative state, you've got to be disciplined, you've got to be focused, and you've got to have people surrounding you that are going to go and support the mission," he told Fox News's Bret Baier.[11]

It's not a needle that he or anyone else can thread, because MAGA voters love Trump not despite but *because* of his baggage—the two impeachments, the multiple criminal indictments, and the civil trials for defamation, fraud, and sexual assault. The same elites who presume to judge him, Trump encourages his base to believe, also look down on them. As he put it himself in 2019, "In reality, they're not after me, they're after you. I'm just in the way."[12]

And then there's Robert F. Kennedy Jr. A lawyer and environmental activist who spearheaded the lawsuits that held General Electric accountable for the Hudson River's PCP contamination decades ago, he styled himself "a Kennedy Democrat" who believes in labor unions and "a strong robust middle class," "racial justice," and "policies that are going to actually help the lowest people on the totem pole."[13] Some mainstream pundits initially took him at his word, but the causes that have engaged him more recently bear scant resemblance to the ones most people associate with his late father and uncle, or for that matter with his campaign manager Dennis Kucinich, a former Cleveland mayor, eight-term congressman, and two-time presidential candidate.

The beliefs that RFK Jr. is best known for today are uncannily like those that animate many MAGA Republicans. He's said that COVID vaccines are the "deadliest" ever made, and that Dr. Anthony S. Fauci profiteered off them as part of a "historic coup d'etat against Western democracy." Vaccine mandates, he said, had made things worse in America than they ever were in Hitler's Germany, where unhappy Jews could always "cross the Alps to Switzerland" or "hide in an attic like Anne Frank did."[14] He's blamed school shootings on antidepressants and claimed, like the arch-conspiracist Alex Jones, that the herbicide atrazine is feminizing teenage boys. He's said that the United States is responsible for Russia's invasion of Ukraine; that the CIA orchestrated John F. Kennedy's assassination; and that Sirhan Sirhan was framed for his father's. Back in 2004, he claimed, in rhetoric that eerily anticipated Trump's, that the presidential election was stolen from John Kerry, and that Bush's reelection was "a massive, coordinated campaign to subvert the will of the people."[15]

But when the time comes to write the inevitable epitaph for his

presidential hopes, most reporters will revisit what he said about
the Jews and COVID at a press event at an Upper East Side restaurant in July 2023. While a diner videotaped him on a cell phone,
RFK speculated that COVID-19 had been engineered "to attack
Caucasians and Black people" and spare "Ashkenazi Jews and Chinese." When the *New York Post* broke the story, he denied that he'd
ever said that COVID was a bioweapon. He'd merely noted, he
explained, that its "furin cleave docking site is most compatible
with Blacks and Caucasians" and thus "serves as a kind of proof of
concept for ethnically targeted bioweapons."

The blowback from Jewish groups was nevertheless instanta-
neous and fierce and inspired a number of think pieces about
the seemingly inevitable link between conspiracism and anti-
Semitism. "Because anti-Semitism has produced centuries of
material pinning humanity's problems on its Jews," Yair Rosenberg wrote in *The Atlantic*, "a person convinced that an invisible
hand is conducting world affairs will eventually discover that it
belongs to an invisible Jew. . . . It is impossible to circulate on the
conspiratorial fringe and not encounter anti-Semitism."[16]

The irony, of course, was that despite polling as high as
20 percent, RFK's candidacy was receiving far less support from
Democrats than it was from independents and Republicans. He
had done Twitter events with Elon Musk and Tulsi Gabbard
and appeared on Joe Rogan's, Russell Brand's, and Bari Weiss's
podcasts, none of them exactly Democrat-friendly venues. Five
million dollars of the $9.8 million his super PAC had raised by
June 2023 was contributed by Timothy Mellon, who'd donated
$20 million to Trump's super PAC America First Action in 2020,
and $53.1 million to Texas governor Greg Abbot's border wall
fund in 2021.[17] Clearly Mellon saw RFK as a spoiler who could
siphon off votes from Biden and allow Trump to gain a plurality.
Steve Bannon and Roger Stone took it a step further and touted

RFK as a potential running mate for Trump.[18] Kennedy himself has said, "I'm proud that President Trump likes me," which makes you wonder if he, like many of the Republicans who are ostensibly running for the presidency, is actually auditioning for that role.[19]

All this raises the question: What happened since 2012 to elevate conspiracy theories, xenophobia, racism, and anti-scientific thinking from the stuff of dog whistles into the main event? Trump has obviously had a lot to do with it, but he is as much a product of the trend as its cause. Nor is he unique. He rose alongside other strongman populists in such far-flung parts of the world as India, where Narendra Modi has built a cult of personality around authoritarian Hindu nationalism; the Philippines, where Rodrigo Duterte's brutal war on drug dealers killed thousands; Brazil, where Jair Bolsonaro was dubbed "the Trump of the Tropics," not to mention Turkey, where Recep Tayyip Erdogan's authoritarian populism has held sway since 2014. There is Hungary's long-serving Viktor Orbán and Russia's Vladimir Putin.

One thing that's changed since I spoke at Powell's Books is social media, which, though rapidly growing, was still relatively young back then (Facebook and Twitter were eight and six years old respectively). Anyone who has studied the Federalist Papers knows that our constitutional republic was deliberately engineered to make it difficult for factions—and especially the demagogues who lead them—to capture a political majority. In the unlikely event that one still did, the Rube Goldberg–like complexities of Congress, the Senate, and the judiciary's roles, plus the many powers reserved to the states, couldn't but dilute and diffuse their ability to impose their will on the country. The advent of mass media like radio and television in the twentieth century gave demagogues like Father Coughlin and Joe McCarthy the ability to broadcast their messages to the entire nation, short-circuiting many of those institutional checks and balances. Algorithmically driven social media now allows them to target inflammatory information and disinformation at precisely the people it will affect the most.

Facebook introduced "Likes" and Twitter introduced the retweet to their systems in 2009. Those Likes and retweets are not only addictive for the people whose posts receive them; they generate data that advertisers, politicians, and propagandists can parse to find out what engages which users the most. As the social psychologist Jonathan Haidt noted in *The Atlantic* in 2022, "posts that trigger emotions—especially anger at out-groups—are the most likely to be shared." As the rancor escalates and metastasizes, it inevitably erodes our trust in our institutions and in one another. Traditional adversaries like Russia and China have weaponized that capability, but we also use it against ourselves to "administer justice with no due process," Haidt wrote, by harassing, shaming, and shunning not just "outsiders," but members of our own groups that stray from the party line.

Algorithmically curated news feeds lock people in epistemic silos, protecting them from arguments and evidence that might soften or even change their views. At the same time, they ensure that the most extreme ideas and the loudest and most aggressive voices are the most widely disseminated. Citing a 2018 study,[20] Haidt notes that the hardest core of conservatives, who represent a small fraction of the public (about 6 percent of the U.S. population) "score highest on beliefs related to authoritarianism. They share a narrative in which America is eternally under threat from enemies outside and subversives within." At the same time, the hardest core of progressive activists (about 8 percent of the U.S. population) advance narratives "in which life at every institution is an eternal battle among identity groups."[21] On the left there are circular firing squads. And on the Republican side there is the race to the bottom between the real Donald Trump and his wannabe successors from his own party.

All of that is true, but it begs the question of where all this rancor is coming from. Social media has only surfaced and exacerbated a tendency that is hardwired into our national identity. Paranoid ideas and hatreds have festered beneath the surfaces of our democracy since its inception, boiling over in times of economic and cultural stress like the one we are living through.

Globalized post-industrial capitalism has been as economically and emotionally devastating for white working-class men as the Gilded Age and the Depression were for farmers and small-town Americans; the cultural and economic differences between cities and rural places are as fraught as they were in the Jackson era. After two-hundred-fifty years, Americans still haven't decided whether they're heirs of the Pilgrims or the Enlightenment, and if we are a racial and cultural melting pot or a beleaguered bastion of white Christian ethnicity. The xenophobia, racism, sexism, religious chauvinism, and flirtations with authoritarian populism that we are hearing today are as old as the republic.

How do we fix this? I'm not sure that we can. If you've read this far, then you know that I don't believe that we will ever see the last of Trumpism, even after Donald Trump leaves the political stage. In time, another demagogue will rise in his place, and use the same narratives that he did to arouse the same kinds of discontented voters.

What keeps me up at night—and what impelled me to write this book—is the worry that we might not recognize his successor until it is too late.

It might be too late already.

August 14, 2023
Brooklyn, New York

Notes

Introduction

1. Jessica Kwong, "Who Is Robert Bowers? Suspect Identified in Pittsburgh Tree of Life Synagogue Shooting," *Newsweek,* October, 27, 2018 (https://www.newsweek.com/who-robert-bowers-suspect-identified-pittsburgh-tree-life-synagogue-shooting-1190440).
2. Nadine Yousif, "Why number of U.S. mass shootings has risen sharply," BBC News, January 26, 2023 (https://www.bbc.com/news/world-us-canada-64377360).
3. Mythili Sampathkumar, "Trump has 'alerted' U.S. border patrol and military that migrant caravan travelling from Mexico is 'national emergency,'" *The Independent,* October 22, 2018 (https://www.independent.co.uk/news/world/americas/us-politics/migrant-caravan-trump-mexico-us-border-patrol-honduras-guatemala-tweet-a8595956.html).
4. Alex Ward, "Trump calls the Pittsburgh shooting 'anti-Semitic' and a 'wicked act of mass murder,'" *Vox,* October 27, 2018 (https://www.vox.com/2018/10/27/18032692/trump-pittsburgh-shooting-synagogue-semitism-murder).
5. https://truthsocial.com/@realDonaldTrump/posts/109177817932811190.
6. "5 of Kanye West's Antisemitic Remarks, Explained," AJC/Global Voice, December 2, 2022 (https://www.ajc.org/news/5-of-kanye-wests-antisemitic-remarks-explained).
7. Theo Wayt, "Kanye West unloads on Josh Kushner over investment in Kim Kardashian's SKIMS," *New York Post,* October 6, 2022 (https://nypost.com

/2022/10/06/kanye-west-unloads-on-josh-kushner-over-investment-in
-kim-kardashians-skims/).

8. http://www.red-network.eu/?i=red-network.en.thesaurus.

9. "Kanye West tweets on 2016 bipolar disorder diagnosis, claims 'was mentally misdiagnosed,'" *Economic Times,* November 4, 2022 (https://economic
times.indiatimes.com/news).

10. Haley Cohen, "Candace Owens claims she's being threatened for supporting Kanye West," *Jerusalem Post,* October 26, 2022 (https://www.jpost.com
/diaspora/antisemitism/article-720602).

11. Adam Kovac, "Trump defends Kanye West in the wake of his own scorn-
ing of American Jews," *Forward,* October 18, 2022 (https://forward.com
/fast-forward).

12. Right Wing Watch, Twitter, September 22, 2022 (https://twitter.com
/RightWingWatch/status/1572963742018674690?ref_src=twsrc%5Etfw
%7Ctwcamp%5Etweetembed%7Ctwterm%5E1572963742018674690
%7Ctwgr%5E969ad28d89b2333bcfd583dda5266d9de256339b%7
Ctwcon%5Es1_&ref_url=https%3A%2F%2Fnewsone.com%2F4415005
%2Fnick-fuentes-pro-trump-video%2F).

13. Ring Wing Watch, Twitter, October 17, 2022 (https://twitter.com
/rightwingwatch/status/1582028599812820992).

14. Katie Glueck, "Mastriano's Attacks on Jewish School Set Off Outcry Over
Antisemitic Signaling," *New York Times,* October 10, 2022 (https://www
.nytimes.com/2022/10/10/us/politics/mastriano-shapiro-antisemitism
.html).

15. Katie Glueck, "In a Race Rife with Antisemitism Concerns, Mastriano
Adviser Calls Shapiro 'At Best a Secular Jew,'" *New York Times,* October 21,
2022 (https://www.nytimes.com/2022/10/21/us/politics/jenna-ellis-josh
-shapiro-jewish.html).

16. Philissa Cramer, "Doug Mastriano's wife: 'We probably love Israel more than
a lot of Jews do,'" Jewish Telegraphic Agency, October 30, 2022 (https://
www.jta.org/2022/10/30/politics/doug-mastrianos-wife-we-probably
-love-israel-more-than-a-lot-of-jews-do).

17. Andrew Lapin, "Ohio GOP candidate defends 'Jew you down' comment
by saying Jews have 'solid money principles,'" Jewish Telegraphic Agency,
October 21, 2022 (https://www.jta.org/2022/10/21/united-states/ohio-gop
-candidate-defends-jew-you-down-comment-by-saying-jews-have-solid
-money-principles).

18. Andrew Lapin, "An evangelical GOP House candidate in Texas wrote a
novel about Anne Frank finding Jesus," Jewish Telegraphic Agency, Octo-

ber 31, 2022 (https://www.jta.org/2022/10/31/politics/an-evangelical-gop
-house-candidate-in-texas-wrote-a-novel-about-anne-frank-finding-jesus).

19. William Buckley, *In Search of Anti-Semitism* (Continuum, 1993).

20. Ryan Chatelain, "Tuberville, Greene slammed for racist rhetoric at Trump
rallies," Spectrum News, October 10, 2022 (https://www.ny1.com/nyc/all
-boroughs/politics/2022/10/10/tommy-tuberville—marjorie-taylor-greene
-push-racist-rhetoric-at-trump-rallies).

21. Michael Hiltzik, "Overt racism and antisemitism have become part of our
political discourse. How did that happen?" *Los Angeles Times,* October 21,
2022 (https://www.latimes.com/business/story/2022-10-21/column-overt
-racism-and-antisemitism-have-become-part-of-our-political-discourse-who
-responsible).

22. Jonathan Weisman, "With Ads, Imagery and Words, Republicans Inject
Race Into Campaigns," *New York Times,* October 25, 2022 (https://www
.nytimes.com/2022/10/25/us/politics/crime-ads-racism-republicans.html).

23. Yasmeen Abutaleb, "What's inside the hate-filled manifesto linked to the El
Paso shooter," *Washington Post,* August 4, 2019 (https://www.washington
post.com/politics).

24. Luke Tress, "Buffalo shooting suspect pushes antisemitic conspiracies,"
Times of Israel, May 15, 2022 (https://www.timesofisrael.com/manifesto
-attributed-to-buffalo-shooting-suspect-pushes-antisemitic-conspiracies/).

25. "Factbook: Excerpts from 1,500-page Norway killer manifesto," Reuters,
July 24, 2011 (https://www.reuters.com/article/us-norway-manifesto-factbox
/factbox-excerpts-from-1500-page-norway-killer-manifesto-idUSTRE
76N14J20110724).

26. Elliot Rodger, *My Twisted World* (https://www.documentcloud.org/docu
ments/1173808-elliot-rodger-manifesto).

27. Jack Holmes, "There Is No 'Motive' for Shooting 9-Year-Old Kids,"
Esquire, March 28, 2023 (https://www.esquire.com/news-politics/a43437954
/nashville-school-shooting-no-motive/).

28. Donald Trump, "Oprah would be first VP choice," interview by Larry
King, CNN, October 7, 1999 (https://www.cnn.com/videos/politics/2018
/01/08/trump-1999-lkl-oprah-vp-sot.cnn).

29. Beth Fouhy, "Trump: Obama a 'Terrible Student' Not Good Enough for Harvard," 4New York, April 25, 2011 (https://www.nbcnewyork.com/news/local
/trump-obama-wasnt-good-enough-to-get-into-ivy-schools/1924291/).

30. Hanne Amanda Trangerud, "The Trump Prophecies and the Mobilization of
Evangelical Voters," *Studies in Religion* 51, no. 2 (2021): 202–222 (https://
journals.sagepub.com/doi/pdf/10.1177/00084298211012698).

31. Tara Isabella Burton, "The biblical story the Christian right uses to defend Trump," *Vox,* March 5, 2018 (https://www.vox.com/identities/2018/3/5/16796892/trump-cyrus-christian-right-bible-cbn-evangelical-propaganda).

32. Andrea Jefferson, "Trump Says He's a Christian, but That He 'Doesn't Need to Ask for Forgiveness' for His Sins," *Political Flare,* December 24, 2019 (https://www.politicalflare.com/2019/12/trump-says-hes-a-christian-but-that-he-doesnt-need-to-ask-for-forgiveness/).

33. Rebecca Shabad, "Donald Trump names his favorite Bible verse," CBS News, April 14, 2016 (https://www.cbsnews.com/news/donald-trump-names-his-favorite-bible-verse/).

34. Dareh Gregorian et al., "Trump shares barrage of QAnon content and other conspiracy theories on his social media platform," NBC News, August 30, 2022 (https://www.nbcnews.com/politics/donald-trump/trump-shares-barrage-qanon-content-conspiracy-theories-social-media-pl-rcna45465).

35. Tanya Lewis, "The 'Shared Psychosis' of Donald Trump and His Loyalists," *Scientific American,* January 11, 2021 (https://www.scientificamerican.com/article/the-shared-psychosis-of-donald-trump-and-his-loyalists/).

36. Mary Panefuss, "Trump Speechwriter Fired After He's Linked to White Nationalist Event," *Huffington Post,* August 20, 2018 (https://www.huffpost.com/entry/white-house-speechwriter-darren-beattie-fired_n_5b7a3db8e4b0a5b1febc9837). Also see Jean Guerrero's *Hatemonger: Stephen Miller, Donald Trump, and the White Nationalist Agenda* (William Morrow, 2020).

37. Eli Watkins and Abby Phillip, "Trump decries immigrants from 'shithole countries' coming to U.S.," CNN, January 12, 2018 (https://www.cnn.com/2018/01/11/politics/immigrants-shithole-countries-trump).

38. Mia Jankowicz, "Mike Lindell set August 13 as the date in his bonkers theory that Trump will be reinstated as president," *Business Insider India,* July 6, 2021 (https://www.businessinsider.in/politics/world).

39. Eric Brooks, "MyPillow CEO Mike Lindell has a new prediction for Trump's return to the Oval Office," KCBS All News, August 23, 2021 (https://www.audacy.com/kcbsradio/news/politics/mike-lindells-new-prediction-for-trumps-oval-office-return).

40. Michael Arceneaux, "Trump is embracing a dangerous racist conspiracy theory about Ashli Babbitt's death," *The Independent,* July 16, 2021 (https://www.independent.co.uk/voices/ashli-babbitt-death-capitol-police-officer-trump-b1885585.html).

41. Robert Kagan, "Our constitutional crisis is already here," *Washington Post,* September 23, 2021 (https://www.washingtonpost.com/opinions).

42. Josh Hafner, "Donald Trump loves the 'poorly educated'—and they love

him," *USA Today,* February 24, 2016 (https://www.usatoday.com/story/news /politics/onpolitics/2016/02/24/donald-trump-nevada-poorly-educated /80860078/).

43. Kai Elwoood-Dieu et al., "Elections 2022: The educational divide that helps explain the midterms," *Politico,* November 17, 2022 (https://www.politico .com/interactives/2022/midterm-election-house-districts-by-education/).

1: Conspiracies and Conspiracy Theories

1. Sally Denton, "Why is so little known about the 1930s coup attempt against FDR?" *The Guardian,* January 11, 2022 (https://www.theguardian.com /commentisfree/2022/jan/11/trump-fdr-roosevelt-coup-attempt-1930s).

2. Mike Caulfield, "The first use of the term conspiracy theory is much earlier— and more interesting—than historians have thought," *Hapgood* (blog); (https:// hapgood.us/2018/12/24/the-first-use-of-the-term-conspiracy-theory-is -much-earlier-and-more-interesting-than-historians-have-thought/).

3. "Speech of A. H. Stephens," Frank Moore, ed., *Rebellion Record: A Diary of American Events, with Documents, Narratives, Illustrative Incidents, Poetry, etc.,* vol. I, (G. P. Putnam, 1861), 45–46 (https://www.americanyawp.com /reader/the-civil-war/alexander-stephens-on-slavery-and-the-confederate -constitution-1861/).

4. Karl Popper, *The Open Society and Its Enemies,* vol. 2 (Princeton University Press, 1971), 104.

5. Howard Sachar, *A History of the Jews in America* (Knopf, 1992), 311.

6. "Glenn Beck: The Puppet Master," aired November 9, 2010, Fox News tran- script (https://www.foxnews.com/story/glenn-beck-the-puppet-master).

7. Quassim Cassam, *Conspiracy Theories* (Polity, 2019), 11.

8. Brian Stelter,"This infamous Steve Bannon quote is key to understanding America's crazy politics," CNN Business, November 16, 2021 (https://www .cnn.com/2021/11/16/media/steve-bannon-reliable-sources/index.html).

9. Edward Craig, ed., *Concise Routledge Encyclopedia of Philosophy* (Routledge, 1999), 170.

10. https://www.cnn.com/videos/politics/2022/09/26/roger-stone-documentary -clips-filmmakers-january-6-lemon-vpx.cnn.

11. Frank Miles, "Geraldo Rivera, Dan Bongino react to US cities in crisis: 'Liberalism is a cancer,'" Fox News, August 20, 2019 (https://www.foxnews .com/media/liberalism-is-a-cancer-bongino-rivera-react-to-liberal-us-cities -in-crisis).

12. Johanna Chisholm, "Marjorie Taylor Greene mocked for hog hunting con-

test as she's seen slaying animals from chopper with rifle," *The Independent*, September 28, 2022 (https://www.independent.co.uk/news/world/americas /us-politics/marjorie-taylor-greene-hog-hunting-video-b2177402.html).

13. Philip Bump, "How a false narrative about Republicans being hunted took root," *Washington Post*, October 3, 2022 (https://www.washingtonpost .com/politics).

14. Arwa Mahdawi, "Jokes about Paul Pelosi aren't just in bad taste. They normalize political violence," *The Guardian*, November 2, 2022 (https://www .theguardian.com/commentisfree).

15. Richard Hofstadter, *The Paranoid Style in American Politics* (Vintage Books, 2008), 23.

16. Elisabeth Zerofsky, "How the Claremont Institute Became a Nerve Center of the American Right," *New York Times Magazine*, August 3, 2022 (https://www.nytimes.com/2022/08/03/magazine/claremont-institute -conservative.html)

17. Glenn Ellmers, "'Conservatism' Is No Longer Enough," *American Mind*, March 24, 2021 (https://americanmind.org/salvo/why-the-claremont-institute -is-not-conservative-and-you-shouldnt-be-either/).

18. "Bill O'Reilly: It's 'Open Season' On Christians and White Men," *Talking Points Memo*, April 14, 2015 (https://talkingpointsmemo.com/livewire /o-reilly-open-season-white-men).

19. Nikki McCann Ramirez, "Tucker Carlson, the face of Fox News, just gave his full endorsement to the white nationalist conspiracy theory that has motivated mass shootings," Media Matters, April 9, 2021 (https://www .mediamatters.org/tucker-carlson/tucker-carlson-face-fox-news-just-gave -his-full-endorsement-white-nationalist).

20. Michael Luciano, "Fox News Host Warns Satanism Is 'Lurking in the Halls' of School, Says It's 'Much More Terrifying' Than Covid," *Mediaite*, January 14, 2022 (https://www.mediaite.com/tv/fox-news-host-warns-satanism -is-lurking-in-the-halls-of-schools-says-its-much-more-terrifying-than-covid/).

21. Larry Cohler-Esses, "George Soros Denounced by Hungary as 'Satan' Seeking to Destroy 'Christian' Europe," *Forward*, October 11, 2017 (https:// forward.com/news).

22. Noah Y. Kim, "The Worst People on the Planet Are Cheering the Reelection of Hungary's Authoritarian Leader," *Mother Jones*, April 4, 2022 (https:// www.motherjones.com/politics).

23. Harry Fletcher, "Tucker Carlson downplays Ukraine conflict by telling Fox viewers to ask: 'Why do I hate Putin?'" *indy100*, February 24, 2022 (https://www.indy100.com/news/tucker-carlson-ukraine-fox-putin).

24. Stephen M. Lepore, "'He's taken over a country for $2 worth of sanctions': Former President Trump doubles down on calling Putin 'smart,'" *Daily Mail*, February 23, 2022 (https://www.dailymail.co.uk/news/article-10545563 /Trump-doubles-calling-Putin-smart-launches-special-military-operation .html).

25. Donald Trump, "Former President Trump Speaks at Conservative Political Action Conference," C-SPAN, February 26, 2022 (https://www.c-span.org /video/?518150-1/pres-trump-criticizes-nato-nations-amid-russian-invasion -ukraine).

26. Adrienne LaFrance, "The Prophecies of Q," *The Atlantic*, June 2020 (https:// www.theatlantic.com/magazine/archive/2020/06/qanon-nothing-can-stop -what-is-coming/610567/).

27. Frank Williams, trans., *The Panarion of Epiphanius of Salamis*, book 1, 2nd ed. (Brill, 2009), 95.

28. Guest post on Charlene L. Edge's blog, April 2023 (https://charleneedge .com/is-qanon-a-cult-what-dont-i-know/). Edge is the author of *Undertow: My Escape from the Fundamentalism and Cult Control of the Way International* (New Wings Press, 2017).

29. Max Boot, "Republicans Are Becoming the QAnon Party," *Washington Post*, August 12, 2020 (https://www.washingtonpost.com/opinions).

30. David Klepper and Ali Swenson, "Trump openly embraces, amplifies QAnon conspiracy theories," AP News, September 16, 2022 (https://apnews.com /article/technology-donald-trump-conspiracy-theories-government -and-politics-db50c6f709b1706886a876ae6ac298e2).

31. Drew Harwell, "QAnon, adrift after Trump's defeat, finds new life in Elon Musk's Twitter," *Washington Post*, December 14, 2022 (https://www.washing tonpost.com/technology).

32. LaFrance, "The Prophecies of Q."

33. Jason Silverstein, "QAnon Is Still Spreading a Bizarre Conspiracy Theory About Adrenochrome," *Men's Health*, March 31, 2022 (https://www.mens health.com/health/a34786868/what-is-adrenochrome-qanon/).

34. "President Trump's mysterious 'calm before the storm' comments," CBS News, October 6, 2017 (https://www.youtube.com/watch?v=iyvhFgCybpg).

35. Week 183, The Weekly List, May 16, 2020 (https://theweeklylist.org/weekly -list/week-183/).

36. "Exposed—Creator of QAnon Speaks for the First Time," One America News Network, September 4, 2018 (https://www.youtube.com/watch?v =aSDqBVVFfsM).

37. Ben Davis, "Is the QAnon Conspiracy the Work of Artist-Activist Prank-

sters? The Evidence for (and Against) a Dangerous Hypothesis," *Artnet News*, August 8, 2018 (https://news.artnet.com/opinion/q-anon-hoax-1329983).

38. Georgi Boorman, "From Trolling to Fleecing: Co-Creator of 'Q' Hoax Explains Its Scary Evolution," *The Federalist*, October 29, 2018 (https://thefederalist.com/2018/10/29/trolling-fleecing-co-creator-q-hoax-explains-dangerous-evolution/).

39. Marc-André Argentino, Twitter, August 8, 2020 (https://twitter.com/_MAArgentino/status/1292245485403635712).

40. Matt Alt, "Why QAnon Flopped in Japan," *New York Times*, March 26, 2021 (https://www.nytimes.com/2021/03/26/opinion/qanon-japan-janon.html).

41. "The Coming Global Tsunami," *Praying Medic* (blog), November 8, 2019 (https://prayingmedic.com/2019/11/08/the-coming-global-tsunami/).

42. E. J. Dickson, "QAnon Followers Think Trump's Covid-19 Tweet Had a Secret Message About Hillary Clinton," *Rolling Stone*, October 2, 2020 (https://www.rollingstone.com/culture/culture-news/qanon-trump-coronavirus-conspiracy-theorists-1070131/).

43. Justin Baragona, "Newsmax Bans Lara Logan After She Goes Full QAnon, Spews Blood Libel on Network," *Yahoo! News*, October 20, 2022 (https://www.yahoo.com/news/lara-logan-goes-full-qanon-170125031.html).

44. Ariel Zilber, "Newsmax cuts ties with Lara Logan after she said world leaders 'dine on the blood of children,'" *New York Post*, October 21, 2022 (https://nypost.com/2022/10/21/newsmax-cuts-ties-with-lara-logan-after-she-said-world-leaders-dine-on-the-blood-of-children/).

45. Ewan Palmer, "Lara Logan Claims Evolution Theory Is a 'Rothschilds' Plot," *Newsweek*, March 29, 2022 (https://www.newsweek.com/lara-logan-rothschild-charles-darwin-evolution-theory-1692813).

46. Umberto Eco, *Foucault's Pendulum*, trans. William Weaver (Harcourt Brace, 1989), 476.

47. Michael Lind, "Rev. Robertson's Grand International Conspiracy Theory," *New York Review of Books*, February 2, 1995; Pat Robertson, *The New World Order* (Word Publishing, 1991).

48. Zach Montellaro, "Trump: Tweet showed 'a Sheriff's Star,' not Star of David," *Politico*, July 4, 2016 (https://www.politico.com/story/2016/07/trump-star-of-david-tweet-225081).

49. Chris Sommerfeldt, "SEE IT: Donald Trump's final campaign ad blasted for peddling in anti-Semitism, conspiracy theories," *Daily News*, November 8, 2016 (https://www.nydailynews.com/news/politics/donald-trump-final-campaign-ad-blasted-anti-semitic-article-1.2863474).

50. Jonathan Chait, "GOP Rep: I Didn't Intend to Blame Jews for the Space-Laser Conspiracy," *New York Intelligencer,* March 18, 2021 (https://nymag .com/intelligencer/2021/03/marjorie-taylor-greene-jewish-space-lasers -rothschilds-didnt-know-anti-semitism.html).

51. Landon Thomas Jr., "Jeffrey Epstein: International Moneyman of Mystery," *New York,* October 28, 2002 (https://nymag.com/nymetro/news /people/n_7912/); For the Epstein-Barr connection, see Dan McGuill, "Did Bill Barr's Father 'Mentor' Jeffrey Epstein and Write a 'Bizarre' Novel?," *Snopes,* October 21, 2020 (https://www.snopes.com/fact-check/bill-barr-jeffrey -epstein-book/).

52. Oz Katerji, "The West's Leftist 'Intellectuals' Who Traffic in Genocide Denial, from Srebrenica to Syria," *Haaretz,* November 24, 2017 (https://www.haaretz .com/opinion).

53. Carmen Reinicke, "56% of Americans can't cover a $1,000 emergency expense with savings," CNBC, January 19, 2022 (https://www.cnbc .com/2022/01/19/56percent-of-americans-cant-cover-a-1000-emergency -expense-with-savings.html).

54. Noah Kirsch, "The 3 Richest Americans Hold More Wealth Than Bottom 50% of the Country, Study Finds," *Forbes,* November 9, 2017 (https://www .forbes.com/sites/noahkirsch/2017/11/09/the-3-richest-americans-hold -more-wealth-than-bottom-50-of-country-study-finds/?sh=841a19c3cf86).

55. "Trends in the Distribution of Family Wealth, 1989 to 2019," Congressional Budget Office (https://www.cbo.gov/publication/58533).

56. Ann Kristin Svendsen, "White Nights in Guyana: Leadership, Conformity and Persuasion in Jonestown and Peoples Temple," Alternative Considerations of Jonestown and Peoples Temple website, San Diego State University (https://jonestown.sdsu.edu/?page_id=33230).

57. Paul Krugman, "The Strange Alliance of Crypto and MAGA Believers," *New York Times,* January 10, 2022 (https://www.nytimes.com/2022/01/10 /opinion/crypto-cryptocurrency-money-conspiracy.html).

58. See for example Michael J. Wood et al., "Dead and Alive: Beliefs in Contradictory Conspiracy Theories," *Journal of the American Psychological Association* 3, no. 6 (2012) (https://doi.org/10.1177/1948550611434786).

2: The Paranoid Style and the Art of the Deal

1. Richard Hofstadter, *The Paranoid Style in American Politics* (Vintage Books, 2008).

2. Daniel Villareal, "QAnon Podcast Airs Bishop Larry Gaiters' Outrageous

Claim of Biden's 'Satanic Sacrifice,'" *Newsweek,* May 10, 2021 (https://www
.newsweek.com/bishop-larry-gaiters-calls-death-bidens-wife-daughter-son
-satanic-sacrifice-1590247).

3. Brandon Gage, "QAnon-Loving Bishop Claims Joe Biden 'Was Executed
Two Years Ago,'" HillReporter.com, June 8, 2021.

4. "Open Letter from Retired Generals and Admirals" (https://img1.wsimg
.com/blobby/go/fb7c7bd8-097d-4e2f-8f12-3442d151b57d/downloads
/2021%20Open%20Letter%20from%20Retired%20Generals%20
and%20Adm.pdf?ver=1621254456411).

5. Bill Glauber, "Ron Johnson called Joe Biden 'a liberal, progressive, socialist,
Marxist.' Can someone be all those things?" *Milwaukee Journal Sentinel,*
June 11, 2021 (https://www.jsonline.com/story/news/politics/2021/06/11
/ron-johnson-joe-biden-a-liberal-progressive-socialist-marxist/7655294002/).

6. Dominick Mastrangelo, "Mark Levin urges Americans to boycott 'woke'
businesses," *The Hill,* July 13, 2021 (https://thehill.com/homenews/media
/562730-mark-levin-urges-americans-to-boycott-woke-businesses/).

7. Byron York, "The Senator from MBNA," *National Review,* August 23, 2008
(https://www.nationalreview.com/2008/08/senator-mbna-byron-york/).

8. Robert A. Pape, "21 Million Americans Say Biden Is 'Illegitimate' and
Trump Should Be Restored by Violence, Survey Finds," *Talking Points Memo,*
September 23, 2021 (https://talkingpointsmemo.com/cafe/21-million
-americans-say-biden-is-illegitimate-and-trump-should-be-restored-by
-violence-survey-finds).

9. Alexander Kacala, "Infowars' Alex Jones has a long history of inflammatory,
anti-LGBTQ speech," NBC News, August 8, 2018 (https://www.nbcnews
.com/feature/nbc-out/infowars-alex-jones-has-long-history-inflammatory
-anti-lgbtq-speech-n898431).

10. Will Sommer, "Trump Praises Right-Wing Conspiracy Theorists at White
House: 'The Crap You Think of Is Unbelievable,'" *Daily Beast,* July 12,
2019 (https://www.thedailybeast.com/trump-praises-right-wing-conspiracy
-theorists-at-white-house-the-crap-you-think-of-is-unbelievable); Oliver
Darcy, "Trump Invites Right-wing Extremists to White House 'Social Media
Summit,'" CNN Business, July 11, 2019 (https://www.cnn.com/2019/07
/10/tech/white-house-social-media-summit/index.html).

11. Khaleda Rahman, "Michael Flynn Could Face Court Martial for Myanmar
Coup Remark: Ex-Trump Official," *Newsweek,* May 31, 2021 (https://www
.newsweek.com/michael-flynn-could-face-court-martial-coup-remark
-1596287).

12. Helene Cooper, "Milley Apologizes for Role in Trump Photo Op: 'I Should

Not Have Been There,'" *New York Times,* September 28, 2021 (https://www.nytimes.com/2020/06/11/us/politics/trump-milley-military-protests-lafayette-square.html).

13. Lloyd Green, "I Alone Can Fix It Review: Donald Trump as Wannabe Führer," *The Guardian,* July 16, 2021 (https://amp.theguardian.com/books/2021/jul/16/i-alone-can-fix-it-review-donald-trump-fuhrer-mark-milley-leonnig-rucker).

14. Chauncey Devega, "Cult expert Steven Hassan: Trump's 'mind control cult' now faces an existential crisis," *Salon,* April 7, 2020 (https://www.salon.com/2020/04/07/cult-expert-steven-hassan-trumps-mind-control-cult-now-faces-an-existential-crisis/).

15. Reid J. Epstein, "The G.O.P. Delivers Its 2020 Platform. It's from 2016," *New York Times,* August 25, 2020 (https://www.nytimes.com/2020/08/25/us/politics/republicans-platform.html).

16. George Wallace, "Segregation Now, Segregation Forever" (https://www.blackpast.org/african-american-history/speeches-african-american-history/1963-george-wallace-segregation-now-segregation-forever/).

17. Matea Gold and James Hohmann, "Charles Koch invokes fight for civil rights as model for political activism," *Washington Post,* August 2, 2015 (https://www.washingtonpost.com/politics).

18. Lawrence Richard, "Ted Cruz slams critical race theory as 'every bit as racist as the klansmen in white sheets,'" *Yahoo! News,* June 18, 2021 (https://news.yahoo.com).

19. "Politicians attack critical race theory without understanding it, experts say," 6News WOWT, May 18, 2021 (https://www.wowt.com/2021/05/18/politicians-attack-critical-race-theory-without-understanding-it-experts-say/).

20. Carol Anderson, "Ferguson isn't about black rage against cops. It's white rage against progress," *Washington Post,* August 29, 2014 (https://www.washingtonpost.com/opinions).

21. Justin Baragona, "Tucker Fearmongers About 'Anti-White Mania' and America Becoming 'Rwanda,'" *Daily Beast,* June 24, 2021 (https://www.thedailybeast.com/tucker-carlson-fearmongers-about-anti-white-mania-and-america-becoming-rwanda).

22. Ewan Palmer, "OAN Reporter Pearson Sharp Denies Calling for Mass Execution of Election 'Traitors,'" *Newsweek,* June 25, 2021 (https://www.newsweek.com/oan-reporter-pearson-sharp-mass-executions-election-treason-denial-1604054)

23. Rick Perlstein, "The Long Con," *The Baffler,* November 2012 (https://thebaffler.com/salvos/the-long-con).

24. Paul Krugman, Twitter, April 19, 2022 (https://twitter.com/paulkrugman /status/1516378634340155396).

25. Adam Serwer, "The Cruelty Is the Point," *The Atlantic,* October 3, 2018 (https://www.theatlantic.com/ideas/).

26. "U.S. Health Care from a Global Perspective, 2019: Higher Spending, Worse Outcomes?" The Commonwealth Fund (https://www.com monwealthfund.org/publications/issue-briefs/2020/jan/us-health-care -global-perspective-2019).

27. "U.S. Health Care from a Global Perspective, 2022: Accelerating Spending, Worsening Outcomes," The Commonwealth Fund (https://www.common wealthfund.org/publications/issue-briefs/2023/jan/us-health-care-global -perspective-2022).

28. Timothy Noah, "Psst. Horatio Alger Was a Pedophile," Substack, April 8, 2022 (https://timothynoah.substack.com/p/psst-horatio-alger-was-a-pedophile).

29. Maureen Breslin, "84 percent of Trump voters are worried about discrimination against whites: poll," *The Hill,* October 8, 2021 (https://thehill.com /homenews/news/575899-84-percent-of-trump-voters-are-worried-about -discrimination-against-whites-poll/).

3: Through the Looking Glass

1. I posted a brief essay about Quinby's manifesto on my blog (www.arthur goldwag.com). The reader comments include links to primary documents, testimonies from people who knew him, and the full text of the manifesto. There are also some really vile anti-Semitic comments that were posted out of the blue.

2. Vernon Stauffer, *New England and the Bavarian Illuminati* (Columbia University Press, 1918).

3. Richard Hofstadter, *The Paranoid Style in American Politics* (Vintage Books, 2008).

4. Kimberlé Crenshaw, "Demarginalizing the Intersection of Race and Sex: A Black Feminist Critique of Antidiscrimination Doctrine, Feminist Theory and Antiracist Politics," *University of Chicago Legal Forum* 1, art. 8 (1989). (https://chicagounbound.uchicago.edu/cgi/viewcontent.cgi?article= 1052&context=uclf).

5. James Boyd, "Nixon's Southern Strategy 'It's All in the Charts,'" *New York Times,* May 17, 1970 (https://www.nytimes.com/packages/html/books /phillips-southern.pdf).

6. Tim Naftali, "Ronald Reagan's Long-Hidden Racist Conversation with

Richard Nixon," *The Atlantic,* July 30, 2019 (https://www.theatlantic.com
/ideas/).

7. "Ronald Reagan's 1980 Neshoba County Fair speech," *Neshoba Democrat*
(https://neshobademocrat.com/stories/ronald-reagans-1980-neshoba
-county-fair-speech,49123).

8. Sheryl Gay Stolberg, "For Gingrich in Power, Pragmatism, Not Purity," *New
York Times,* December 20, 2011 (https://www.nytimes.com/2011/12/21/us
/politics/the-long-run-conservatives-remain-suspicious-of-gingrich.html).

9. "Language: A Key Mechanism of Control," *Fair,* February 1, 1995 (https://
fair.org/home/language-a-key-mechanism-of-control/).

10. Patrick Joseph Buchanan, "Culture War Speech: Address to the Republican
National Convention," August 17, 1992, Voices of Democracy: The U.S.
Oratory Project (https://voicesofdemocracy.umd.edu/buchanan-culture-war
-speech-speech-text/).

11. Michael Barkun, *A Culture of Conspiracy* (University of California Press,
2013).

12. Fox News, "McVeigh's April 26 Letter to Fox News," January 13, 2015
(https://www.foxnews.com/story/mcveighs-apr-26-letter-to-fox-news).

13. Susan Faludi, *The Terror Dream: Myth and Misogyny in an Insecure America*
(Picador, 2008), 12.

14. Hofstadter, *The Paranoid Style.*

15. "Limbaugh Says Obama's Economic 'Role Model' Is Robert Mugabe, Who
'Took the White People's Farms,'" Media Matters, August 4, 2011 (https://
www.mediamatters.org/rush-limbaugh/limbaugh-says-obamas-economic
-role-model-robert-mugabe-who-took-white-peoples-farms).

16. Dinesh D'Souza, "How Obama Thinks," *Forbes,* September 9, 2010
(https://www.forbes.com/forbes/2010/0927/politics-socialism-capitalism
-private-enterprises-obama-business-problem.html?sh=7e7d13342217).

17. Eustace Clarence Mullins, *Mullins' New History of the Jews* (The International Institute of Jewish Studies, 1968), 49 (https://citeseerx.ist.psu.edu
/document?repid=rep1&type=pdf&doi=1f70eda7de60e6c384474fb93667
ce683ecdc7ec).

18. GlennBeck.com, radio clips, March 24, 2010 (https://www.glennbeck
.com/content/articles/article/198/38320/).

19. Arthur Goldwag, "Putting Donald Trump on the Couch," *New York Times,*
September 1, 2015 (https://www.nytimes.com/2015/09/01/opinion/putting
-donald-trump-on-the-couch.html).

20. Jared Taylor, "Africa in Our Midst," *American Renaissance,* October 2005
(https://www.amren.com/archives/back-issues/october-2005/).

21. See Arthur Goldwag, "National Press Club Hosts White Nationalist Event," SPLC *Hatewatch,* September 11, 2011 (https://www.splcenter.org/hatewatch /2011/09/11/national-press-club-hosts-white-nationalist-event); Daniel Lombroso and Yoni Appelbaum, " 'Hail Trump!': White Nationalists Salute the President-Elect," *The Atlantic,* November 21, 2016 (https://www.theatlantic .com/politics/).

22. Michael Minnicino, "The New Dark Age," *Fidelio,* Winter 1992 (https:// archive.schillerinstitute.com/fid_91-96/921_frankfurt.html).

23. Samuel Moyn, "The Alt Right's Favorite Meme Is 100 Years Old," *New York Times,* November 13, 2018 (https://www.nytimes.com/2018/11/13/opinion /cultural-marxism-anti-semitism.html).

24. Tweet from Eduardo Bolsonaro, August 4, 2018 (https://twitter.com /BolsonaroSP/status/1025718449425788929).

25. Marco Rubio, U.S. Senator for Florida, press release, May 26, 2021 (https://www.rubio.senate.gov/public/index.cfm/2021/5/icymi-rubio-joins -fox-friends).

26. Rachel Scully, "DeSantis Defines 'Woke' as 'A War on the Truth' After Trump said People 'Can't Define It,'" *The Hill,* June 3, 2023 (https://thehill .com).

4: Cognitive Dissonance

1. Amy Mitchell et al., "Misinformation and Competing Views of Reality Abounded Throughout 2020," Pew Research Center, February 21, 2021 (https://www.pewresearch.org/journalism/2021/02/22/misinformation -and-competing-views-of-reality-abounded-throughout-2020/).

2. Philip Bump, "A New Poll Result Reveals Sharp Pessimism on America's Political Right," *Washington Post,* February 24, 2021 (https://www .washingtonpost.com/politics/2021/02/24/new-poll-result-reveals-sharp -pessimism-americas-political-right/).

3. Jose A. Del Real, "They're Worried Their Mom Is Becoming a Conspiracy Theorist. She Thinks They're the Ones Living in a Fantasy World," *Washington Post,* March 12, 2021 (https://www.washingtonpost.com/nation).

4. Leon Festinger, Henry W. Riecken, and Stanley Schachter, *When Prophecy Fails: A Social and Psychological Study of a Modern Group That Predicted the Destruction of the World* (Harper & Row, 1957), 3.

5. David J. Halperin, "Sabbatai Zevi, Metatron, and Mehmed: Myth and History in Seventeenth-Century Judaism," reprinted from *The Seductiveness of*

Jewish Myth: Challenge or Response?, ed. S. Daniel Breslauer (New York Press, 1997); (https://www.davidhalperin.net/wp-content/uploads/2015/01/Sabbatai-Zevi-Metatron-and-Mehmed.pdf).

6. Cynthia Ozick, "Slouching Toward Smyrna," *New York Times Book Review,* February 24, 1974 (https://timesmachine.nytimes.com/timesmachine/1974/02/24/148799472.html?pageNumber=329).

7. Festinger, Riecken, and Schachter, *When Prophecy Fails,* 56.

8. Festinger, Riecken, and Schachter, *When Prophecy Fails,* 168.

9. Festinger, Riecken, and Schachter, *When Prophecy Fails,* 233.

10. The Truth About Ellen G. White website (https://www.ellengwhitetruth.com/life-times/two-great-disappointments/the-great-disappointment).

11. Festinger, Riecken, and Schachter, *When Prophecy Fails,* 38–39.

12. Martin's story is told in Jerome Clark, "The Odyssey of Sister Thedra," a chapter of *Alien Worlds: Social and Religious Dimensions of Extraterrestrial Contact,* ed. Diana G. Tumminia (Syracuse University Press, 2007) (https://www.google.com/books/).

13. Aetherius Society website (https://www.aetherius.org/).

14. George W. Van Tassel, *I Rode a Flying Saucer: The Mystery of the Flying Saucer Revealed* (1952, reprinted by Saucerian Publisher, 2020), 39.

15. David Moye, "Unarius, UFO Cult, Gets Profiled in 'Children of the Stars' Documentary," *Huffpost,* February 1, 2014 (https://www.huffpost.com/entry/unarius-documentary_n_4697049).

16. William Dudley Pelley, *Star Guests: Design for Mortality* (Soulcraft Chapels, 1950), 242.

17. Quoted by Clay S. Jenkinson, "Is Balloon Panic a New Sputnik Crisis?" *Governing,* February 19, 2023 (https://www.governing.com/context/is-balloon-panic-a-new-sputnik-crisis).

18. Mayhill Fowler, "Obama: No Surprise That Hard-Pressed Pennsylvanians Turn Bitter," *Huffington Post,* November 17, 2008 (https://www.huffpost.com/entry/obama-no-surprise-that-ha_b_96188).

19. Katie Reilly, "Read Hillary Clinton's 'Basket of Deplorables' Remarks About Donald Trump Supporters," *Time,* September 10, 2016 (https://time.com/4486502/hillary-clinton-basket-of-deplorables-transcript/).

20. Jim Tankersley, "A 'Main Street' Tax Speech Becomes a Trump Riff on the Rich," *New York Times,* November 29, 2017 (https://www.nytimes.com/2017/11/29/us/politics/a-main-street-tax-speech-becomes-a-trump-riff-on-the-rich.html).

21. Emma Stefansky, " 'You All Just Got a Lot Richer,' Trump Tells Friends at

Mar-a-Lago After Signing Tax Overhaul," *Vanity Fair,* December 24, 2017 (https://www.vanityfair.com/news/2017/12/you-all-just-got-a-lot-richer -trump-tells-friends-at-mar-a-lago-after-signing-tax-overhaul).

22. C. G. Lord et al., "Biased Assimilation and Attitude Polarization: The Effects of Prior Theories on Subsequently Considered Evidence," *Journal of Personality and Social Psychology* 37, no. 11 (1979); (https://psycnet.apa.org /doi/10.1037/0022-3514.37.11.2098).

23. Ronald Brownstein, "The Post-racial Republicans," *The Atlantic,* June 24, 2023 (https://www.theatlantic.com/ideas/archive/2023/06/nikki-haley -tim-scott-2024-election-racial-inequity/674511/).

24. Peter Baker and Maggie Haberman, "A Presidency Increasingly Guided by Suspicion and Distrust," *New York Times* (https://www.nytimes.com/2020 /02/15/us/politics/trump-distrust-paranoia.html).

25. Jordyn Phelps, "President Trump Tees Up 2020 Fight with Swipes at Biden," ABC News (https://abc13.com/president-trump-tees-up-2020-fight-with -swipes-at-biden/5232113/).

26. "Donald Trump Laura Ingraham Interview Transcript August 31: Says People 'in the Dark Shadows' Controlling Biden," rev. transcript (https://www .rev.com/blog/transcripts/).

27. "Donald Trump's RNC Speech," transcript, CNN, August 28, 2020 (https:// edition.cnn.com/2020/08/28/politics/donald-trump-speech-transcript /index.html).

28. "Trump warns Democrats will 'destroy' suburbs," Associated Press Videos, July 16, 2020 (https://news.yahoo.com/).

29. Christian Britschgi, "Trump Warns Biden Will Destroy Washington Monument, Christmas, Easter, Suburbs, Borders, and the American Dream," *Reason,* November 2, 2020 (https://reason.com).

30. Thomas Colson, "Trump suggests Joe Biden will try to take the word Christmas 'out of the vocabulary,'" *Insider,* December 7, 2020 (https://www .businessinsider.com/trump-suggests-biden-will-take-christmas-out-of-the -vocabulary-2020-12?op=1).

31. *Trump University Playbook,* 2010, 100 (https://static.politico.com/25/88 /783a0dca43a0a898f3973da0086f/trump-university-playbook.pdf).

32. Jason Szep and Linda So, "Trump Campaign Demonized Two Georgia Election Workers—And Death Threats Followed," Reuters, December 1, 2021 (https://www.reuters.com/investigates/special-report/usa-election-threats -georgia/).

33. Alan Feurer, "Giuliani Concedes He Made False Statements About Geor-

gia Election Workers," *New York Times,* July 26, 2023 (https://www.nytimes .com/2023/07/26/us/politics/giuliani-georgia-election-workers.html).

34. Brett Samuels, "Trump Attacks Pence as Protesters Force Their Way into Capitol," *The Hill,* January 6, 2021 (https://thehill.com/homenews /administration/532942-trump-attacks-pence-as-protesters-force-their -wayinto-capitol/).

35. Drew Harwell and Craig Timberg, "'My Faith Is Shaken': The QAnon Conspiracy Theory Faces a Post-Trump Identity Crisis," *Washington Post,* November 20, 2020 (https://www.washingtonpost.com/technology).

36. "Trump says there will be an 'orderly transition' of power, acknowledges defeat," *PBS News Hour,* January 7, 2021 (https://www.pbs.org/newshour /politics/trump-disagrees-with-the-outcome-of-the-election-but-that-there -will-be-an-orderly-transition-of-power).

37. noah, "RED1: Just As Q Predicted 3 Years Ago, Trump Permanently REMOVED from Twitter! It's Happening!" January 8, 2021 (https://welove trump.com/2021/01/08/red1-just-as-q-predicted-3-years-ago-trump -permanently-removed-from-twitter-its-happening/).

38. Found in the comment thread of Project War Path's Facebook page (https://m.facebook.com/ProjectWP5326/photos/a.2353076718153252 /3224970334297215/?type=3&_rdr).

39. Drew Harwell and Craig Timberg, "QAnon believers grapple with doubt, spin new theories as Trump era ends," *Washington Post,* January 20, 2021 (https://www.washingtonpost.com/technology).

40. Drew Harwell and Craig Timberg, "A QAnon revelation suggests the truth of Q's identity was right there all along," *Washington Post,* April 5, 2021 (https://www.washingtonpost.com/technology).

41. Ewan Palmer, "QAnon Already Turning Back on March 4 Theory as Day of Donald Trump Prophecy Arrives," *Newsweek,* March 4, 2021 (https://www .newsweek.com/qanon-march-4-trump-president-inaugruation-1573690).

42. Pritha Paul, "QAnon theory claims Joe Biden is 'Donald Trump wearing a mask,' Internet asks 'explain the elegant physique,'" MEAWW, January 31, 2021 (https://meaww.com/q-anon-theory-claiming-biden-really-trump -wearing-potus-mask-mocked-explain-elegant-physique).

43. "Understanding QAnon's Connection to American Politics, Religion, and Media Consumption," May 27, 2021 (https://www.prri.org/research/qanon -conspiracy-american-politics-report/).

44. Charles C. W. Cooke, "Maggie Haberman Is Right," *National Review,* June 3, 2021 (https://www.nationalreview.com/2021/06/maggie-haberman-is-right/).

45. "Understanding QAnon's Connection to American Politics, Religion, and Media Consumption."

46. David Brooks, "The Rotting of the Republican Mind," *New York Times,* November 26, 2020 (https://www.nytimes.com/2020/11/26/opinion /republican-disinformation.html).

47. Kurt Andersen, "How America Lost Its Mind," *The Atlantic,* September 2017 (https://www.theatlantic.com/magazine/).

48. Cass R. Sunstein and Adrian Vermeule, "Conspiracy Theories," Coase-Sandor Working Paper Series in Law and Economics, 2008 (https://chicago unbound.uchicago.edu/law_and_economics/119/).

5: The Deepest Bias(es)

1. Theron Mohamed, "'The American Dream isn't a private club with a cover charge': Alexandria Ocasio-Cortez trashes Trump's wealth test for immigrants," *Business Insider India,* January 28, 2020 (https://www.businessinsider.in).

2. Arthur Goldwag, "The National Policy Institute Conference: Immigrants Ruining America," *Hatewatch,* September 12, 2011 (https://www .splcenter.org/hatewatch/2011/09/12/national-policy-institute-conference -immigrants-ruining-america).

3. Martin A. Lee, "American Black Muslims, Neo-Nazis, Foreign Muslim Extremists Join Forces," *Intelligence Report,* March 5, 2002 (https:// www.splcenter.org/fighting-hate/intelligence-report/2002/american-black -muslims-neo-nazis-foreign-muslim-extremists-join-forces).

4. Joseph Loconte, "An American Defense of Britain's Constitutional Monarchy," *National Review,* March 18, 2021 (https://www.nationalreview.com /2021/03/an-american-defense-of-britains-constitutional-monarchy/).

5. "Thomas Jefferson: On the Breeding of Kings," *People's World,* April 28, 2011 (https://www.peoplesworld.org/article/thomas-jefferson-on-the-breeding -of-kings/).

6. Adrienne LaFrance, "A Skeleton, a Catholic Relic, and a Mystery About American Origins," *The Atlantic,* July 28, 2015 (https://www.theatlantic.com/national/).

7. William Carlos Williams, *In the American Grain* (New Directions, 1925, 1933).

8. John Foxe and John Cumming, *Foxe's Book of Martyrs: The Acts and Monuments of the Church,* vol. 3 (G. Virtue, 1844), 68.

9. Erin Lee Isaac, "'Our Enemy, Who for Our Religion . . . Abhored Us': The Establishment and Maintenance of 18th-Century Anti-Catholicism in North America," *University of Saskatchewan Undergraduate Research Jour-*

nal 4, no. 2 (2018); (https://pdfs.semanticscholar.org/78fb/74bf75b3cf18fa 53a651980d59ccd5405374.pdf).

10. John Tracy Ellis, *American Catholicism* (University of Chicago Press, 1956, 1969), 10, 151.

11. Robert Emmett Curran, *Papist Devils: Catholics in British America, 1574–1783* (Catholic University of America Press, 2014), 202.

12. Curran, *Papist Devils,* 212, 216.

13. Rebecca Ryskind Teti, "In Good Company: George Washington Among the Catholics," Catholic News Agency, February 16, 2010 (https://www.catholic newsagency.com/column/51127/george-washington-among-the-catholics).

14. Samuel Finley Breese Morse, *Foreign Conspiracy Against the Liberties of the United States* (Ripley, 1835), 68.

15. Lyman Beecher, *A Plea for the West* (Truman and Smith, 1835), 60–61.

16. Charles H. Brown, "Young Editor Whitman: An Individualist in Journalism," *Journalism and Mass Communication Quarterly* 27, no. 2 (1950), 141–48 (https://journals.sagepub.com/doi/10.1177/107769905002700203).

17. See David H. Bennett, *The Party of Fear: The American Far Right from Nativism to the Militia Movement* (University of North Carolina Press, 1988) for more on nativism.

18. Roy P. Basler, ed., *The Collected Works of Abraham Lincoln,* vol. 2 (New Brunswick, NJ, 1953), 320–23.

19. David Brion Davis, *The Fear of Conspiracy: Images of Un-American Subversion from the Revolution to the Present* (Cornell, 1971 and 2008), 111.

20. Mark S. Massa, S.J., "Anti-Catholicism in the United States," *Oxford Research Encyclopedia of American History,* June 9, 2016 (https://doi.org /10.1093/acrefore/9780199329175.013.316).

21. The full text of the oath can be found at the Indiana State Library digital archive (https://indianamemory.contentdm.oclc.org/digital/collection /p16066coll69/id/211).

22. Thomas J. Shelley, " 'What the Hell Is an Encyclical?': Governor Alfred E. Smith, Charles C. Marshall, Esq., and Father Francis P. Duffy," *U.S. Catholic Historian* 14, no. 2 (Spring 1997); (https://www.jstor.org/stable /25154585?read-now=1&seq=11#page_scan_tab_contents).

23. Robert A. Slayton, "When a Catholic Terrified the Heartland," *New York Times,* December 10, 2011 (https://archive.nytimes.com/campaignstops .blogs.nytimes.com/2011/12/10/when-a-catholic-terrified-the-heartland/).

24. Grenda Blair, "How Norman Vincent Peale Taught Donald Trump to Worship Himself," *Politico,* October 6, 2015 (https://www.politico.com/maga zine/story/2015/10/donald-trump-2016-norman-vincent-peale-213220/).

25. Dave Roos, "How John F. Kennedy Overcame Anti-Catholic Bias to Win the Presidency," History Channel, November 20, 2019 (https://www.history.com /news/jfk-catholic-president).

26. Gregory A. Smith, "8 Facts About Catholics and Politics in the U.S.," Pew Research Center, September 15, 2020 (https://www.pewresearch.org /fact-tank/2020/09/15/8-facts-about-catholics-and-politics-in-the-u-s/).

27. Amy Coney Barrett and John. H. Garvey, "Catholic Judges in Capital Cases," 81 *Marquette Law Review* 303 (1997–1998), (https://scholarship.law .nd.edu/law_faculty_scholarship/527/).

28. "'The dogma lives loudly within you': Revisiting Barrett's confirmation hearing," *New York Times,* September 26, 2020 (https://www.nytimes .com/2020/09/26/us/politics/the-dogma-lives-loudly-within-you-revisiting -barretts-confirmation-hearing.html).

29. Linda Greenhouse, "Grievance Conservatives Are Here to Stay," *New York Review of Books,* July 1, 2021 (https://www.nybooks.com/articles /2021/07/01/grievance-conservatives-are-here-to-stay/).

30. Jim-Kouri, "Pope Francis' Friendship with Soros Leads to Pontiff's Support of Socialism," *Conservative Base,* September 5, 2019 (https://conservativebase .com/pope-francis-friendship-with-soros-leads-to-pontiffs-support-of -socialism/).

31. Eric Jon Phelps, "Morris Dees: Jesuit Temporal Coadjutor and Founder of Southern Poverty Law Center: Update," Vatican Assassins website, December 2, 2011 (https://vaticanassassins.org/2011/12/02/morris-dees-jesuit -temporal-coadjutor-founder-of-southern-poverty-law-center-update/).

32. "The Papacy vs. The United States of America," *Endr Times* (blog), April 13, 2008 (https://endrtimes.blogspot.com/2008/04/papacy-vs-united-states-of -america.html).

33. Charles Chiniquy, *Fifty Years in the Church of Rome* (Protestant Literature Depository, 1886); (https://www.biblebelievers.com/chiniquy/index.html).

34. "The Occhionero Conspiracy: The Pope, the Clintons, Obama and an Italian President and Prime Minister Attempted a Coup Against Trump," *Millennium Report* (blog), June 3, 2019 (http://themillenniumreport.com).

35. Bill McCormick, S.J., "Marjorie Taylor Greene Showed That the Most Brutal Anti-Catholicism Can Come from Catholics," *America: The Jesuit Review,* April 29, 2022 (https://www.americamagazine.org/politics-society /2022/04/29/marjorie-taylor-greene-catholic-242915).

36. Representative Marjorie Taylor Greene, Twitter, April 27, 2022 (https:// twitter.com/RepMTG/status/1519422483929182209?ref_src=twsrc%5E tfw%7Ctwcamp%5Etweetembed%7Ctwterm%5E15194224839291822

09%7Ctwgr%5E%7Ctwcon%5Es1_&ref_url=https%3A%2F%2Fwww
.insider.com%2Fcontrolled-by-satan-marjorie-taylor-greene-blasts-catholic
-leaders-2022-4).

37. Karen Liebreich, "The Catholic Church has a long history of child sexual
abuse and coverups," *Washington Post,* February 18, 2019 (https://www
.washingtonpost.com/opinions).

38. Alison Kinney, "How the Klan Got Its Hood," *New Republic,* January 8,
2016 (https://newrepublic.com/article/127242/klan-got-hood).

39. John Quincy Adams, *Letters on Freemasonry* (1833, reprinted by Rivercrest,
2001).

40. Alexis de Tocqueville, *Democracy in America,* vol. 2, trans. Henry Reeve,
Esq. (J & H. G. Langley, 1841), 114.

41. When I researched *The New Hate,* the book was excerpted at a website run
by Acacia Press, which specialized in anti-Masonic publications. Unfortunately, the site (and the press) no longer appear to exist.

42. "Humanum Genus": Encyclical of Pope Leo XIII on Freemasonry (https://
www.vatican.va/content/leo-xiii/en/encyclicals/documents/hf_l-xiii_enc
_18840420_humanum-genus.html).

43. I drew these quotes from an online edition of the *Protocols,* which I found
at Scribd (https://www.scribd.com/document/211655861/The-Protocols
-of-the-Learned-Elders-of-Zion-ENG).

44. A multivolume compilation of *The Dearborn Independent* was published as
The International Jew. A full-text ebook can be found at Project Gutenberg
(https://www.gutenberg.org/files/37539/37539-8.txt).

45. Raymond Fendrick, " 'Heinrich' Ford Idol of Bavaria Fascisti Chief,"
Chicago Tribune, March 7, 1923 (https://twitter.com/100YearsAgoLive
/status/1633226943372881920/photo/1).

46. Thomas Jefferson, *Notes on the State of Virginia,* ed. William Peden (University of North Carolina Press, 1954), query 17 (https://press-pubs.uchicago
.edu/founders/documents/amendI_religions40.html).

47. Jonathan Evans, "U.S. adults are more religious than Western Europeans,"
Pew Research Center, September 5, 2018 (https://www.pewresearch.org
/fact-tank/2018/09/05/u-s-adults-are-more-religious-than-western
-europeans/).

6: Farm and City, Church and State

1. J. Hector St. John de Crèvecoeur, *Letters from an American Farmer* (Fox,
Duffield & Company, 1904); (https://books.google.com).

2. Jeffrey G. Williamson and Peter Lindert, "Unequal Gains: American Growth and Inequality Since 1700," *VoxEU,* June 16, 2016 (https://cepr .org/voxeu/columns/unequal-gains-american-growth-and-inequality-1700).

3. From the Founders Online website at the National Archives: Letter to John Jay from Thomas Jefferson, August 23, 1785 (https://founders.archives .gov/?q=Thomas%20Jefferson%20to%20John%20Jay%201785%20culti vators%20of%20the%20earth&s=1111311111&sa=&r=4&sr=); Letter from Thomas Jefferson to James Madison, December 20, 1787 (https:// founders.archives.gov/documents/Jefferson/01-12-02-0454).

4. Richard Hofstadter, *The Age of Reform* (Vintage, 1955), 24.

5. Hofstadter, *The Age of Reform,* 34–35.

6. William Jennings Bryan Democratic National Convention address, 1896. Text and audio at American Rhetoric Online Speech Bank (https://www .americanrhetoric.com/speeches/williamjenningsbryan1896dnc.htm).

7. Mrs. Sarah E. V. Emery, *Seven Financial Conspiracies Which Have Enslaved the American People* (1887, reprinted by Forgotten Books, 2018), 9–10.

8. Populist Party Platform of 1892, The American Presidency Project (https:// www.presidency.ucsb.edu/documents/populist-party-platform-1892).

9. William Hope Harvey, *Coin's Financial School* (1894, reprinted by Forgotten Books, 2009).

10. William Faulkner, *The Sound and the Fury* (Vintage, 1929 and 1984), 191.

11. Bryan Democratic National Convention address.

12. Bryan Democratic National Convention address.

13. Ta-Nehisi Coates, "A History of Liberal White Racism, Continued," *The Atlantic,* April 18, 2013 (https://www.theatlantic.com/politics/).

14. Philip Bump, "The selective socialism of Donald Trump: Farmers, yes. Poor families, no," *Washington Post,* July 23, 2019 (https://www.washing tonpost.com/politics).

15. "Trump: 'All Democrat-Run Cities Are Going to Hell,'" Bloomberg Quick-take (https://www.youtube.com/watch?v=_AUUX3rjv5M).

16. Carolyn Dimitri et al., "The 20th Century Transformation of U.S. Agriculture and Farm Policy," USDA Economic Information Bulletin no. 3, June 2005 (https://www.ers.usda.gov/webdocs/publications/44197/13566_eib3_1 _.pdf).

17. Richard Florida, *The Rise of the Creative Class Revisited* (Basic Books, 2012), 44–48.

18. Muzaffar Chishti et al., "Fifty Years On, the 1965 Immigration and Nationality Act Continues to Reshape the United States," Migration Policy Institute, October 15, 2015 (https://www.migrationpolicy.org/article/fifty

-years-1965-immigration-and-nationality-act-continues-reshape-united
-states).

19. William H. Frey, "The Nation Is Diversifying Even Faster Than Predicted,
According to New Census Data," Brookings Institution, July 1, 2020 (https://
www.brookings.edu/research/new-census-data-shows-the-nation-is
-diversifying-even-faster-than-predicted/).

20. William H. Frey, "The US Will Become 'Minority White' in 2045, Census
Predicts," Brookings Institution, March 14, 2018 (https://www.brookings
.edu/articles/the-us-will-become-minority-white-in-2045-census-projects/).

21. Jordan Weissmann, "Vast Stretches of America Are Shrinking. Almost All
of Them Voted for Trump," *Slate*, August 14, 2021 (https://slate.com/news
-and-politics/2021/08/2020-census-shrinking-counties-voted-trump.html).

22. Mark Muro, Sifan Liu, "Another Clinton-Trump Divide: High-Output
America vs Low-Output America," Brookings Institution, November 29,
2016 (https://www.brookings.edu/articles/another-clinton-trump-divide
-high-output-america-vs-low-output-america/).

23. Howard Schneider, "Much of 'Trump Country' Was in Recession During
2016 Campaign: Data," Reuters, December 18, 2019 (https://www.reuters
.com/article/us-usa-economy-counties-idUSKBN1YM0HC).

24. J. M. Berger, "Alt History," *The Atlantic*, September 16, 2016 (https://www
.theatlantic.com/politics/).

25. Ibram X. Kendi, "The Mantra of White Supremacy," *The Atlantic*, November 30, 2021 (https://www.theatlantic.com/ideas/).

26. About David Lane, Southern Poverty Law Center (https://www.splcenter
.org/fighting-hate/extremist-files/individual/david-lane).

27. Anne Case and Angus Deaton, *Deaths of Despair and the Future of Capitalism* (Princeton University Press, 2020), 166.

28. Case and Deaton, *Deaths of Despair*, 187.

29. Gregory A. Smith, "More White Americans Adopted Than Shed Evangelical
Label During Trump Presidency, Especially His Supporters," Pew Research
Center, September 15, 2021 (https://www.pewresearch.org/fact-tank).

30. Ryan Burge, "Why 'Evangelical' Is Becoming Another Word for 'Republican,'" *New York Times*, October 26, 2021 (https://www.nytimes.com/2021
/10/26/opinion/evangelical-republican.html).

31. Jeremy W. Peters and Elizabeth Dias, "Paula White, Newest White House
Aide, Is a Uniquely Trumpian Pastor," *New York Times*, November 2, 2019
(https://www.nytimes.com/2019/11/02/us/politics/paula-white-trump
.html).

32. Tom Gjelten, "How Positive Thinking, Prosperity Gospel Define Don-

ald Trump's Faith Outlook," NPR, August 3, 2016 (https://www.npr.org/2016/08/03/488513585/how-positive-thinking-prosperity-gospel-define-donald-trumps-faith-outlook).

33. Jeff Sharlet, " 'He's the Chosen One to Run America': Inside the Cult of Trump, His Rallies Are Church and He Is the Gospel," *Vanity Fair,* June 18, 2020 (https://www.vanityfair.com/news).

34. Philip S. Gorski and Samuel L. Perry, *The Flag and the Cross: White Christian Nationalism and the Threat to American Democracy* (Oxford University Press, 2022), 7.

35. Gorski and Perry, *The Flag and the Cross,* 88.

36. Jack Jenkins, "The Insurrectionists' Senate Floor Prayer Highlights a Curious Trumpian Ecumenicism," Religion News Service, February 25, 2021 (https://religionnews.com).

37. Jenkins, "The Insurrectionists' Senate Floor Prayer."

38. Sarah Jones, "White Christian Nationalism 'Is a Fundamental Threat to Democracy,' " *Intelligencer,* June 4, 2022 (https://nymag.com/intelligencer/2022/06/white-christian-nationalism-is-a-threat-to-democracy.html).

39. Alan Charles Raul, "For Republicans, Less Purity and More Reality," *Washington Post,* November 8, 2012 (https://www.washingtonpost.com/opinions).

40. Shushannah Walshe, "RNC Completes 'Autopsy' on 2012 Loss, Calls for Inclusion Not Policy Change," ABC News, March 18, 2013 (https://abcnews.go.com/Politics).

41. Dave Troy, "The Real Republican Adversary? Population Density," *Dave Troy* (blog), November 19, 2012 (https://davetroy.com/posts/the-real-republican-adversary-population-density).

42. Dave Troy, "Paranoia on Parade: How Goldbugs, Libertarians and Religious Extremists Brought America to the Brink," *Washington Spectator,* June 27, 2022 (https://washingtonspectator.org/paranoia-on-parade/).

43. Paul Boyer and Stephen Nissenbaum, *Salem Possessed: The Social Origins of Witchcraft* (Harvard University Press, 1974), xiii.

44. Boyer and Nissenbaum, *Salem Possessed,* 30.

45. Taylor Ardrey, "Far-right pundits baselessly claim Hurricane Ian was created by the 'deep state' to target Gov. Ron DeSantis and other red states: 'They are angry with us,' " *Insider,* October 1, 2022 (https://www.insider.com/far-right-pundits-deep-state-made-hurricane-ian-to-target-desantis-2022-10).

46. Aila Slisco, "Ron DeSantis Says Media Wanted Ian to Hit Florida for 'Political Agenda,' " *Newsweek,* October 5, 2022 (https://www.newsweek.com/ron-desantis-says-media-wanted-ian-hit-florida-political-agenda-1748975).

7: Into the Fire

1. Devlin Barrett and Carol D. Leonnig, "Material on foreign nation's nuclear capabilities seized at Trump's Mar-a-Lago," *Washington Post,* September 6, 2022 (https://www.washingtonpost.com/national-security).
2. "Remarks by President Biden on the Continued Battle for the Soul of the Nation," September 1, 2022 (https://www.whitehouse.gov/briefing-room /speeches-remarks/2022/09/01/remarks-by-president-bidenon-the -continued-battle-for-the-soul-of-the-nation/).
3. Matt Keeley, "Read Everything Donald Trump Said at His First Rally After Mar-a-Lago Raid," *Newsweek,* September 3, 2022 (https://www.newsweek .com/read-everything-donald-trump-said-his-first-rally-after-mar-lago-raid -1739683).
4. Dan Mangan, "Steve Bannon's podcast barred from Twitter after he made beheading comment about Fauci, FBI Director Wray," CNBC, November 5, 2020 (https://www.cnbc.com/2020/11/05/steve-bannon-makes-beheading -comment-about-fauci-on-war-room-podcast-.html).
5. "General Michael Flynn and Family Speak at Jericho March in DC, 12/12/20," Right Side Broadcasting Network (https://www.youtube.com /watch?v=romt1iWW4Oc).
6. Rod Dreher, "What I Saw at the Jericho March," *American Conservative,* December 12, 2020 (https://www.theamericanconservative.com/what-i -saw-at-the-jericho-march/).

Afterword

1. Jacques Berlinerblau, "Why Does Santorum Despise the Separation of Church and State?," Berkeley Center for Religion, Peace & World Affairs, Georgetown University, February 17, 2012 (https://berkleycenter.georgetown .edu/posts/why-does-santorum-despise-the-separation-of-church-and -state).
2. Debbie Elliott, "'Food Stamp President': Race Code, Or Just Politics?," National Public Radio, January 17, 2012 (https://www.npr.org/2012/01/17/145312069 /newts-food-stamp-president-racial-or-just-politics).
3. David Espo, "Newt Gingrich Scores Upset Victory in South Carolina Primary," *Florida Times Union,* January 21, 2012 (https://www.jacksonville .com/story/news/nation-world/2012/01/22/newt-gingrich-scores-upset -victory-south-carolina-primary/15878095007/).
4. National Journal, *The Atlantic,* July 12, 2012 (https://www.theatlantic

.com/politics/archive/2012/07/romney-after-naacp-if-you-want-more
-free-stuff-vote-for-obama/428103/).

5. Jake Tapper, Bradley Blackburn, and Devin Dwyer, "Pew Poll Finds 1 in
5 Americans Wrongly Believe Barack Obama is a Muslim," ABC News,
August 19, 2010 (https://abcnews.go.com/WN/pew-poll-18-percent
-americans-president-obama-muslim/story?id=11437070).

6. Ben Samuels, "Trump Compares 'Marxist Thugs' FBI to Gestapo, Germany's
Nazi-era Secret Police," *Haaretz*, January 18, 2023 (https://www.haaretz.com
/us-news/2023-01-18/ty-article/.premium/trump-compares-marxist-thugs
-fbi-to-gestapo-germanys-nazi-era-secret-police/00000185-c5d2-da66-a1bf
-fddae22d0000).

7. Kieran Corcoran, "Trump Trashed the US Military for Becoming 'Woke' a
Few Hours After Claiming He Actually Hates that Term," *Insider*, June 2,
2023 (https://www.businessinsider.com/trump-said-disney-woke-4-days
-before-saying-hates-term-2023-6).

8. David Smith, "'I am Your Retribution': Trump Rules Supreme at CPAC as he
Relaunches Bid for White House," *The Guardian*, March 4, 2023 (https://www
.theguardian.com/us-news/2023/mar/05/i-am-your-retribution-trump
-rules-supreme-at-cpac-as-he-relaunches-bid-for-white-house).

9. Julia Mueller, "Trump Slams Bill Barr as 'A Coward Who Didn't Do His
Job," *The Hill*, June 11, 2023 (https://thehill.com/blogs/blog-briefing
-room/4044744-trump-slams-bill-barr-as-a-coward-who-didnt-do-his-job/).

10. Ryan Bort, "Trump Says His Hand-Picked Chief of Staff Was 'Born With
a Very Small Brain," *Rolling Stone*, June 16, 2023 (https://www.rolling
stone.com/politics/politics-news/trump-john-kelly-chief-of-staff-small
-brain-1234773043/).

11. Ashley Carnahan, "DeSantis says Trump Can't Win in a General Election: 'Those
Are Just the Realities," Fox News, July 31, 2023 (https://www.foxnews.com
/media/desantis-says-trump-cant-win-general-election-those-just-realities).

12. Michael Goodwin, "Donald Trump's 'they're after you' tweet says it all,"
New York Post, December 21, 2019 (https://nypost.com/2019/12/21
/donald-trumps-theyre-after-you-tweet-says-it-all-goodwin/).

13. David Remnick, "The Alternative Facts of Robert F. Kennedy, Jr.," *The
New Yorker*, July 7, 2023 (https://www.newyorker.com/news/q-and-a/the
-alternative-facts-of-robert-f-kennedy-jr).

14. AP story, "RFK Jr. Remarks on Anne Frank, Vaccines Draw Condemnation,"
Politico, January 24, 2022 (https://www.politico.com/news/2022/01/24
/robert-kennedy-holocaust-vaccines-00001548).

15. Anjali Huynh, "5 Noteworthy Falsehoods Robert F. Kennedy, Jr. Has Promoted," *New York Times,* July 6, 2023 (https://www.nytimes.com/2023/07/06/us/politics/rfk-conspiracy-theories-fact-check.html).

16. Yair Rosenberg, "The Most Shocking Aspect of RFK Jr.'s Anti-Semitism," *The Atlantic,* July 16, 2023 (https://www.theatlantic.com/ideas/archive/2023/07/rfk-kennedy-covid-anti-semitism/674727/).

17. Mary Yang, "Robert F. Kennedy Jr's Campaign Bankrolled by Republican Mega-Donor," *The Guardian,* August 2, 2023 (https://www.theguardian.com/us-news/2023/aug/02/robert-f-kennedy-jr-republican-donor-super-pac).

18. Alex Seitz-Wald, "Why Steve Bannon and Alex Jones Love Robert F. Kennedy, Jr.," NBC News, April 28, 2023 (https://www.nbcnews.com/politics/2024-election/steve-bannon-alex-jones-love-robert-f-kennedy-jr-rcna82057).

19. Charisma Madarang, "Robert F. Kennedy Jr. Says He's 'Proud' Trump Likes Him," *Rolling Stone,* June 29, 2023 (https://www.rollingstone.com/politics/politics-news/robert-f-kennedy-jr-proud-trump-likes-him-town-hall-1234780451/).

20. Stephen Hawkins, Daniel Yudkin, Miriam Juan-Torres, Tim Dixon, "Hidden Tribes: A Study of America's Polarized Landscape," More in Common, 2018 (https://hiddentribes.us/media/qfpekz4g/hidden_tribes_report.pdf).

21. Jonathan Haidt, "Why the Past 10 Years of American Life Have Been Uniquely Stupid," *The Atlantic,* April 11, 2022 (https://www.theatlantic.com/magazine/archive/2022/05/social-media-democracy-trust-babel/629369/).

Index

B

Babbitt, Ashli, 23

baby formula shortage, 18n

Bankman-Fried, Sam, 61

Bannon, Steve, 127, 199, 216, 228–29

  Brazil's Bolsonaro and, 101–2

  "flood the zone with shit" strategy, 38–39, 67

  indictment of, 76

  as Trump chief strategist, 76, 166n

Barkun, Michael

  A Culture of Conspiracy, 93–94

Barnes, Mandela, 10

Barnum, P. T., 77

Barr, William, 57, 225

Barrett, Amy Coney, 157–59, 158n

Barruel, Abbé Augustin, 96

  Memoirs Illustrating the History of Jacobinism, 54

Beck, Glenn, 37, 38, 38n, 97–98, 102

Beecher, Lyman, 149, 154

  A Plea for the West, 149

Behold a Pale Horse (Cooper), 56

Bell, Daniel, 40

Bell, Derrick, 74

Bennett, Alex, 84

Biarritz (Retcliffe), 53

Biden, Joe, 8, 21, 22, 23, 41, 41n, 66, 126, 207, 211, 220

  accused of Marxism, 66, 67

  capitalism and, 66

  Catholicism of, 157

  confidential documents and, 205–6n

  conspiracy theories and, 63, 64

  election 2020 and, 68, 71, 74–75, 124, 126, 131

  fitness of, 66, 122

  open letter from the military warning about, 65–66

  plagiarism scandal, 66

  presidency of, 206

  speeches targeting Trump and MAGA, 206, 217

  voters for, 24, 104

Bilbo, Theodore, 184, 184n

bimetalism, 60, 60n

bin Laden, Osama, 61, 95

Birth of a Nation (film), 164

Black Hebrew Israelites, 4n, 169n

Blankfein, Lloyd, 55

Blavatsky, Madame, 116

Blisset, Luther, 50

  Q, 50

Blum, Richard, 56

Bohemian Club, 31–32

Bolsonaro, Eduardo, 102

Bolsonaro, Jair, 229

Bolton, John, 225

Bongino, Dan, 40

bootstrapping, 80, 141

Boston Marathon bombings, 30, 69

Bowers, Robert, 3, 4–5, 4n

Boyer, Paul

  Salem Possessed, 199–202

Bradshaw, Sally, 197

Bragg, Alvin, 38n